Studies in the Psychosocial

Series Editors
Stephen Frosh
Department of Psychosocial Studies
Birkbeck, University of London
London, UK

Raluca Soreanu
Psychosocial and Psychoanalytic Studies
University of Essex
Colchester, UK

Hannah Zeavin
University of California, Berkeley
Berkeley, USA

Studies in the Psychosocial seeks to investigate the ways in which psychic and social processes demand to be understood as always implicated in each other, as mutually constitutive, co-produced, or abstracted levels of a single dialectical process. As such it can be understood as an interdisciplinary field in search of transdisciplinary objects of knowledge. Studies in the Psychosocial is also distinguished by its emphasis on affect, the irrational and unconscious processes, often, but not necessarily, understood psychoanalytically. Studies in the Psychosocial aims to foster the development of this field by publishing high quality and innovative monographs and edited collections. The series welcomes submissions from a range of theoretical perspectives and disciplinary orientations, including sociology, social and critical psychology, political science, postcolonial studies, feminist studies, queer studies, management and organization studies, cultural and media studies and psychoanalysis. However, in keeping with the inter- or transdisciplinary character of psychosocial analysis, books in the series will generally pass beyond their points of origin to generate concepts, understandings and forms of investigation that are distinctively psychosocial in character.

Julie Macken

Australia's Schism in the Soul

Colonialism, Immigration Detention and a Nation's Failure to Mourn

Julie Macken
Western Sydney University
Sydney, NSW, Australia

ISSN 2662-2629 ISSN 2662-2637 (electronic)
Studies in the Psychosocial
ISBN 978-3-031-93812-2 ISBN 978-3-031-93813-9 (eBook)
https://doi.org/10.1007/978-3-031-93813-9

© The Editor(s) (if applicable) and The Author(s), under exclusive license to Springer Nature Switzerland AG 2025

This work is subject to copyright. All rights are solely and exclusively licensed by the Publisher, whether the whole or part of the material is concerned, specifically the rights of translation, reprinting, reuse of illustrations, recitation, broadcasting, reproduction on microfilms or in any other physical way, and transmission or information storage and retrieval, electronic adaptation, computer software, or by similar or dissimilar methodology now known or hereafter developed.
The use of general descriptive names, registered names, trademarks, service marks, etc. in this publication does not imply, even in the absence of a specific statement, that such names are exempt from the relevant protective laws and regulations and therefore free for general use.
The publisher, the authors and the editors are safe to assume that the advice and information in this book are believed to be true and accurate at the date of publication. Neither the publisher nor the authors or the editors give a warranty, expressed or implied, with respect to the material contained herein or for any errors or omissions that may have been made. The publisher remains neutral with regard to jurisdictional claims in published maps and institutional affiliations.

Cover credit: Jonathan Wood

This Palgrave Macmillan imprint is published by the registered company Springer Nature Switzerland AG.
The registered company address is: Gewerbestrasse 11, 6330 Cham, Switzerland

If disposing of this product, please recycle the paper.

*This is dedicated to those who have lived and those who have died in Australia's immigration detention regime. In honour of the hope that drove you, in recognition of the pain that assailed you and the harm we have done to you, to your mothers, to your nanas, to the men, women and children who cherished you so deeply.
I am so sorry.*

Acknowledgements

I would like to acknowledge the friends and colleagues who have offered various forms of assistance and support during this project. Thanks must begin at the beginning with the support of my father, Jim Macken, and brilliant mother, Ann Daniel.

Jim encouraged me with vitally needed support, with clear guidance and with laughs from the beginning until his end in September 2019. Ever reminding me that the healing is always in the collective. My mother, Ann Daniel, made this work not only possible but necessary. She has been an extraordinary model of scholarship, tenacity, love and enduring creativity. Her kindness and grace sustains me.

My sister Mary Macken-Horarik for her capacity to make me feel excited by my work while reminding me there is still much to be done. My brother Jamie Macken was the one I turned to, to ask if this was possible. His answer set me off on this journey. Rebecca Macken for her support and insightful reading and commentary. My wonderful partner and husband of many decades, Jon Haynes, for his dinners, for creating the space I needed and for giving me not only a lever but a place to stand. Lily Macken-Haynes is the best daughter I could have asked for—with her hugs, her videos, her eye rolls and love.

It was my enormous good fortune to have a small army of brilliant woman to guide this work. My supervisors Linda Briskman, Rimple Mehta and Sonia Tascon are three women who always led by example and who were as kind as they are brilliant. Allison Weir and Magdalena Zolkos were generous from the first day and Judith Pickering for her insight, constancy and companionship on so many of these truly crazy journeys. Peter Bansel, Joumanah El Matrah, Daniel Perell and Susan Mowbray made thinking strange things so exciting.

Victoria Chance was everything I hoped for and needed in an editor and friend. She provided a safety net I never knew I needed—but did—and I am indebted to her patience and forensic attention to detail. Indeed, none of my friends have escaped the ups and downs of this adventure. You know who you are and how much I have put you through. Thank you for your comradeship and your friendship.

Finally, I have always thought books should include a playlist because I know this owes much to the musicians and singers who lifted, soothed and transported me during the years of research and writing. Although too numerous to name them all I owe a debt to Missy Higgins, Gang of Youths, Briggs, Archie Roach, Paul Kelly and Florence and the Machine. Thank you.

Contents

1	**Linking the 'No' Vote to 'Stop the Boats'**	1
	References	8
2	**A Sickened Sovereignty**	9
	An Imagined Nation	10
	Just How Crazy Are We?	11
	Mourning and Melancholia	12
	Periods of Mourning	15
	The Seduction of Melancholia	18
	Operationalising Abuse	20
	Devolving into the Paranoid-Schizoid Phase	22
	The Racist Nature of the Split	23
	Putting the Nation on the Couch	25
	Overcoming Melancholia	29
	References	31
3	**A Dream in Three Parts: A Nation in Pieces (1778–1972)**	33
	Was It Genocide?	37
	Denial, Disappearance and the 'Great Australian Silence'	41
	Australian Stories: Colonial Myth	43
	Splitting the Nation, Killing the (m)Other	46

	The Melancholic Narrative Falters and Mourning Breaks Through	47
	References	55
4	**Waiting with Baseball Bats (1972–1996)**	59
	An Unlikely Leader	62
	The End of the Symbolic	64
	Splits Appear as Melancholia Tightens Its Grip	65
	The Opposite of Love Is Not Hate, It's Indifference	67
	References	73
5	**Is It Torture?**	77
	Particularities of Torture	79
	A Contested Accusation	81
	The Camps	84
	Anatomy of a Death in Custody	86
	Moving the Camps Out of Site/Sight: A Timeline	89
	What the Doctors Found	94
	References	104
6	**Words Make Worlds**	107
	Meet the Media	109
	Disappearing the Asylum Seeker	111
	We Weren't Always This Fragile	114
	The Subtle Art of Criminalising Movement	116
	Wounded Sovereignty	120
	When a Picture Lies	122
	Secrecy and Disclosure	129
	Access to Facts	131
	References	134
7	**Privatising Abuse**	137
	Before Privatisation	139
	Changing the Nation: Less Heart Less Soul	139
	Meet the Detainers	143
	Was It Always Going to End in Tears?	149

Torture Prevention	151
Australia's Privatised Immigration Detention Regime	152
What If …?	159
Cruelty and Denial Are the Point	161
When the Private Was Made Public	164
References	166

8 Mania or Mourning — 171
- A Changing of the Guard — 173
- Moments of Fear and Love — 174
- Body Swap — 175
- Mourning Requires More than Death — 178
- Reality Interrupts Relaxation — 179
- Imagine This! — 181
- Operationalising Imagination — 183
- References — 191

9 Conclusion: What Is to Be Done? — 193
- Finding Our Way Back to Mourning — 195
- Return to Mourning — 197
- Policy as Healing — 199
- Creating Subjects of Care — 201
- #LetThemStay and Why Names and Faces Matter — 202
- Disturbance as Transcendence — 204
- References — 208

Epilogue — 211

Index — 213

Abbreviations

AAL   Australian Aborigines League
ABC   Australian Broadcasting Corporation
ACM   Australasian Correctional Management
ALP   Australian Labor Party
APODs   Alternative Places of Detention
APS   Australian Public Service
ASIO   Australian Security Intelligence Organisation
AFR   *The Australian Financial Review*
AIATSI Australian Institute of Aboriginal and Torres Strait Island Studies
APA   Aborigines Progressive Association
CIDT   Cruel, Inhuman, or Degrading Treatment
CPSU   Community Public Sector Union
DIMA   Department of Immigration and Multicultural Affairs (1996–2001)
DIMIA   Department of Immigration and Multicultural and Indigenous Affairs (2001–2006)
EU   European Union
HREOC   Human Rights and Equal Opportunity Commission
MEAA   Media Entertainment and Arts Alliance
MOU   Memorandum of Understanding
MU   management unit
NBIA   No Business in Abuse

OPCAT	Optional Protocol to the Convention against Torture and other Cruel, Inhuman and Degrading Treatment or Punishment
PNG	Papua New Guinea
SAS	Special Air Service
SBS	Special Broadcasting Service
TPV	Temporary Protection Visa
UNHCR	United Nations High Commissioner for Refugees
UNSW	University of New South Wales
UTS	University of Technology Sydney

1

Linking the 'No' Vote to 'Stop the Boats'

To this day we are still like walking ghosts, utterly broken and hopeless. We are hollowed out and devoid of any enthusiasm for life, and we are stuck in animalistic state of existence because that is what we have become.
— a father, and asylum seeker, in The Nauru Regional Processing Centre, 2016

I am writing this as Aboriginal and Torres Strait Islander peoples emerge from a week of mourning. They, with twenty-seven million other Australians, have witnessed this October 2023 the majority of the nation vote down a request for an Indigenous voice to Parliament[1] be included in the Australian Constitution. It feels like a moment suspended: as history herself draws a long, deep breath. First Nations people quietly hold the time of Sorry Business and contemplate what may follow.

The campaign, framed simply as 'Yes' or 'No', was bruising for those Aboriginal and Torres Strait Islander peoples campaigning for a 'Yes' vote.

---

[1] The Voice would have been a permanent advisory body that would give advice to the government about issues that affect First Nations peoples.

Lies, dissembling and racist trolling of spokespeople intensified as the weeks rolled by. In the end, many leaders of the 'Yes' campaign chose to spend the referendum results night with family and friends rather than at official receptions, such was the exhaustion, the heartbreak, the anger.

Predictably, non-Indigenous Australians are not so quiet. The forty per cent of people that voted 'Yes' are struggling to understand exactly what happened in this Australia's most recent referendum. How has such a humble request, 'a call for the establishment of a First Nations Voice enshrined in the Constitution', been rejected by six in every ten Australians? The result has not only destroyed the hopes of millions who saw this change as a small first step towards meaningful and honest reconciliation with Aboriginal and Torres Strait Islander people, but it also reveals the Australian Constitution to be based on a calculated lie. Bernard Keane wrote in *Crikey* on 16 October that the dominant 'No' vote is

> a rejection of historical fact in favour of white fantasy. The foundational document of Australia now deliberately, purposefully, with the endorsement of Australian voters, denies the foundational act of the Australian polity, the dispossession of First Peoples. (Keane, 2023)

That denial of historic fact, which has underpinned Australia's colonisation since 1788, has generated a bitter and ugly referendum campaign and result; it has also added fuel to the ongoing assault on the rights of all people who disrupt the Australian colonial 'White fantasy' by simply existing in or in relation to Australia, including those who seek Australia's protection as refugees. I believe we will find reasons for the defeat of this referendum buried under the same psycho-affective landscape that has created and operationalised the documented abuse of those who have come seeking Australia's protection over the last twenty-five years. The abuse and dispossession of First Nations people, both historic and very recent, is intimately related to the abuse of those who now seek asylum here. To explain this linkage we need to read the nation psychologically as well as politically, economically and rhetorically. We need to trace the nation's psychological state from 1788 to today, with respect to the violence of Australia's colonisation and the collective national denial of it. To begin to understand this denial, we can look closely at some moments when the affective field of the nation's politics was briefly transformed into something more hopeful and self-aware.

This book began as research into why the Australian state abuses and even tortures some people who come by boat seeking asylum. The first time I heard Australia accused of state-sanctioned torture was in September 2002 when, as a senior writer with *the Australian Financial Review (AFR)*, I wandered into a darkened conference room hosting Australia's first Mental Health Alliance for Refugees conference and sat down at the back to listen. Over several hours, psychiatrists discussed in grim detail the verified mental health impacts of Australia's policy of mandatory and indefinite detention of asylum seekers and refugees. Horrific impacts included people becoming paralysed and blind due to trauma, taking so much medication they slept for twenty hours a day, and attempting suicide—even children. In the conference's final presentation, Professor Michael Dudley from the University of New South Wales stood centre stage and summarised their findings, saying, 'What all of this describes is state-sanctioned torture. Australia is torturing refugees in these camps'.

I walked back to my office stunned by these revelations. But what came next left me unmoored. I mentioned to a colleague that I had spent the day in a conference wherein senior medicos had pronounced Australia guilty of state-sanctioned torture of refugees and that I intended to file a news story about it. My colleague stared at me for an uncomfortable thirty seconds before opining that the newspaper would never run a story like that because, apparently, Australia doesn't torture people—it's not who we are.

I never wrote that story for the *AFR*, but in the next two decades other writers for newspapers, blogs, reports, Senate Inquiries, medical journals and so on did draw attention to the mounting evidence supporting Professor Dudley's claim that day: that Australia was, and is, state-sanctioning torture of refugees. A 2015 report by United Nations Special Rapporteur Juan Mendez (2015) found that

> the Government of Australia ... has violated the right of the asylum seekers, including children, to be free from torture or cruel, inhuman or degrading treatment, as provided by articles 1 and 16 of the Convention Against Torture.

A year later, Amnesty International (2016) reported that refugees held in Australian facilities in the small island country of Nauru were attempting suicide, some by self-immolation. Women were unable to parent or feed their infants. Many refugees were unwilling or unable to leave their tents—if they did they were often attacked by locals. This 2016 Amnesty report concluded:

> The conditions on Nauru – refugees' severe mental anguish, the intentional nature of the system, and the fact that the goal of offshore processing is to intimidate or coerce people to achieve a specific outcome — amounts [sic] to torture.

Testimony about the brutal impact of Australia's policies can also be found in the writings of asylum seekers and refugees themselves, in volumes such as *Human Rights Overboard* edited by Linda Briskman et al. (2008); *No Friend but the Mountains* by Behrouz Boochani (2018); and *Writing through Fences* edited by Hani Abdile et al. (2021). There is ample evidence and attestation that the Australian state has been using the bodies of desperate people as a message board that says, '*Turn Back, You Are Going the Wrong Way*'.

My colleague's assertion that 'It's not who we are'—and his response grounded in the confidence of a 'good' Australia and a 'we' that could be relied upon to not torture other people—left me wondering where the truth might lie, especially as Australia's treatment of refugees has deteriorated further since 2002. Our offshore immigration detention camps, emptied in 2007 by the Rudd Labor government, were reopened and refilled in 2012 by the Gillard Labor government. At the time of writing, it appears the Albanese Labor government has reopened the camp in Nauru and detained at least a hundred people there. The Refugee Council of Australia cites that in these camps people are being sexually assaulted and beaten, and are dying from medical neglect, suicide and murder.

I have spent the last twenty-five years researching Australia's abuse of asylum seekers. Like a grey nurse shark to bait, I have circled the issue, tried to take chunks out of it, stalked and tackled it from numerous points of view. As a journalist I reported the abuse, expecting that if people knew what was happening, the policy and situation would change. I wrote stories about the financial cost, as the spending grew to billions of dollars while incompetence and mismanagement were apparent. These made no difference. As a political consultant, my face pressed up against the window of power, I saw decent people paralysed and curiously unable to apprehend or even imagine what was happening in offshore detention. I began to realise that the Coalition[2] and the Labor Party don't have this policy: this policy has them. As an activist and communicator I experimented with ways of discussing the issue. Many advocates believe that they will more effectively engage people using language such as 'they are just like you and me', rather than graphic descriptions of cruelty or complicity. Others want to bring attention to the human rights abuses in the camps believing that raising awareness of such cruelty will scandalise the electorate and force change. Whichever approach was taken, it didn't matter. Despite the commitment of thousands of clever, compassionate and hardworking activists, academics, nurses, nuns, lawyers and regular citizens,[3] change only ever occurred at the margins and it never endured. The substantial failure of this resistance over twenty-five years and the way the stories so quickly slip from view led me to ask: could the driver for this Australian cruelty be unconscious? Is that why it evades detection, confrontation, dissolution?

Judith Butler, philosopher and gender theorist, argues in *Precarious Life* (2004, p. 41) that while nations and individual psyches are not the same, 'both can be described as "subjects", albeit of different orders'. Just as an individual's mental health is both revealed and determined by what they do, so too is the psyche of a nation revealed and determined by its collective action (and inaction). I began to look to the literature and practice of psychotherapy and psychoanalysis to understand the Australian electorate's paradoxical sanctimonious condonement of, and lack of curiosity about, the immigration detention complex; the growing contempt for any public gestures that were considered 'symbolic'; and the

---

[2] The Liberal–National Coalition, commonly known simply as the Coalition, is an alliance of centre-right political parties that forms one of the two major groupings in Australian federal politics. The two partners in the Coalition are the Liberal Party of Australia and the National Party of Australia.

[3] Including the Mums4Refugees and the Grandmothers for Refugees.

deadening, banal, flat tone used in Australian politics to discuss subjects that normally, globally, demand sweeping rhetoric and persuasive meaning-making. I argue that it is the regressive, infantile psychological state of Australia as a nation that has generated these phenomena and their attendant human rights abuses. My claims are supported by the works of two historic figures in the analysis of the psyche: Sigmund Freud and Melanie Klein.

Freud's classification of mourning and its malignant sibling, melancholia, offers one way of comprehending the power and fury that can be embodied in a deadpan denial and disavowal of reality. His framework of interpretation allows us to trace what happened to this nation's vitality, curiosity and capacity to love, especially in the period from the early 1970s to the mid-1990s. As I read his descriptions of the melancholic, I recognised what we had witnessed in the broader political landscape and leadership. Then, Klein's account of why/how we split ourselves into mutually exclusive 'good' and 'bad' parts, and her development of the paranoid-schizoid position which explains the victim-complex of the bully, illuminate the defensive posturing of pathological narcissism. In this framework, the finite process of mourning retains vitality and erotic energy because it remains in contact with the reality of love and loss, life and death; melancholic denial of the painful realities of love and loss results, rather, in shallow, lifeless, thin attachments. Realistic reflection and subsequent truth-telling are the antidote to this destructive, narcissistic state of mind. In psychotherapeutic terms, the Australian people need to face the truth about colonisation in order to address the submerged fear of non-White people that steers the nation's politics on an almost lifeless autopilot.

This ongoing psychic state of melancholia was harnessed by the campaign for 'No' with its slogan 'If you don't know, vote no', a slogan described by Dr. Allan Patience (2023), fellow in political science at the University of Melbourne, as 'ignorant, ethically despicable, and antidemocratic'. Calling on a populace to negate progress and conversation purely because of apathy or lack of curiosity—not knowing or wishing to know the experience of others—is an extraordinary political paean to ignorance and buried fear. As Freud would probably attest, what we 'don't know' can really make us sick; as thousands of asylum seekers and First Nations people have experienced, what we collectively pretend to not-know can actually kill.

Australia is a fragile, divided, anxious nation. We vote for policies that destroy the sacred core of people, of children—simply to assuage and manage our own fear. We are unable to accept the reality of Australia's colonial violence and we all continue to pay a dangerously high price for this delusion. As for any person caught in a life of lies and denial, our world has become an unsafe place to be.

This is a terrible moment for Australia's First Nations people and their allies. But it is a moment rich in revelation for those willing to look closely at unfolding events. We are, according to Professor Louise Newman of the Monash University Centre for Developmental Psychiatry and Psychology (see Chap. 5), 'in the midst of the collapse of collective values'. Or, in the words of child psychiatrist, John Jureidini (see also Chap. 5), it could alternatively be a moment when a large part of the nation rejects 'the moral antidepressant it's on, because it is numbing the state's capacity to take responsibility for this behaviour and face up to the bad things it's done'. This could be the moment we all imagine the pain of powerlessness and that we begin to become capable of hearing the truth of historical and ongoing colonisation and bearing the sorrow. If we do not take this chance, we will continue to be marooned in a state of melancholia.

In the following chapters I explore the impact of widespread melancholic malady in Australia from colonisation to present day. Throughout this time there have been moments of real heroism and creativity as well as suffering. There have been two centuries of resistance from Aboriginal and Torres Strait Islander peoples. There has been a resistance movement to the inhumane treatment of asylum seekers, and the organised fury of women and of climate activists as they demand justice and reason from those in power. Arguably, reality, with its unfinished business, is coming ready-or-not for this nation.

References

Abdile, H., Boochani, B., Galbraith, J., & Tofighian, O. (Eds.). (2021). Writing through fences: Archipelago of letters. *Southerly, 79*(2).

Amnesty International. (2016). *Island of despair: Australia's "processing" of refugees on Nauru*. https://www.amnesty.org.au/island-of-despair-nauru-refugee-report-2016/

Boochani, B. (2018). *No friend but the mountains: Writing from Manus prison* (O. Tofighian, Trans.). Picador, Pan Macmillan.

Briskman, L., Latham, S., & Goddard, C. (2008). *Human rights overboard: Seeking asylum in Australia*. Scribe.

Butler, J. (2004). *Precarious life: The powers of mourning and violence*. Verso.

Keane, B. (2023, October 16). Australia is now a legal fiction. *Crikey*. https://www.crikey.com.au/2023/10/16/voice-to-parliament-first-nations-peoples-constitution/

Méndez, J. E. (2015). *Report of the Special Rapporteur on torture and other cruel, inhuman or degrading treatment or punishment. Addendum: Observations on communications 146 transmitted to governments and replies received*. Office of the United Nations High Commissioner for Human Rights. https://ap.ohchr.org/documents/dpage_e.aspx?si=A/HRC/28/68/Add.1

Patience, A. (2023, October 15). Australian politics has reached a dead end. *Pearls and Irritations*. https://johnmenadue.com/australian-politics-has-reached-a-dead-end/

2

A Sickened Sovereignty

I come to this story as a White Australian whose forebears arrived five generations ago. My father's family came here, in part, so my great-great-grandmother, Mary Macken, could evade retaliation by the British forces in Ireland, and in part, so her husband, Mark Foy, could make a new life and fortune in the goldfields of Ballarat and later in his shops. My maternal forebears came from Ireland four generations ago as economic migrants in search of freedom from hunger and poverty. My background is marginal to the story, but I want to acknowledge that I write from the privileged perspective of a White Australian—a position of privilege that I have as a result of birth. My citizenship is secure, my appearance allows me to move unchallenged, I assume I have a right to speak out and I assume the law will protect me—because it was created by people like me. This is not the case for many like my young Somali friend who spent years on Nauru suffering the predations of that camp. She can make no such assumptions, despite now living in Australia for five years. In a very real sense she and I inhabit a different nation.

There is a wealth of material—research, data and documentation—on the lives of people who come to Australia seeking protection. But if we want to look at the relationship between the Australian state and the abuse and torture of asylum seekers and refugees meted out in its name, we also need to examine the actions, motives and behaviours of the state which, to date, have gone largely unexamined. This lack of curiosity and analysis is not only dangerous for asylum seekers, it is ultimately destructive for us, the citizens of Australia.

I turned to a psychoanalytic frame when I found that the conscious worlds of politics, race, opportunism and economics didn't explain the known/unknown quality in the national conversation—the lack of curiosity and the depravity of the abuse itself. Sensing an unconscious driver behind both policy and practice, I turn to a psychoanalytic frame.

I am of course not the first to attempt to read the contemporary Australian state, from a psychoanalytic perspective. Ghassan Hage's *Against Paranoid Nationalism* (2003), Jennifer Rutherford's *The Gauche Intruder* (2002) and Anthony Burke's *In Fear of Security* (2001) are profound contributions to understanding how Australia became dangerous for those seeking protection and how the nation attempts to manage its paranoia; taken together these works sketch a cultural, political and moral position of White Australia. Their authors chart the nation's shift from human rights advocacy to human rights abuse through various lenses: fear of insecurity, unresolved collective aggression and the corrosive power of endless anxiety and worrying. But now, the Australian practice of torture in the context of asylum demands its own specific study.

An Imagined Nation

Australia's abuse of asylum seekers is operationalised through its media, through its privatised immigration regime, and through a co-opted national imagination. Benedict Anderson, an Anglo-Irish political scientist and historian, defines a 'nation' as an imagined political community:

> *imagined* because the members of even the smallest nation will never know most of their fellow-members, meet them, or even hear of them, yet in the minds of each lives the image of their communion. (1983, p. 6, italics in original)

Anderson footnotes Robert Seton-Watson's remark that 'a nation exists when a significant number of people in a community consider themselves to form a nation, or behave as if they formed one' (1983, p. 6). Based on these definitions, 'Australia' exists as the collective imagination of the political community. Certainly, this collective effort is scaffolded by colonial artefacts in the Australian Constitution. It is a nation made of blood and treasure: millions of people pay taxes; ninety-five thousand bodies were sacrificed in its name in the First and Second World Wars. To put one's body on the line for a homeland might seem wholly physical and pragmatic, evidence that this country is more than a figment of a shared imagination. But that misjudges the power of the imagination.

To properly site this national crisis, one must look back to the foundational crisis that created Australia: the dispossession and denial of the existence of Aboriginal and Torres Strait Islander peoples. Prior to 1778, this continent was a place imagined, sung and dreamed up by more than two hundred and fifty separate nations. Yet one of the first acts of imagination by the colonisers was to declare the country nobody's land: *Terra Nullius*. Such was the power of this imaginative invocation that with its declaration the British attempted to disappear the oldest cultures on Earth, comprising over a million people speaking two-hundred and fifty languages, and systems of land management and ecology that had sustained populations for more than sixty-five thousand years. Such is the power of the imagination. This is why imagination needs to be taken into account and understood as a force that has roots buried deeply in the unconscious.

Just How Crazy Are We?

A review of any federal election campaign will assuage doubts about the existence of a national imagination—an imagination always in a state of flux and contest. To watch a political campaign at full clip, from within or without, is to see the construction of an imagined nation just waiting for the citizens to vote themselves into it. These campaigns lay bare the bones of the leader's national—nationalist—hopes; they reveal the foundational stories of both the nation and the leaders. Political campaigns project the hopes, values and fears of the community, and attempt to foretell a path into a safe and prosperous future for the majority of the citizenship. Relying on recreations of 'us' and 'them', they spend millions getting the best advertising experience because they are built on the imagination: an imagination with roots in the shared psycho-affective landscape of the dominant culture. In this sense the political community is created out of a carefully curated use of imaginative talismans and archetypes. Like a pea and cup game, this psychic development can be subtle and swift, making it nearly impossible to catch the sleight of hand that delivers the unthought known (Bollas, 2017). Through the use of advertising billboards and flyers, slogans and videos, the best practitioners are able to conjure a sense, image, snatch of memory, almost a smell that transports us back to the pre-linguistic state. The alchemical process in the construction of this imagined political community pulls straight from the unconscious. Imagination matters because it gives access to the subconscious and the possibility of working psychoanalytically with our most destructive impulses.

Mourning and Melancholia

By the early 2000s I had become increasingly aware of some peculiar aspects of this developing scandal, the way the horrifying reports of conditions within the camps slipped from view, John Howard's fury when asked to address the wounds of colonisation in symbolic fashion by, among other gestures, issuing an official apology to Indigenous Australians. Howard's policy towards refugees, too, was driven by a need to control the symbolic, its belligerence further enabled by a chilling lack of curiosity on the part of the electorate. By the early 2000s Australia's immigration camps, both onshore and offshore, were beginning to constellate as psychotic pockets filled with the nation's unnamed fears and sadism. They were sites literally and metaphorically severed from the conscious life of the nation. Their existence might burst through into national consciousness momentarily when the human trauma within them overwhelmed the razor wire of their boundary fences. But for the most part reports slid from view with indecent speed and the realities of the camps were reframed in the collective imagination to one-dimensional, nondescript buffers against evil. These were liminal places inhabited by unknown and unknowable ghosts: necessary, yet dreamlike and indistinct.

In psychoanalysing an individual (rather than a nation), the treatment would draw any psychotic, deviated aspects of the mind back towards the conscious mind. This process would make conscious that which had been unconscious, meaning the individual can use language and thought and dialogue to try to understand the conditions and emotions that created the psychosis in the first place and work through, rather than act out of, for example, fear or narcissism. This is a process of integrating those parts of the psyche that appear to be entirely severed from the conscious mind of the patient. In this difficult and painstaking process the person moves to wholeness of mind. But how to do that when the 'patient' is a nation? I think we begin by trying to create a frame to understand where we are now. To do that we must also retrace our collective steps and see clearly where we have been.

A hundred years after its first publication, Sigmund Freud's 'Mourning and Melancholia' (1957) offers a surprisingly contemporary guide to understanding the extraordinary psychological transition that has occurred in the Australian electorate since the mid-1990s. 'Mourning and Melancholia' explores loss and loss-avoidance. Freud wrote it in 1915 when his two sons were fighting in the First World War and the European ideal was drowning in the mud and madness of Flanders Fields. The massive loss of life in the First World War meant that the healthy process of grieving the dead, lost sovereignty and the lost dreams of European superiority were live questions in the mental health community, as well as in hospitals full of shell-shocked, psychotic soldiers and grieving widows.

In the paper 'Mourning and Melancholia' Freud grapples with psychological states that are basic to the human condition. He asks why, during periods of grief and loss, do some people recover and not others? How is it that some people can hold on through the destabilising distress of this liminal state, a threshold moment of betwixt and between, to emerge capable of love and life? Why do other people stall and collapse into narcissism, lifelessness and compulsive repetition? He says he wrote the paper 'to throw some light on the nature of melancholia by comparing it with the normal affect of mourning'. For Freud, a critical element of mourning is the mourner's ability to stay in contact with reality: to recognise that someone has died and that their death is important enough to grieve, and to acknowledge that the deceased was loved and known—that they mattered. Freud says mourning is more than passive acceptance of a death. Despite the enormous pain and disorientation of loss, the mourner is not willing to avoid or deny it. By staying in connection with the truth of their loss, the mourner remains in contact with truth and therefore reality. In contrast, a refusal to confront a death, or a denial of its importance, leads to a state of pathological melancholia.

A century after it was written, it is easy to forget that ideas we take for granted today had not been thought until Freud thought them. These ideas include the human psyche's capacity to split parts of itself off and then wage war on the rest; that a person can be totally committed to life while sabotaging the drives necessary for life; that a person can have a deep hatred for a person they also love. Freud not only imagines the state of the psyche but, like a detective, goes in search of subtle ways in which the unconscious mind seeks to hide some of its most destructive moves.

Freud was first to begin theorising about the dynamic of splitting within the psyche; Melanie Klein took this notion and developed a more sophisticated and rigorous theory that became known as object relations. Klein's 1946 paper 'Notes on Some Schizoid Mechanisms' was presented in London a few months after the bombs had stopped falling there. A child psychiatrist, Klein's patients were the children of London who were experiencing the dread that comes from the fear of disintegration and having one's secure relations and systems shattered.

Klein professed the idea that, from infancy, we are caught up in a process of psyche-splitting intended to manage the dread of annihilation, as 'one of the earliest ego mechanisms and defences against anxiety'. She argued that life begins with our relationship to objects. The first important object in life, the mother's breast, initiates the first object relation in life, and the infant begins their life's work of managing unspeakable anxiety. This first object is conceptually split into 'good' and 'bad'. The infant's *phantasie*—this is the German spelling of a word that carries all the menace of a Grimms' fairy-tale—is that the good breast is always available with an abundance of nourishment and it is thus loved and idealised as perfect. The bad breast doesn't arrive on time, is frustrating, or is not nourishing, and onto this breast the baby projects her hate and fury. In this way goodness is protected from badness by their being conceptualised as comprising separate objects. At this stage the infant does not know where she begins and ends. The world, including the mother, is an extension of the babe, which is why the psychic life begins with narcissism—everything is not about the baby, it is literally the baby. This splitting of the phantasie of the all-good mother and the all-bad mother—without realising they are one and the same—is the earliest way to manage rejection, abandonment, pain or discomfort. It is a primitive stage in development.

Klein's ideas have endured in part because they are tough and chunky (Sedgwick, 2007, p. 625). Ideas such as binary splitting (all-good–all-bad), projection (attributing something that is within oneself to an external person or object), introjection (incorporating within oneself a representation of an external object or person) and a paranoid/schizoid position (the term she used to describe the infant's primitive psyche) are now commonly used and understood.

Periods of Mourning

Mourning presupposes a death, and in my conceptualisation what died—or needed to be finally buried—was the national foundational myth of the good and peaceful settler. This is the fiction that Australia was 'an empty land' waiting for the civilising touch of the British Empire; the idea that the land was settled, not violently colonised through musket, massacres, rape and poisonings against the populations of Australia's Aboriginal and Torres Strait Island peoples. From the early 1970s an emerging recognition of the violent nature of Australia's colonisation began to permeate the mainstream. This new awareness was prematurely foreclosed by reactionary politicians in the mid-1990s, leaving a kind of 'stillborn' mourning in its place which devolved into melancholic denial characterised by evasion and occlusion. From this perspective, in this book I apply Freud's rubrics of mourning and melancholia to three periods in White Australia's development.

Firstly, the arrival of the British forces in 1778. The violent colonisation of Australia led to a scale of death that eventually covered the entire nation. Aboriginal and Torres Strait Islander peoples lost land, language, culture, hundreds of thousands of lives and eventually children. This began a period of violence and dispossession that would continue for over two centuries and that continues in many forms today. In the face of so much loss it is a testament to an extraordinary capacity for survival on the part of Aboriginal and Torres Strait Islander people that so much has survived.

While these Frist Nations peoples fought back, grieved and buried their dead, the White Australians of the period engaged in ongoing frontier violence and theft, and began the process of psychologically covering their tracks through the propagation of the myth of the kindly settler. Official denial of the very existence of Aboriginal and Torres Strait Islander peoples through the principle of *Terra Nullius*, sometimes used in international law to justify claims that territory may be acquired solely by an entity's occupation of it, put denial at the heart of the emerging nation and provided the denialist basis for a melancholia in the new colony that will be explained later in the chapter.

Secondly, I characterise as a time of emergent mourning in Australia the period 1972–1996, beginning under the prime ministership of Gough Whitlam. The violence of Australia's colonisation began to bleed through into national conversations and debates. For the first time in White Australia's brief history the call to mourn nationally and publicly was heard by White Australia. As the brutalities of colonisation were first publicly spoken about in the early years of the Whitlam government, White Australians were offered a lifeful reconnection with reality through the process of sifting through, reflecting on and interrogating the past. This move towards national mourning, and the truth-telling (Allam & Evershed, 2019) that anchored and inspired it, led to an extraordinary period of creativity in public policy, the arts and legislation. Questions of national identity fomented storytelling, dialogue, contested histories, and a diversity of expressions and enactments.

Artefacts and images—theatre, media, women's liberation, land rights, debate surrounding a newly independent Australian character—from the early 1970s to the mid-1990s show a profound transformation in Australia as the truth of a violent colonisation jostled to displace the foundational *phantasie* of the non-violent settler. In two decades of enormous upheaval, groups previously rendered powerless, primarily Aboriginal and Torres Strait Islanders, women and multicultural communities, demanded seats at the table of national decision-making. There was a sense in which White Australia was finally being told to leave home, stand on its own feet, become a Republic, engage as an equal in the Asia-Pacific and get over its pining for the Motherland England.

Prime Minister Paul Keating heralded the hightide mark of this public performance of mourning in his 1992 'Redfern Speech' in which, on behalf of the non-Aboriginal and Torres Strait Islander population, he took full, unequivocal responsibility for the ruin wreaked on First Nations peoples by the first settlers and all subsequent generations (see Chap. 3). But, as Freud cautions, mourning is hard work. A time of profound disturbance and destabilisation, it breaks us open and breaks our hearts. After more than twenty years of trying to imagine a new national narrative that acknowledged the truth of foundational violence and the need to make restitution, many Australians at this time were restless and angry. National identity, who owned it, how it was formed, indeed who was truly Australian, were central debates in the 1996 federal election. Keating and his supporters watched the tide quickly turn when, in the 1996 federal election campaign, the electorate was given the option of not confronting the past but volunteering for a more comfortable and relaxed national story. Liberal Party leader John Howard won this election with a sweeping majority and the nation regressed to a time of intense melancholia that I am calling a third period of national psychic development which persists to the present day.

Disavowal and denial were hallmarks of the Howard government. Howard spent much of his political capital denying the need first to reject, and then to mourn the loss of the White Australian settler *phantasie*. The period from 1996 onwards has evinced a growing indifference to the circumstances and the pain of the Other in Australia and abroad. This is a distinguishing psychological feature of melancholia as Freud defines it: 'cessation of interest in the outside world, loss of the capacity to love'. This loss of national love was made possible by a loss of imagination and empathy deftly exploited by Howard and the prime ministers that have followed him.

The Seduction of Melancholia

Freud describes melancholia as 'pathological and essentially a disease of narcissism'. While mourning is navigated by symbolic and metaphoric means which demand imagination and empathy, the melancholics' world is ruled by pragmatic concerns. Unlike those in mourning, who are absorbed in memories of their lost love/s and may weep and talk at length about their positive attributes, the melancholic will weep and talk endlessly of what the loss means for them, how it has literally reduced them. Their focus is on their own impoverishment, carrying an affect of outrage rather than sorrow—not 'we have lost a beloved person/idea/leader', but 'how dare they die/leave/disappoint me?'. Melancholia is powerfully seductive because it enables a person (or a nation) to avoid the most painful aspects of a loss, which are connected to love. Because of their denial of the death or its importance, the melancholic is psychologically severed from reality and their external life is devitalised and superficial and lacking in the power of the metaphoric and symbolic.

John Howard's prime ministership was characterised by his consistent refusal to countenance the symbolic: reconciliation with Aboriginal and Torres Strait Islander peoples; acknowledgement of climate change; ethics of joining the Iraq war. His belligerent public refusal to make any kind of symbolic gesture was tolerated by a populace which appeared to uncritically accommodate his bellicosity. Indeed, watching Howard grow visibly angry at the idea of treating a national issue symbolically made me reflect on Freud's work. Symbolic work is, of course, how we work through things psychologically. So, what would the opposite of that look like? I tried to understand the language of splitting, of us versus them, and the methodical process of demonising asylum seekers and their children that became particularly apparent through successive federal election campaigns.

Howard made this psychological path clear within months of winning the 1996 election. His opening address at the Australian Reconciliation Convention in May 1997 went straight to the difference between mourning and melancholia—and between the previous Keating government and his own—when he said that '[r]econciliation will not work if it puts a higher value on symbolic gestures and overblown promises rather than the practical needs of Aboriginal and Torres Strait Islander people' (Howard, 2001). Howard's demand to elevate the practical above the symbolic gave him greater control of the national agenda—particularly in relation to Aboriginal and Torres Strait Islanders' issues—and it stripped the vitality, the potential and the lifefullness from those conversations.

The devitalised, fixed psychic state of melancholia is at times interrupted by a manic defensive reaction which Freud called melancholia's 'most remarkable characteristic', since mania and melancholia have opposite symptoms. A muscular response, mania occurs when the melancholic breaks free from the lifelessness of their malady, and it may service the liberation of emotional energy. To Freud, both disordered states (mania and melancholia) are 'wrestling with the same "complex". But ... in melancholia the ego has succumbed to the complex whereas in mania it has mastered it or pushed it aside'. In 2019, Prime Minister Scott Morrison displayed an example of this manic response when he refused to return from a holiday in Hawaii while Australia confronted a nationwide bushfire crisis. (Famously, his glib explanation was, 'mate, I don't hold a hose'.) Morrison's denial of the Australian state of emergency was compounded by a further series of manic responses that all went awry. When he returned from Hawaii a few days later, his first photo opportunity at the fires was marred by his own demand that a young woman and an exhausted older man shake his hand, even as they tried to refuse. He went so far as to create a much-derided video commercial that put himself at the heart of the drama and took it upon himself to involve the army reserves without consulting those in charge of the crisis response, the New South Wales Rural Fire Service. In these responses we can sense the manic and anti-relational edginess of melancholia and observe its devolution into intransigent narcissism.

Operationalising Abuse

In Freud's description, the psychological state of melancholia has within it not just narcissism but also a sadism that seeks an outlet. In Australia, this psychological state provided an unconscious need to demonise, punish and abuse asylum seekers. The government initiated a number of strategies to put this into practice. These strategies include reframing asylum seekers as a threat to Australia's national security rather than people fleeing persecution; occluding the faces of asylum seekers and disappearing thousands of people into offshore detention giving the state almost total control of the narrative; privatising and outsourcing the administration of the camps to the private sector allowing the state to claim a 'hands off' approach while manipulating and managing a sometimes-overwhelmed media. These strategies were aided and abetted by the effective production of state propaganda that framed those seeking Australia's protection as a dangerous and non-valid Other. An unconscious urge to sadism has energised the state's decisions, converting its melancholia from a dark ambition of a sickened sovereignty to a globally recognised hard-line treatment of potential refugees.

Over the last twenty-five years Australia has been transformed by its own immigration policy. There is an interlocking and spiralling relationship between population and policy—between the politicians who continue to strengthen the policy, especially during each successive election period, and the electorate that votes it into action. Privatising detention centres transformed them from sites of potential political intervention into sites of de-politicised economic activity. Since then, Australia has become a pioneer in externalising its responsibilities as regards political asylum, redefining its borders to shift functions that are normally—and were previously—undertaken by a state within its own territory so that they are now performed outside its territory by private profiteers. Privatising the camps put most aspects of their operations, including the people held in them, almost completely beyond the reach of media and advocates. It prevented the general public from gaining a clear picture of the condition of the camps and provided the state with plausible deniability for any abuse conducted within.

Australia's treatment of asylum seekers, now known as the Pacific Solution (or the Australian Solution), is fast becoming a major intellectual property export. In August 2022, the UK government's Nationality and Borders Bill received Royal Assent for flights sending their asylum seekers to Rwanda. Denmark has passed a law allowing relocation of asylum seekers outside the European Union and is in talks with Rwanda to strike a similar deal.

The externalisation of border controls by a state seeking to assert its national sovereignty is inherently contradictory. For instance, John Howard announced during the launch of the Australian Liberal Party's 2001 election campaign: 'We will decide who comes to this country and the circumstances in which they come'—yet a short time later, he removed large parts of those borders he'd said he would protect. He did this when he passed legislation that re-defined Christmas Island, Ashmore and Cartier Islands, Cocos (Keeling) Islands and Australian sea and resources installations as well as any other external territories or state or territory islands, as 'excised offshore places'. This legislation was also retrospective.

The objective of excising areas from the Australian migration zone was to ensure that asylum seekers who landed in an excised area were only able to apply for refugee status to the United Nations High Commissioner for Refugees (UNHCR), not to Australia. Suvendrini Perera (2009), a renowned cultural scholar, has commented that the intense focus on the particularities and preciousness of Australia's border has acted as a public performance of sovereignty whilst paradoxically reflecting Australia's 'retraction and dis-location'. Australia is not alone in these tensions, but its response to them is particular to its own history.

The changes wrought by this national failure are not limited to the persecution of asylum seekers. They can also be found in the nation's stalled political capacity: the failure to realise a mature reconciliation with Aboriginal and Torres Strait Islander people as again evidenced by the failure of the referendum on the Voice to Parliament; the apparent inability to take real action to prevent extreme climate change and to create strategies to prevent an ongoing and catastrophic species extinction, desertification, salination of once productive land; and, finally, the historic collapse of trust in institutions. These are political problems emanating from the same shadowland of melancholia.

Devolving into the Paranoid-Schizoid Phase

The next foot to fall as the psyche retreats into the narcissism of melancholia is a devolution into our most primitive psychic state, a state where 'you are either for us or against us'. At the 'for' end of the binary, Klein's concept of introjection goes some way to explaining the development of ascribing to Australians all good values and motives. For instance, when a crisis in the form of wild weather or natural disaster occurs and the community acts to care for and protect those impacted, at some point a reporter or politician will observe that that is what 'Australians' do, as if those of other nationalities do not act in the same way. From the mid-1990s onwards it became apparent that the all-good Australian was in large measure created by the emergence of the all-bad 'un-Australian'. The *Macquarie Dictionary* first included 'un-Australian' in its 2001 federation edition in response, according to its publisher Sue Butler, to a 'burst' of use among politicians such as John Howard and Pauline Hanson (15 March 2005). By 2005 the word had become so widespread that *Macquarie* decided to update the definition in its fourth edition. That year, a Media Monitors survey of metropolitan Australian newspapers found that usage of 'un-Australian' increased from 68 uses in 1995 to 406 in 2000 and 571 in 2005. Joseph Pugliese, a scholar of 'un-Australian Cultural Studies' at Macquarie University, told *The Sydney Morning Herald* that a sense of belonging was at stake and that this 'divisive term, one that's predicated on an "us and them" mentality' was used with the intention to 'to discriminate between individuals and groups that refuse to conform to the dominant culture'.[1]

Philosopher Jessica Whyte points out that exclusion is enshrined in the Australian Constitution, but citizenship is not, a fact 'that gave legal sanction to Australia's mandatory detention regime'. Justice Gaudron from the High Court 'argued that the category of the alien could not necessarily be assumed to be synonymous with "non-citizen", as alien was the more fundamental category. Hence, it can be argued that the decision to declare some people aliens, and hence exclude them, is the decision that enables others to be considered citizens. A citizen in Australia can

---

[1] SMH, 15 March 2005.

therefore be considered a "non-alien". Exclusion precedes belonging' (Gaudron in Whyte, 2008).

An 'alien' to this country can be considered as utterly foreign and unworthy of rights and dignities due on the spectrum of citizenship. Hence, 'un-Australians' are almost non-people who risk sliding into legal oblivion.

The Racist Nature of the Split

Klein believed life came down to a struggle between love and hate and that this was an experiential, visceral struggle. Perhaps that's why Klein was also the first analyst to argue that envy—as opposed to greed and hate—carried the greatest power for destruction.

Envy is associated with anxiety, in the sense that envy and anxiety stand as a barrier to the reconciliation of good and bad in the 'depressive position'. Depressive position is the term Klein gave to the mental constellation the infant eventually achieves when they are able to reconcile the merging of the 'good mother' and 'bad mother'. If the infant is able to bear this merging and establish a whole mother, they begin to care for the welfare of their loved person, the mother integrated. This moment and insight creates remorse, sadness and love because with this new awareness the baby/nation recognises the harm done and the need to make amends for those harms. It is a moment, repeated through life, when the ego's capacity is enlarged and the world is more richly and realistically perceived. Maturation is thus closely linked to loss and mourning.

Arguably, envy compounds the anxiety associated with reparation in the depressive position—the position from which we begin to make amends for harm done. We perceive others as possessing something good that has been stolen from us—jobs, cultures, ways of life. We try to take it back, but we cannot have it all (greed), so we destroy it (envy). In seeking to ethnically cleanse 'others', we are in fact cleansing ourselves, ridding ourselves of the discomfort of envy. Envy drives the racist to destroy the good that he cannot have. The racist, unable to enjoy cultural difference, is a manifestation of envy, making bad what is good and destroying what he cannot have because he is unable to accept and share.

The defence mechanism of splitting explains why—from the state's point of view—it is so imperative that asylum seekers are loaded up with the abject material of Australia's anxiety—anxiety about being 'swamped', about invasion from the north, about losing control of its borders, anxiety that another nation will do to us what the colonisers did to First Nations peoples—before being expelled offshore. Psychoanalyst Robert Hinshelwood noted that Klein viewed projected identification 'as a central mechanism of defense [which] involves splitting the ego and disposing of unwanted parts of the self by projecting them onto a person who is identified as the other and then phantasizing about controlling those parts in the other person' (Hinshelwood, 1998).

Envious projection is how we attempt to overcome anxiety and dread by pushing 'badness' onto someone outside of ourselves. In seeking to control others, we are in fact attempting to gain control over ourselves, ridding ourselves of the discomfort of envy.

This is what the Australian state has been doing since colonisation. Earlier, its projections had been directed at Aboriginal and Torres Strait Islander peoples. When First Nations peoples collectively refused the projection, the colonisers' anxieties were redirected onto asylum seekers: tellingly, they focused on those arriving by boat as had the colonisers. An example of splitting can be seen in a 2019 comment from the then Minister for Home Affairs Peter Dutton, as reported in *The Guardian:*

> Dutton said he was sure that some of the 1,000 or so people from offshore processing who had come to Australia for medical treatment over the years were of 'bad character'. 'I don't think there is any question about that', he said. He would not provide details of those cases, nor would he say what 'bad character' meant. (Davidson, 2019)

Read as splitting in the melancholic state, we see here how melancholia can create a victim mentality in even the most powerful people. In the same interview, the minister further illuminated how splitting can be used to invert the power relationship.

> There are people who have claimed that they've been raped and come to Australia to seek an abortion because they couldn't get an abortion on Nauru. They arrived in Australia and then decided they were not going to

have an abortion. They have the baby here and the moment they step off the plane their lawyers lodge papers in the federal court which injuncts us from sending them back. (Davidson, 2019)

Here one of the most powerful men in Australia is complaining that young women who have experienced unspeakable trauma are controlling the narrative, manipulating and even generating trauma to achieve the near-impossible task of getting out of Nauru and settling in Australia. Rather than Dutton admitting to controlling the story, he splits what he instinctively knows is a negative impulse (because it is his own) and projects malicious control onto a perceived enemy, regardless of any other social dynamics evident on any register. These comments are then normalised in public fora.

This is no accident, nor is it simply clever politics. It is how an anxious nation like Australia manages its dread. A fear of disintegration was roiling to the surface in the closing years of the Keating government. Interrogations of who and what constituted Australia and Australian had mounted along with anxious questions about the validity of the national anthem, national holiday, flag, allegiances and history. There is no doubt many felt this as a shattering of national coherence. Having embarked on the work of mourning the violence of colonisation, but then failing to complete that mourning, Australia needed an Other to carry the unwanted parts of the incoherent nation. The state's projection of the nation's abject material onto asylum seekers, an utterly powerless group of people, was a co-option of the rising anxiety for political purposes. Split-off not just from community but also from humanity, asylum seekers and refugees have been Othered and vilified, loaded up with the abject psychic material of Australia's stillborn mourning and stranded at sea carrying this corrosive cargo.

Putting the Nation on the Couch

I propose that Australia needs to be understood psychoanalytically as well as geopolitically, legally and ideologically to explore this subterranean world. In this book I focus on the psychoanalytic, specifically the movement between mourning and melancholia and the splitting that can result from these psycho-affective terrains. Some may challenge the legitimacy of analysing a nation psychoanalytically in the same way an individual can be understood psychologically. As Judith Butler suggests, 'Nations are not the same as individuals' psyches, but both can be described as "subjects", albeit of different orders' (2004, p. 41). To make sense of the subjects it is important to recognise the 'different orders'. Beginning with the emergence of melancholia as a psycho-affective state,

> There is a growing body of historical, international and sociological literature that examines and reveals the impact melancholia has on social formations, racism and national forgetting. As Freud himself noted (1917), melancholia is a slippery concept, 'whose definition fluctuates even in descriptive psychiatry, takes on various clinical forms the grouping together of which into a single unity does not seem to be established with certainty' Over a century later, the term melancholia is a historically laden term, at times in peril of collapsing under the weight of this history. Diagnosis of an individual suffering melancholia is complex, diagnosing a state, a people, a reaction to historic events such as colonisation and war is even more complex and more prone to slippage between the personal and the political, the clinical and the sociological.

I recognise the danger and the difficulty of the task. But I propose that it is possible to track melancholia—as described by Freud (1917)—as it appears in the acts, the media and the politics of the state and specific communities. It is substantive enough, particular enough, to recognise it and 'diagnose' it. Broadly, this approach follows the work of many others who considered the psychological state of the nation and how it relates to the malady of melancholia.

For instance, the Mitscherlich's *The Inability to Mourn* (1984) is a psychoanalytic exploration of post-war West German melancholic reaction to the loss of Hitler and radical loss of moral legitimacy. The authors track how the German people defended against the guilt, shame and remorse they felt in the aftermath of Nazi atrocities and the death of Hitler. They ask in the opening chapter who is responsible for the horror of Nazi Germany and answer in way that reveals the foundational role played by denial of historic fact in the formation of a national melancholia.

In actual fact all levels of society, and especially those in positions of leadership—that is, industrialists, judges, university professors—had given the regime their decisive and enthusiastic support; yet, with its failure, they regarded themselves as automatically absolved from any personal responsibility (p. 15).

This refusal or inability to mourn for harm done, the dream of a greater Germany destroyed, demanded a forgetting on the part of the nation; by avoiding the hard psychological work of mourning with its confrontation with reality and the brutality held within such a confrontation, the German people were left with a numbing of political, social and creative capacity. In Freudian terms, 'a profoundly painful dejection, cessation of interest in the outside world, loss of the capacity to love' (Freud, 1917, p. 244). They were marooned in a collective narcissism that threatened to strand future generations in this melancholic state. In the end it was the people's capacity to avoid melancholia by nationally 'working through' and remembering the collective complicity with its cargo of shame and remorse. This working through depended on the German people remembering the eagerness with which they fused with the Fuhrer's promises and their own fantasies of omnipotence.

Paul Gilroy's *Postcolonial Melancholia* (2004) uses Freud's work, 'Mourning and Melancholia' and applies it to the collective pathology of neo-imperialism in post-colonial England. He sees melancholia expressing itself in the violence directed against asylum seekers, black citizens and immigrants. But perhaps Gilroy's greatest contribution here is his understanding that the inability to value, even love, the multicultural reality that has sprung up with the tenacity of weeds through the nation's cracks, is also evidence of a melancholic state. Written in 2004 Gilroy would probably not be surprised to see melancholia, with its attendant 'cessation of interest in the outside world, loss of the capacity to love' in the recent decision on the part of the conservative UK government to 'Stop the Boats' and transfer asylum seekers to Rwanda. On the 29th of June 2023, Suella Braverman told MPs she would do 'whatever it takes to stop the boats'. Her comments echo the nasty catch phrase of her Australian counterparts.

It is not only the 'different orders' that make this psychological state contested. Questions about its always-and-every-time negative impact on social formation are challenged in Ranjanna Khanna's book *Dark Continents: Psychoanalysis and Colonialism* (2003); Khanna argues,

> that melancholia emerges from colonialism in a manner that allows critique ... Unlike arguments concerning melancholic affectation, described by Wolf Lepenies, Walter Benjamin, and Wendy Brown as disabling in terms of imagining a politically different future, the affect of melancholia—as theorized by Freud and by Abraham and Torok—points the way toward a political future free of the failures of postcolonial states and misguided biopolitics.

This challenge to the absence of redemption and hope within the melancholic fugue is developed by the work of Wolf Lepenies when he suggests melancholia is the wound that counters 'the Enlightenment impulse to improve the world' (Lepenies, 1992 p. 197). For Lepenies the 'wound' has value in its capacity to challenge the structure, certainty and purity of the Enlightenment. Its value as far as Lepenies is concerned, is the generation of rebellion and critique of happiness. In *Melancholy and Society* (1992), he argues melancholy has played a critical role in galvanising political dissent and traces the emergence of melancholia through the social classes of the Renaissance, the French aristocracy and the middle classes of eighteenth-century Germany. But, *Melancholy and Society* is not a clinical examination of melancholia but rather a social and hypothetical study of melancholia—it is about society, not pathology. It locates the emergence of a kind of miasma of melancholia as classes or people experience a loss of power and relevance. It is the reaction and treatment of loss in a huge variety of settings that drives the state of melancholia.

Tammy Clewell's essay 'Mourning beyond Melancholia' (2004) tracks the development of Freud's thinking as he reflects on the cultural ideals lost by the war in 'Thoughts for the Times' (1915). She observes that Freud, confronted by the loss of ideals of progress, humanity's capacity to curb its own violence and transcend national boundaries, does not turn to mourning as a way to explain it as he did in 'On Transience'. Rather he takes a new line of thought suggesting all these ideals 'were based on an illusion to which we had given way. In reality our fellow citizens have not sunk so low as we feared, because they had never risen so high as we believed' (p. 285).

So, the nature and boundaries of melancholia are contested. While I acknowledge the depth and breadth of previous scholarship, for the purposes of this book—and because I am drawing specifically on the work of Freud found in his paper, 'Mourning and Melancholia' (1917)—it is legitimate to use his 1917 work and the parameters of that paper to trace Australia's development psychologically in this state. Because I am using that paper, and in contrast to Khanna and Lepenines, I see no way to read melancholia as a positive or potentially transformative state. The opposite seems true as Freud describes melancholia with its stuck, narcissistic state full of profoundly painful dejection and lack of love.

Overcoming Melancholia

Behrouz Boochani, a Kurdish-Iranian journalist who was held by Australia for four years in offshore detention in Papua New Guinea (PNG), wrote from Manus Island Detention Centre amidst protests that caused the camp's closure in 2017:

> We have reminded a majority of the Australian public that throughout their history they have only ever imagined that their democracy and freedom has been created on the basis of principles of humanity.
>
> If a majority of Australians were to reflect deeply on our resistance and sympathise with us, they would come to realise something about how they imagined themselves to be until now. They would undergo a kind of self-realisation regarding their illusions of moral superiority. And they would be forced to self-analyse in relation to the principles and values they hold dear at this point in time and realise that they are not connected to a mythical moral past.

Prime Minister Anthony Albanese's election in 2022 was considered by many to be a portent of hope, an occasion alive with promise. On 21 May 2022, Albanese began his federal election victory speech with an

Acknowledgement of Country and a commitment to the Uluru Statement from the Heart.[2] The Labor Party's win came after three years of the Covid-19 pandemic, and after devastating bushfires (2019–2020) and historic floods (early 2022). These had been years of death and dying. They had also seen growing numbers of protests for women's safety and equality, for an end to Aboriginal and Torres Strait Islander deaths in custody, and for action to avert a climate crisis. The fall of Afghanistan to the Taliban in 2021, and war between Russia and Ukraine, again raised the possibility for new Australian approaches to providing asylum. How might we read these years? These political protests may be a harbinger of the reality of historical and world events returning to the purview of the Australian electorate. But if that is so, how do we understand the loss of the 'Yes' vote? How do we understand the Labor government maintaining an immigration policy that has produced worldwide censure and disgust? And in the closing months of 2024, how do we make sense of the Albanese-Labor government passing the most brutal and extreme anti-asylum seeker legislation yet (see Human Rights Law Centre)?[3]

As a nation, we are still caught in the grip of a malignant melancholia that forestalls deep and restorative change. The seduction of melancholia, of a relaxed and comfortable life built on lies, is compelling. One of the many problems with splitting is that the nation is impoverished by the process: it makes Australia a shallow, narcissistic state capable of extreme abuse. Twenty-odd years after inventing the Pacific Solution I had hoped that we might find our way back to mourning, to the erotic vitality that is unleashed as the truth of Australia's colonisation is revealed. It is my hope that we may become a nation that refuses to treat the most vulnerable with cruelty and contempt; that it is possible for Australia to stop torturing asylum seekers, and finally live in right relationship with First Nations peoples and the country itself. But for me to hope for a possible return to the nation-building project of mourning and, in the process, again become capable of imagination and empathy and love, I have to acknowledge that to return to the Australia of the 1970s to 1990s is to again become becalmed and stranded in a melancholia that dominates

---

[2] https://ulurustatement.org/the-statement/view-the-statement/
[3] https://www.hrlc.org.au/reports-news-commentary/2024/11/8/deportation-surveillance

today. In the end to believe in the possibility of mourning is to accept I have no idea where this may take us even as I know that the journey into not-knowing is vital if we are to recover from this schism in the soul of the nation.

References

Allam, L., & Evershed, N. (2019, March 4). The killing times: The massacres of Aboriginal people Australia must confront. *The Guardian*. https://www.theguardian.com/australia-news/2019/mar/04/the-killing-times-the-massacres-of-aboriginal-people-australia-must-confront
Anderson, B. (1983). *Imagined communities: Reflections on the origin and spread of nationalism*. Verso Books.
Butler, J. (2004). *Precarious life: The powers of mourning and violence*. Verso.
Bollas, C. (2017). *The shadow of the object: Psychoanalysis of the unthought known*. Taylor & Francis Group.
Boochani, B. (2017, December 9–15). A letter from Manus Island. The Saturday Paper. https://www.thesaturdaypaper.com.au/news/politics/2017/12/09/letter-manus-reynoldsisland/15127380005617
Clewell, T. (2004). Mourning beyond melancholia: Freud's psychoanalysis of loss. *Journal of the American Psychoanalytic Association, 52*(1), 43–67.
Davidson, H. (2019, June 20). Peter Dutton says women using rape and abortion claims as ploy to get to Australia. *The Guardian*. https://www.theguardian.com/australia-news/2019/jun/20/peter-dutton-says-women-using-and-abortion-claims-as-ploy-to-get-to-australia
Freud, S. (1957). Mourning and melancholia. In J. Strachey (Ed.), *The standard edition of the complete psychological works of Sigmund Freud* (Vol. XIV, pp. 237–258). Hogarth Press. (Original work published 1917).
Gilroy, P. (2004). *Postcolonial Melancholia*. Columbia University Press.
Hinshelwood, R. D. (1998). *A dictionary of Kleinian thought*. Free Association Books.
Howard, J. (2001, November 2). *Address at the launch of 'a stronger Tasmania policy'*. PM Transcripts: Transcripts from the Prime Ministers of Australia. Department of the Prime Minister and Cabinet. https://pmtranscripts.pmc.gov.au/release/transcript-12332
Khanna, R. (2003). *Dark continents: Psychoanalysis and colonialism*. Duke University Press.

Lepenies, W. (1992) *Melancholy and society.* Harvard University Press, 1992. *Social Forces, 72*(3), 906–907. The University of North Carolina Press. https://doi.org/10.1093/sf/72.3.906

Mitscherlich, A., & Mitscherlich, M. (1984). *The inability to mourn.* Grove Press.

Perera, S. (2009). *Australia and the insular imagination: Beaches, borders, boats and bodies.* Palgrave Macmillan.

Sedgwick, E. K. (2007). Melanie Klein and the difference affect makes. *South Atlantic Quarterly, 106*(3), 625–642. https://doi.org/10.1215/00382876/2007/020

Whyte, J. (2008). Its silent working was a delusion. In J. Clemens, N. Heron, & A. Murray (Eds.), *The work of Giorgio Agamben: Law literature life* (pp. 66–81). Edinburgh University Press.

3

A Dream in Three Parts: A Nation in Pieces (1778–1972)

The following is a waking dream Professor Judy Atkinson (2003), a woman of Jiman, Bundjalung and Celtic-German descent, recorded in 1993. It transported the dreamer back to the time of Australia's colonisation.

> Then I saw my great-grannie and grannie, sitting with many other old, old women whom I did not know. They beckoned to me to come to them. So, I went through the throng of people to where they were sitting. We began to talk. I was so happy to see them but I could feel a great sadness around them and in them. I went into their sadness and suddenly – suddenly, we were in another time and another place, and we were running, running in terror through the bush, running in terror from the thundering horses and the guns of the white men. Tremendous fear – tremendous terror. I now know what it feels like to be a hunted animal with no place to hide … Exhaustion … We couldn't run any more. Crawling under scrub, scrub that had been our home, our heart place, our nurturing companion over many lifetimes, to hide and rest. After a while as we lay in our terror, I heard a voice … my voice. 'The children! The children … Where are the children?' In the terror of our flight, we had lost our children. And so … we women began to look for our children. The children, our lifeblood, our

spiritline, representing our future generations. Such intense sorrow, such a depth of pain, as one by one we found our children ... broken ... ravished (sic)... wounded ... the children, the children ... searching, searching ... We found our children, battered ... bloodied ... crushed ... violated. Gathering them to us, gathering them to us. And so ... we women began our grieving for our children, with our children.

It is fitting to begin this chapter with a dreamscape littered by broken bodies past and future—with howls of pain and shattered hearts. Australia's colonisation was bloody. Ignoring that reality has led to a multitude of wrongs. But before I continue, it is important to acknowledge that approaching the condition of one's soul or one's nation psychoanalytically is a brave and sometimes desperate path to take. It's usually taken when other ways of understanding pain, cruelty and loss have been inadequate. Often, at the outset of the journey, there is a quiet, unspoken hope on the part of the patient that psychoanalysis will deliver a degree of control and agency. The cool, shimmering mirage of insight and independence beckons. Sadly, psychological authenticity is rarely elegant or linear, or past. It is almost always buried in the blood and tears, scorched earth and shattered relationships of an ever-present past—in this case, our personal past and our nation's.

As Professor Atkins' dream demonstrates, mourning is an embodied and messy business of sorrow and lostness. Despite the years that pass, it is always in the present—a present comprised of past and future as time folds in on itself. It is relational and finds expression in love and curiosity, in performance and ritual, and in the groaning incoherence of pain. Mourning will not be contained as it bleeds into our dreams and waking lives. It will eventually be heard and seen. Indeed, the bloody footprints of Australia's colonisation make it possible to track powerful affective states through the last two hundred and thirty years and to identify where they diverge from the energy of mourning to the inertia of melancholia.

Modern Australia's melancholia, its most recent expression being the rejection of the Indigenous Voice to Parliament, began with denial of the violence of colonisation and the losses wrought upon First Nations peoples by colonising forces and subsequent generations of settlers. As Judith Butler (2002) argues in *Antigone's Claim*, 'where there is no public

3 A Dream in Three Parts: A Nation in Pieces (1778–1972)   35

recognition or discourse through which such [losses] might be named and mourned, then melancholia takes on cultural dimensions'. I am proposing that there is a psychological relationship between the violence and torture carried out in the colonisation of Australia and the country's cruel and inhumane treatment of refugees and asylum seekers: that the failure to mourn the first has given rise to the second. This link was illustrated by Professor Lowitja O'Donoghue, a Yankunytjatjara woman, at a public forum in Adelaide in 2003, where she spoke as an Aboriginal Elder and as parental figure to some young asylum seekers on temporary protection visas (TPVs).

> I have heard their stories. I have felt their pain. So, it's also as an adopted 'mother' that I speak. The pain of some of my friends – some families and 'my boys' – is not unlike the pain of my own people. How is it that this nation's First Peoples, and its last peoples, should suffer similar indignity? Is it why they share the same Minister in Federal Government. Sorry Minister! Sorry Prime Minister! But I smell something rather more sinister in the air.

Crystal McKinnon (2020), Amangu woman, historian and a critical Indigenous studies scholar from the Yamatji Nation, argues that when considering the experiences of people seeking asylum alongside the experiences of Indigenous people, the breadth of the carceral colonial state is revealed.

> To see contemporary practices of incarceration and detention of asylum seekers as exceptional removes them from the historical and contemporary context of global systems of imperialism and racial capital, which have made people refugees and asylum seekers and forced people to flee their homes. It removes the local context and histories too, erasing the ongoing colonial violence against Indigenous people.

To track that process from 'this nation's First Peoples, and its last peoples' I take up the red string offered by Ariadne in one hand and curiosity in the other to enter the labyrinth of our own national psyche and go in search of the Minotaur, a monster of our own creation and our own monstrousness. Like string, this psychoanalytic frame at times feels frighteningly insubstantial. But, also like string, it may take us to a place where we begin to understand what we have done to the 'Other', and to our own capacity to love and imagine and grieve.

It is a string entwined with Freud's understanding of mourning and melancholia, with Klein's knotty insight into the management of terror by an infant nation (see Chap. 2) and a string dyed red by Judith Butler's invocation of the politics of mourning and melancholia as embodied and public (see also Chap. 8). As Butler (2002) argues, 'where there is no public recognition or discourse through which such [losses] might be named and mourned, then melancholia takes on cultural dimensions' (p. 171). But before entering the labyrinth the string must be anchored deeply in the reality of a violent colonisation that now spans over two hundred years.

A word of caution is important at this point. As observed by Dr. Liam Gillespie, Lecturer in Criminology at the School of Social and Political Sciences in a personal communication, it is not possible—and is assimilationist—to attempt to apply a Western, psychoanalytic theory of mourning to First Nations peoples' mourning of dislocation from country. Aboriginal and Torres Strait Islander people subscribe (and subscribed) to entirely different ontologies, epistemologies and ethical systems. These cannot be subsumed or understood through Freudian psychoanalysis or Klein's object relations because the ideas that underpin Western notions of loss and objects are fundamentally incommensurate with Indigenous ontologies, subjectivities and connection to country and waters, which are relational in an entirely different way.

The starting point is itself occupying almost dimensionally different space. Moreton-Robinson's account of the logics of 'the white possessive' (2015) sketches the outline of those differences.

The ontological incommensurables between the concepts of Indigenous sovereignties and state sovereignty reside in two different epistemologies. In its transition from the divine to the secular, patriarchal White sovereignty is artificial, it is not predestined nor is it immutable, and its ontological and epistemological reach does not control Mother Earth and her resilient existents, Indigenous sovereignties (Moreton-Robinson, 2021, p. 267).

Was It Genocide?

However, in the story of Australia the starting point is colonial violence. The fact that martial force was applied on Aboriginal and Torres Strait Islander peoples with the arrival of colonising British forces in 1778 is not generally contested. However, the nature, intention and extent of the death and destruction have been persistently queried. Was it so violent, deliberate and sweeping as to constitute genocide? It was not, according to the British forces that first occupied the country, or to Archie Cameron, Liberal Member for Barker, in the 1949 parliamentary debate on Australia's ratification of the Convention on the Prevention and Punishment of the Crime of Genocide:

> No one in his *[sic]* right senses believes that the Commonwealth of Australia will be called before the bar of public opinion, if there is such a thing, and asked to answer for any of the things which are enumerated in this convention.

Cameron's opinion is shared by former Prime Minister John Howard (term of office 1996–2007), who at the 1997 Australian Reconciliation Convention described Australia's founding colonial aggressions as mere historical 'blemishes'. Historian Patrick Wolfe (2006) argues that 'the primary motive for elimination is not race (or religion, ethnicity, grade of civilisation, etc.) but access to territory', and as historian Jan Kociumbas (2004, p. 99) notes, 'this land has long been painted by historians as the "quiet continent", its indigenes dreamily awaiting discovery by the civilized British'. Further, the very idea of genocide has seemed preposterous in context of the British Empire in the eighteenth century: an expanding wonderland of modernity and Enlightenment.

However, many others, including the Australian Human Rights Commission, describe it as genocide. First Nations scholar Professor Larissa Behrendt reasons that by the early 1900s, genocidal, state-sanctioned massacres had reduced the First Nations population from an estimated 1–1.5 million before invasion to less than 100,000 (Miller et al., 2012, p. 175). Such massacres were investigated by *Guardian* reporters Loreena Allam and Nick Evershed in the 2019 article 'The

Killing Times', and included dawn raids (Allam & Evershed, 2019) and the deliberate poisoning of flour and waterholes (Lydon, 1996). The combination of gun and horse, previously unknown on the continent, and the arrival of ever more British troops and convicts, meant that Aboriginal and Torres Strait Islander resistance was overwhelmed. Secondary effects of the massacres further reduced the populations. Introduced diseases such as measles, whooping cough, influenza, tuberculosis and smallpox, previously unknown in the Aboriginal and Torres Strait Islander population, wiped out whole communities. The 1845 parliamentary *Report from the Select Committee on the Condition of the Aborigines*[1] details the impact of the sexual abuse of Aboriginal women and children by White settlers, and how this resulted in widespread venereal diseases, sterility and deaths after just sixty years of colonisation.

Taking children—some being only infants—from their parents, families and communities was another very effective strategy employed by the colonial powers, and it is an ongoing practice. *Bringing Them Home*, a 1997 report from the National Inquiry into the Separation of Aboriginal and Torres Strait Islander Children from their Families, states that

> when a child was forcibly removed that child's entire community lost, often permanently, its chance to perpetuate itself in that child. The inquiry concluded that this was a primary objective of forcible removals and is the reason they amount to genocide. ... The Australian practice of Indigenous child removal involved both systematic racial discrimination and genocide as defined by international law. Yet it continued to be practised as official policy long after being clearly prohibited by treaties to which Australia had voluntarily subscribed.

When *Bringing Them Home* was released in 1997, Aboriginal and Torres Strait Islander children represented one in every five children living in out-of-home care. Today they are one in every three.[2] The Inquiry heard

---

[1] The report, published by the New South Wales Legislative Council, can be viewed at https://hunterlivinghistories.com/wp-content/uploads/2018/01/1845-condition-of-the-aborigines.pdf

[2] In 2018–2019, 51,500 Indigenous children received child protection services, a rate of 156 per 1000 Indigenous children—an increase from 42,900 or 134 per 1000 in 2014–2015. The number and rate of Indigenous children in out-of-home care also increased from 15,500 to 18,000, and from 48 to 54 per 1000 Indigenous children. Australian Institute of Health and Welfare.

confidential evidence from people around the country, including this person in Tasmania who was placed in state care in 1936 at two months of age:

> It would have been lovely to have known a father and a mother, to know parents even for a little while, just to have had the opportunity of having a mother tuck you into bed and give you a good-night kiss – but it was never to be. (Confidential evidence 65)

The intergenerational trauma and isolation grinds down through the years in the lives of Aboriginal and Torres Strait Islander people.

Some estimates of the cost in lives of those frontier wars are relatively vague, for instance, in this account given by historian Henry Reynolds (2006, p. 126):

> For the continent as a whole it is reasonable to suppose that at least 20,000 Aborigines were killed as a direct result of conflict with the settlers. Secondary effects of the invasion – disease, deprivation, disruption – were responsible for the premature deaths of many more although it is almost impossible to arrive at a realistic figure.

The colonisers may have lost count—or have decided quite literally that these deaths did not count—but Aboriginal and Torres Strait Islander people knew their living and their dead. Massacres (Allam & Evershed, 2019), dawn raids, poisoning flour and waterholes (Lydon, 1996), the theft of land, children and culture are all part of the history of British colonisation of Australia.

Long before Western scholarship began investigating the public and performative nature of mourning (e.g. Butler, 2004, 2005, 2009; Derrida, 1994; Honig, 2001, 2009; Stow, 2011; Zizek, 2000). Rona Glynn-McDonald (2019), a Kaytetye woman from Central Australia and CEO of Common Ground, describes the collective nature of Sorry Business:

> Aboriginal and Torres Strait Islander societies are based around the concept of community rather than the individual. This means that an experience of

loss impacts whole communities just as much as the individuals within them. For First Nations people, overcoming grief is a unique and complex process. It seeks to ensure that as a community we can move past death and commemorate those we have lost with consideration and celebration.

It is beyond the scope of this book to investigate Sorry Business more closely, especially as the writer is not Indigenous—but it could be that the spiritual, psychological and communal strength derived from honouring Sorry Business forms a central plank in the ongoing resistance to the continuing colonisation of Australia. Sorry Business obligations call kin home to family and Country, time and time again, and in this way relationships and ceremony are kept alive even under occupation and dislocation.

The Australian National Mental Health Commission (NMHC) states that '[g]rief and loss remain at the heart of the life experience of Aboriginal people and communities, and we need to authentically acknowledge this' (NMHC, 2013, p. 3). This may explain why, in 1938, Aboriginals and Torres Strait Islanders called for a national day that officially recognised the need to mourn as a whole country. On 26 January 1938, while most Australians were celebrating one hundred and fifty years of colonisation, a group of First Nations women and men gathered at Australia Hall in Sydney and announced the following document and resolution.

> WE, representing THE ABORIGINES OF AUSTRALIA, assembled in Conference at the Australian Hall, Sydney, on the 26th day of January, 1938, this being the 150th Anniversary of the whitemen's seizure of our country, HEREBY MAKE PROTEST against the callous treatment of our people by the whitemen during the past 150 years, AND WE APPEAL to the Australian Nation of today to make new laws for the education and care of Aborigines, and we ask for a new policy which will raise our people to FULL CITIZENS STATUS and EQUALITY WITHIN THE COMMUNITY. (Australian Institute of Aboriginal and Torres Strait Islander Studies, 2021, capitalisation in original)

The institution of this first Day of Mourning was the culmination of years of work by the Australian Aborigines League (AAL) and the

Aborigines Progressive Association (APA).³ Over the following eighty years, Aboriginals and Torres Strait Islanders have continued to recognise the need to conduct the ceremony and protocols of Sorry Business: to mourn the loss of family, children, country, language, culture and history.

This mourning accepts the acute reality of death. It does not attempt to deny the past or to minimise the pain of it by occluding the love between the surviving and the dead. Butler's (2004) critique of Freud's concept of mourning is that Freud saw a process of substitution rather than transformation. Aboriginal and Torres Strait Islander grief is indeed a process of ongoing transformation throughout the decades, building a body of work and power and lifefullness; it harnesses the inherently political nature of public and communal performance. The healing achieved by mourning is centred in relationships and relatedness to the community, country. In this place the truth of dependency on family, community and nation is like breath: it is taken in and let out in a shared vulnerability.

Denial, Disappearance and the 'Great Australian Silence'

When anthropologist Bill Stanner (2009) used the term 'the great Australian silence' in his 1968 Boyer Lectures to describe the omission of Aboriginal and Torres Strait Islander voices from the historical account of colonisation, he observed, 'the native question is rising into great importance, the melancholy footnote is turning into a whole chapter of Australian history, and the codicil is becoming a major theme in the Australian story' (2009, p. 176). I suggest there are two problems with his observation. The first is that 'the great Australian silence' was on the side

---

³ The Australian Aborigines' League was established in Melbourne in 1933 by William Cooper, Margaret Tucker, Eric Onus and others. In a letter to the editor of the *West Australian* newspaper (22 November 1938, p. 9), Cooper wrote 'The plea of our league is a fair deal for the dark race'. The League campaigned for the repeal of discriminatory legislation and for programmes to 'uplift the aboriginal race'. The Aborigines Progressive Association, an all-Aboriginal body, was formed in 1937 in New South Wales with Jack Patten as president and Bill Ferguson as secretary. It had three aims: full citizenship rights for Aboriginal Australians, Aboriginal representation in parliament and abolition of the New South Wales Aborigines' Protection Board (National Museum of Australia).

of White Australia as noted by scholars Frances Peters-Little, Ann McGrath, Ingereth Macfarlane (Peters-Little et al., 2006) who found 'many non-Indigenous historians have been so focussed upon revising and interpreting the Indigenous "silences" of the official archival records that they have not heard the racket being made by Indigenous artists, performers, biographers, poets, filmmakers and even footballers and their spectators'. Silence may be, as it were, in the ear of the beholder.

With chilling similarities to the treatment of refugees and asylum seekers, this silence was made possible by removing Aboriginal and Torres Strait Islander people to far-flung missions beyond the ken of most urban Australians.

Second, the proverbial 'melancholy footnote' can be more accurately psychoanalytically interpreted as referring to a melancholia within White Australia than one within Aboriginal and Torres Strait Islander peoples. As Freud observed, the most notable difference between mourning and melancholia is that the mourner does not deny a death's solemnity, whereas the melancholic person begins from the premise of denial—minimising the death in the sense that 'yes, they died, but I didn't love them very much'. Early in the emergence of this modern state of Australia, the psychological paths of First Nations and colonisers diverged.

The denial that is a precondition of melancholia began in Australia with the arrival of Captain James Cook and his undertaking to disappear the roughly two hundred and fifty Indigenous nations who inhabited the lands at the time. Having sailed three thousand kilometres along the mainland's east coast and undoubtedly seen Aboriginal people as he stopped for water and repairs, he stood on a smaller island in the north, opposite what is now called Cape York and, with a volley of gunfire, claimed possession of the entire continent. He was lauded in European history as the man who 'discovered' Australia from that day on. To 'discover' a land already inhabited ignores any conception of Indigenous sovereignty.

The colonisation and ongoing settlement of Australia was made possible by the denial of Aboriginal and Torres Strait Islander people and the British occupation of the land. A freeman, John Batman, attempted to establish a treaty in order to buy land from First Nations people in what became known as Port Phillip. New South Wales governor Sir Richard

Bourke quashed his attempt with the Proclamation of Terra Nullius issued by the Colonial Office on 10 October 1835. This meant in effect all people—including Aboriginal and Torres Strait Islander people—found occupying land without the authority of the government would be considered illegal trespassers. The proclamation canonised and reinforced the lie that the land had been nobody's before it was 'discovered' and effectively ethnically cleansed by the British.

Two and a half centuries later, Australia's sovereignty is still unsettled and fragile. We might imagine what Australia would be like today if the British had sought and managed to make a high-level treaty that recognised the First Nations custodians of this land and incorporated their existing practices and laws in collaboratively stewarding this country. It is conceivable that not one single element of current Australian politics would be the same. It is possible to imagine this primarily because First Nations peoples understanding of ownership and sovereignty does not turn on 'discovery', but on integration. The Uluru Statement from the Heart (2017) says:

> This sovereignty is a spiritual notion: the ancestral tie between the land, or 'mother nature', and the Aboriginal and Torres Strait Islander peoples who were born therefrom, remain attached thereto, and must one day return thither to be united with our ancestors. This link is the basis of the ownership of the soil, or better, of sovereignty. It has never been ceded or extinguished and co-exists with the sovereignty of the Crown.

British colonisers did not have a language, let alone a cultural point of reference, by which to comprehend or welcome such a sophisticated and profound concept of sovereignty.

Australian Stories: Colonial Myth

There is no doubt that early British colonisers of Australia felt anxiety and existential dread about being exiled to a place so completely foreign and hostile to them. White Australia's state of melancholia can be detected as emerging since the very early days of colonisation. Convicts, misfits, soldiers and adventurers, these colonisers were often the last, the lost and the least of the British Empire. Now, for many different reasons, they were stranded far from home.

As an individual's psyche is revealed by what they do and think, the Australian nation's subjectivity is revealed by the stories it tells about itself. It is worth investigating how far these stories deviate from 'reality' and how they instruct us in what Australia allows and accepts in its treatment of Others. Evidence of the nation's dominant psychological condition can be seen in its political campaigns and health campaigns, and in the now-constant use of the terms 'un-Australian' and 'Australian values'. Melancholia is prevalent in what the majority of Australians remember and what is forgotten, what is valorised and what is disdained; these are sustained and supported by 'Australian stories'.

Unlike in other British colonies, in Australia colonial anxiety was not solely focused on original inhabitants but was also projected onto the landscape itself. The fear of being lost, disappeared or devoured by the Australian bush is explored in Peter Pierce's 1999 book *The Country of Lost Children: An Australian Anxiety*, which traces through art, literature and media 'the apprehensions of [Anglo-European settlers] about having sought to settle in a place where they might never be at peace' (pp. xi–xii). Art historian Iain McLean (1998) sees this irredeemable lack of peace in the works of D.H. Lawrence, for whom the land itself was stricken and 'the spirit of the place' evoked 'the icy sensation of terror',

> so phantom-like, so ghostly ... so deathly still ... the tree trunks like naked pale aborigines among the dark-soaked foliage ... Not a sign of life — not a vestige. Yet something. Something big and aware and hidden! ... there was something among the trees ... a presence. He looked at the weird, white, dead trees, and into the hollow distances of the bush. (p. 8 -9)

This dismal state weaves its way also through the writings of Patrick White, for instance, in his novels *The Aunt's Story*, *Happy Valley* and *Tree of Man* in which

3 A Dream in Three Parts: A Nation in Pieces (1778–1972)

melancholy operates to undercut the readers' identification with cultural chauvinism and white mythmaking ... Melancholies are famously aware of the moral failings of the self, and in White's oeuvre we find remarkably acute analyses of the failings of the self as nation. White's genius does not reside in the often berating and castigating voice of the narrator – in itself a melancholic flagellation – but in a melancholy sustained in multiple registers that exposes the national self as faltering at every turn. (Rutherford, 2010, p.128)

Australian melancholy was the subject of a 2015 exhibition *Weird Melancholy: The Australian Gothic* at the Potter Museum of Art, for which curator Suzette Wearne borrowed the title from novelist Marcus Clarke's famous description of the Australian outback. Clarke's writings are imbued with this gloom: his short story 'Holiday Peak' (1896) opens with a narrator riding with barely contained, 'indescribable' dread through 'white, bare, and ghastly gums ... lonely pools begirt with shivering reeds and haunted by the melancholy bittern'. Australian melancholy can be seen in films like *Picnic at Hanging Rock* (Peter Weir, 1975) and *Wolf Creek* (Greg McLean, 2005)—such films act out the colonial fear of never belonging and the feeling of being severed from the landscape, the former film through the oft-repeated nineteenth-century trope of the lost Australian child. Ross Gibson's book *Seven Versions of an Australian Badland* (2002) picks up this underlying fear of the country by probing the idea that places can become repositories of 'bad' people and bad ghosts. Foreshadowing the future creation of offshore immigration camps as places of not-Australia, Gibson wrote:

> Thus arose the image of the central Queensland Badlands, a no-go area for White Australia, a tract which, like the dead centre, could be cordoned off from sociability and everyday consciousness; a tract of Australia which was paradoxically and usefully not-Australia. (2002, pp. 169–170)

As will be made clear in Chap. 9, these contemporary places of excision and detention take on an even more haunting duplicity by being constructed on traditional Aboriginal lands.

Splitting the Nation, Killing the (m)Other

Melancholia is not only a state of denial of reality, and therefore shallow and lacking vitality, it is also a stuck, primitive state of psychological development. In Klein's work into the infant paranoid-schizoid phase, she describes infants as terrorised by life's complexity, ambiguity and threat, and as managing to split off psycho-affective parts of themselves to manage this terror. Klein saw the psychological world as being fluid, one of positions rather than a fixed state. And as the name suggests, the position is constructed by defences, attitudes that change throughout life. But it would be wrong to assume the patient/nation moves from one state to another in an ascent of maturation and insight. In Klein's world the paranoid-schizoid position was always available and if the nation/patient was put under enough pressure—real or imagined—this splitting would re-emerge. This is what happened in Australia.

This psycho-affective state, and the splitting that manifested through it, played itself out politically and culturally. One of the complexities and dangers of splitting off the 'bad' or unwanted parts of the psyche is that the splitting will continue as more aspects/people are sliced off in pursuit of safety and stability. Having effectively disappeared Aboriginal and Torres Strait Islander people and secured ownership of the continent in its entirety, the purge of the other non-Anglo people picked up in pace and politics. This was a purge managed by splitting off the abjected material of early colonial life—the disease, promiscuity and 'foreignness' onto non-Anglo arrivals such as Chinese miners. The riots at Lambing Flats are an example and an event that both embodied and inspired the desire for a White Australia and a White Australia policy. As historian Karen Schamberger explained to *The Guardian* (Harris, 2018),

> [In] the broader mentality of settler colonialism, the way that the colonies were settled, you had to get rid of Aboriginal people, and you had to dominate the landscape in such a way that nothing else was going to challenge your authority. So when there were people who were clearly different, who worked in ways that European miners didn't understand, who were successful in ways that made them envious, they had to demonise them. (Schamberger in Harris, 2018)

The Lambing Flat riots were a series of violent anti-Chinese demonstrations that took place in the Burrangong region of New South Wales (now a four-hour drive from Sydney) from 1860 to 1861. They occurred on the goldfields at Spring Creek, Stoney Creek, Back Creek, Wombat, Blackguard Gully, Tipperary Gully and Lambing Flat. They culminated in a catastrophic attack on Chinese miners.

> On the day of the largest riot, over 3,000 Australian, European-born and American miners marched from Tipperary Gully through different goldfields. They cut off the queue [pigtails] from Chinese miners, scalped some of them. They burnt the Chinese miners' tents, brutalised them. (Schamberger in Harris, 2018)

Like so many other 'ungrievable' deaths (Butler, 2004 [see Chapter 7]), the number of Chinese miners killed is not known. Only one rioter was convicted, and two unconvicted rioters were later elected to parliament. The riots were used as a basis for the first Act of Parliament in the newly federated nation: the *Immigration Restriction Act 1901*, better known as the White Australia policy.[4] The Australian Constitution (1900) that enabled the Act included a statement that denied the human existence of First Nations people—'Aborigines not to be counted in reckoning population'—and provided that the Commonwealth would legislate for any race except Australia's Indigenous.

The Melancholic Narrative Falters and Mourning Breaks Through

Butler (2003, p. 469) pinpoints a schism between the mourning and melancholic states by referencing Walter Benjamin:

---

[4] Decisions around who and what constituted 'White' would be revisited after the Second World War, when Britain began to discourage British citizens from emigrating as they were needed in Britain to rebuild the war-torn country. Desperate for workers for the same reason, the Australian Government expanded its White Australia policy by allowing some migration of 'displaced persons' (due to war) from Europe. Baltic people were the first group chosen as they were reassuringly fair-skinned and fitted White Australian aesthetic ideals. Australia's first immigration minister, Arthur Calwell, scoured post-war Europe for these potential workers whom he characterised as 'Beautiful Balts'. Around 170,000 Baltic immigrants arrived in Australia between 1947 and 1952.

In The Origin of German Tragic Drama, Benjamin explains that a certain problem of loss emerges when established narratives begin to falter, suggesting that narrative functioned once as a way of containing loss.

It is not really possible to pinpoint the exact date the narrative began to falter and bend. Was it the gravitational force of Aboriginal and Torres Strait Islander people's capacity to resist, to hold on to reality, to keep reminding the nation of the truth of colonisation that gave White Australia the strength to begin to face the past?

Certainly, the reality of Australia's violent colonisation kept materialising through the frontier wars and political and cultural performances of political activism and resistance. The foundation of the Aboriginal League in 1933, the 1963 Yirrkala bark petitions[5] and the Freedom Ride were all moments when the real events of colonisation and discrimination were spoken and chronicled aloud against the denial of White Australia. The Freedom Ride 1965 was a bus tour of western and coastal towns across New South Wales, organised by a group of students from the University of Sydney. They planned to draw public attention to the poor state of Aboriginal health, education and housing. The students had formed into a body called Student Action for Aborigines (SAFA) in 1964 in order to plan this fifteen-day trip and ensure media coverage. Charles Perkins, an Arrernte and Kalkadoon man born in Alice Springs and an arts student at the university, was the elected president of SAFA. Jim Spigelman, one of the students on the Freedom Ride, told the BBC years later of its potency and impact.

> This was the first-time indigenous affairs had been front-page news in Australia on a more or less continuous basis for a few weeks … It convinced a very wide section of the public that things were very, very bad in the treatment of indigenous Australians, both in terms of their poverty and also in terms of active discrimination. (Spigelman in Perkins, 1975)

---

[5] On 13 March 1963 the Australian Government took more than three hundred square kilometres of land from the Yolngu people in Arnhem Land so that mining company Gominco could extract bauxite. Work started without talking to these people about their land. Requesting an inquiry and asserting their ownership of the land, the Yolngu created petitions using painted designs to proclaim Yolngu law, depicting traditional relations to land. Inside the painted frame they added typed text in English and Gumatj languages. These petitions were the first petitions to use traditional forms and combine bark painting with text typed on paper. The Yolngu sent the petitions to the Commonwealth Parliament in August 1963 (Korff, 2020a).

3 A Dream in Three Parts: A Nation in Pieces (1778–1972)   49

Following the Freedom Ride and its nationwide publicity, the 1967 referendum proposed to include Aboriginal people in the National Census and to allow the Commonwealth Government to make laws for Aboriginal people (Korff, 2020b). Unlike the referendum for a Voice to Parliament in 2023, this referendum was successful and First Nations peoples were given the vote.

These are all legitimate sites of the foundering of the national narrative of denial, but another important site is the Wave Hill Walk-off. On 20 August 1966, Vincent Lingiari led a walk-off of two hundred Gurindji, Mudburra and Warlpiri workers from Wave Hill cattle station in the Northern Territory of Australia, a moment immortalised in Kev Carmody and Paul Kelly's song *From Little Things Big Things Grow*. After fighting to get their land back for nine years, in 1975 the prime minister arrived out of a clear blue sky to speak and treat with Lingiari, a Traditional Owner of the land, and to authorise the return of a portion of it to the Gurindji nation.

An iconic photograph was taken of this meeting by the first Indigenous press photographer, Mervyn Bishop. The image of Prime Minister Gough Whitlam—a physically imposing man who arrived in the sweltering Northern Territory wearing a well-cut suit—carefully pouring red sand into the weathered hands of slightly built Lingiari to signify the transfer of land title is evocative and powerful. Together these two men captured a spirit of change and movement in the hearts and minds of non-Indigenous Australia: this symbolic transfer of earth was the beginning of the end of the foundational lie of Australia's colonisation. In this moment it is possible to see a loosening of the stranglehold of melancholic denial and disavowal. The myth of *Terra Nullius* is symbolically rendered dead by the gesture of transferring land *back* to Aboriginal people. Reality, in its vitality and chaos and creativity, is re-established and 'reality testing' is underway. As Whitlam poured the red dirt, he said:

> Vincent Lingiari I solemnly hand to you these deeds as proof, in Australian law, that these lands belong to the Gurindji people and I put into your hands part of the earth itself as a sign that this land will be the possession of you and your children forever. (Whitlam in McKeon, 2016)

Lingiari's response, with its kindness and gentle forgiveness, calls forth our best selves, our best elders. Lingiari calls White Australia to friendship as if they were rebellious but redeemable youngsters. After having endured so much pain, theft and cruelty, it is an extraordinary gesture of generosity and hospitality and embodies the transformative momentum that Butler (after Freud) attributes to the work of mourning.

> Let us live happily together as mates, let us not make it hard for each other ... We want to live in a better way together, Aboriginals and white men, let us not fight over anything, let us be mates. (Lingiari in McKeon, 2016)

Both these leaders enabled the Australian community to watch and imagine and sink into the possibility of another way of being. They took responsibility for the public performance of mourning and created room for observers to cognitively and affectively reckon with the lives and spirits of Others.

Whitlam understood that denial of Aboriginal and Torres Strait Islander peoples' pain and their relationship to country morally impoverished Australia. In his 1972 policy speech 'It's Time', he began making relationship and interdependence a central component of the national imagination.

> We will legislate to give Aborigines land rights – not just because their case is beyond argument, but because all of us as Australians are diminished while the Aborigines are denied their rightful place in this nation. (Whitlam, 1972)

'It's Time' was Labor's campaign slogan. It was an iconic campaign that captured the public imagination with the promise of universal healthcare, access to free tertiary education and the beginnings of reconciliation.

In the next twenty years, throughout the prime ministerships of Gough Whitlam (Labor), Malcolm Fraser (Liberal), Bob Hawke (Labor) and Paul Keating (Labor), burying the foundational settler myth was a national project. Even resistant White Australia policy adherents were increasingly drawn to the project's nourishment and life. Mourning was finally flowing in the business of nation-building and recognising with remorse the harm done to Aboriginal and Torres Strait Islander people. The process took on political dimensions and materiality in landmark events such as the bipartisan support for the *Aboriginal Land Rights (Northern Territory) Act 1976* under the Fraser Liberal government. This was the first piece of legislation that allowed for Aboriginal and Torres Strait Islander people to claim land title if they could prove traditional association.

In 1988, the question of sovereignty dominated national debate as Australians tried to agree on how to acknowledge two hundred years of colonisation in its bicentennial celebrations. On 26 January over forty thousand people, including First Nations people from across the country and non-Indigenous supporters, staged the largest protest march in Sydney since the Vietnam moratorium. Standing at Central Station in Sydney's business district, supporters awaited First Nations people making their way down from Redfern. A deafening roar went up from the crowd as Aboriginal and Torres Strait Islander peoples appeared at the top of Elizabeth Street. The protesters then marched together through Sydney chanting for land rights. The march ended at Hyde Park where several prominent Aboriginal leaders and activists spoke, among them activist Gary Foley: 'Let's hope Bob Hawke and his Government gets this message loud and clear from all these people here today. It's so magnificent to see black and white Australians together in harmony. This is what Australia could and should be like' (Deadly Story, 2017). Foley was right. That march again created the space for all Australians to imagine a different nation. The 1988 'Bicentennial celebrations' triggered heated debates about who and what was Australia and Australian.

With the foundational myth now in its death throes, it should have come as no surprise that debate and fear around national identity dominated. Was the real Australia being celebrated in an historic and peaceful re-enactment of the arrival of the First Fleet at Botany Bay? Was the truth the grinding poverty, disease and dispossession revealed in John Pilger's three-part documentary, *The Last Dream*? Or was it in the throes of a spiritual malady as argued by anthropologist, Julie Marcus (1988):

There is an uneasiness about the Australian bicentenary celebrations that exacerbates the usual swings of political mood. But it would be wrong, I think, to attribute the uneasiness to a slowly awakening consciousness of the reality of settlement, or to a realization that the prosperity of some rests upon the exploitation of others. The uneasiness flows from a fear that the emptiness of Australia's inner space may well correspond to a cultural and spiritual emptiness. (p. 4)

Also during the bicentennial year, the Barunga Statement, calling for self-management and land rights for Aboriginal and Torres Strait Islander peoples, was presented to Prime Minister Bob Hawke, who indicated his support for a treaty. Of course, the fact of a treaty confirms the existence of war and resistance and invasion. Its words would finally negate notions of an empty land belonging to no one, that was peacefully settled. Four years later, on 3 June 1992, the High Court handed down its decision that *Terra Nullius* should not have been applied to Australia. The Mabo Case was a significant legal case in Australia that recognised the land rights of the Meriam people, traditional owners of the Murray Island Group (comprising the islands of Mer, Dauer and Waier) in the Torres Strait. The decision, known as the Mabo decision, recognised that Aboriginal and Torres Strait Islander peoples have rights to this land, that existed before the British arrived and can still exist today.

Then, in what was to become a central focus of mourning in Australia, the Keating Labor government asked the Human Rights and Equal Opportunity Commission to carry out the National Inquiry into the Separation of Aboriginal and Torres Strait Islander Children from their Families (1997). Having re-established the prior existence of Aboriginal and Torres Strait Islander peoples through the Mabo decision, this Inquiry would weigh and measure the cost extracted by colonial settler governments from Aboriginal and Torres Strait Islander families. A published example of confidential evidence given at this Inquiry describes a forcible removal of children from their family that occurred in Western Australia in 1935, shortly after Sister Kate's Orphanage, Perth, was opened to receive 'lighter skinned' Aboriginal children who might be subsumed into White Australia:

3 A Dream in Three Parts: A Nation in Pieces (1778–1972)   53

I was at the post office with my Mum and Auntie [and cousin]. They put us in the police ute and said they were taking us to Broome. They put the mums in there as well. But when we'd gone [about ten miles] they stopped and threw the mothers out of the car. We jumped on our mothers' backs, crying, trying not to be left behind. But the policemen pulled us off and threw us back in the car. They pushed the mothers away and drove off, while our mothers were chasing the car, running and crying after us. We were screaming in the back of that car. When we got to Broome they put me and my cousin in the Broome lock-up. We were only ten years old. We were in the lock-up for two days waiting for the boat to Perth. (chapter ten)

The results of this National Inquiry were published in the *Bringing Them Home* report. Revealing the trauma, heartache and ongoing pain of the Stolen Generation,[6] ironically the report would become a lightning rod for the emerging voices of denial and melancholia post-1996. Nevertheless, during the final years of the Keating government and up until the 1996 election, the fact that White Australia had a Black history became more than just a protest badge—it became part of the secondary school curriculum. This period of honest mourning culminated in Keating's Redfern Speech in December 1992.

Often voted one of the best speeches made by an Australian, Keating delivered the speech standing on a shaky stage under the hot summer sun of a December afternoon in a park in the inner-city suburb of Redfern. To invoke mourning and melancholia is to say that something, or someone, has been lost. Whether he knew it or not, in the Redfern speech Keating was burying the foundational myth of the 'good' White Australia and bringing the dispossessed out of the shadows to witness the burial.

Redfern is a good place to contemplate these things. Just a mile or two from the place where the first European settlers landed, in too many ways it tells us that their failure to bring much more than devastation and demoralisation to Aboriginal Australia continues to be our failure. … That

---

[6] In Australia, between 1910 and the 1970s*, governments, churches and welfare bodies forcibly removed many Aboriginal and Torres Strait Islander children from their families. These children became known as the Stolen Generations. Their removal was sanctioned by various government policies (AIATSIS 2022a), which have left a legacy of trauma and loss that continues to affect First Nations communities, families and individuals today (Australians Together).

is perhaps the point of this Year of the World's Indigenous People: to bring the dispossessed out of the shadows, to recognise that they are part of us, and that we cannot give indigenous Australians up without giving up many of our own most deeply held values, much of our own identity – and our own humanity.

Mourning is a process of slowly reintegrating the psyche or some would say the soul. This restorative process is not primarily concerned with right or wrong, but with being made whole again. In this speech Keating articulated non-Indigenous Australia's psychological interdependency with Aboriginal and Torres Strait Islander people—there is no 'us' of substance without 'them'. He called on modern Australia to hold itself to account for its violent nature and not hide behind a façade of benign innocence. There is the seed of healing in recognising

> that it was we who did the dispossessing. We took the traditional lands and smashed the traditional way of life. We brought the diseases. The alcohol. We committed the murders. We took the children from their mothers. We practiced discrimination and exclusion. It was our ignorance and our prejudice. And our failure to imagine these things being done to us.

In this speech there is none of the knowing/not-knowing complication of a melancholia wherein reality is disavowed. The speech reveals the perpetrator and the victim in a conscious process and outlines their interrelatedness. Significantly, Keating calls on the imaginative powers of his audience:

> It might help us if we non-Aboriginal Australians imagined ourselves dispossessed of land we had lived on for fifty thousand years – and then imagined ourselves told that it had never been ours. Imagine if ours was the oldest culture in the world and we were told that it was worthless. Imagine if we had resisted this settlement, suffered and died in the defence of our land, and then were told in history books that we had given up without a fight. Imagine if non-Aboriginal Australians had served their country in peace and war and were then ignored in history books. Imagine if our feats on sporting fields had inspired admiration and patriotism and yet did nothing to diminish prejudice. Imagine if our spiritual life was denied and

ridiculed. Imagine if we had suffered the injustice and then were blamed for it. It seems to me that if we can imagine the injustice we can imagine its opposite. And we can have justice. (Keating, 1992)

Keating's speech reconnected the national narrative with real history in all its ugliness, and in doing so it liberated erotic energy—cathexis in Freud's terms—and imagination via empathy and communal grief and horror.

We work through mourning symbolically and psychologically. Symbolism takes on an enormous variety of forms in language, performance, ritual, imagery and music. From 1972 through 1996 there was an explosion of uniquely Australian art and culture. This included strong, internationally artworks from Indigenous troupes like Bangarra Dance Company and Black Theatre, and combative national debates about Australia becoming a republic, floating the dollar, removing tariffs, protecting wild places such as Franklin River and creating Kakadu Park, increasing involvement in Asia, and forgoing the ANZAC legend in the interest of the triumphant Kokoda engagement. They were the years of the Mabo decision, the Royal Commission into Black Deaths in Custody and the historic *Bringing Them Home* report. A great deal of action occurred at the national level and within communities. In mourning there is movement and change—it passes through us, and in its passing it metabolises grief to produce new people, new possibilities, potentially a new nation.

References

Allam, L., & Evershed, N. (2019, March 4). The killing times: The massacres of Aboriginal people Australia must confront. *The Guardian.* https://www.theguardian.com/australia-news/2019/mar/04/the-killing-times-the-massacres-of-aboriginal-people-australia-must-confront

Atkinson, J. (2003). *Trauma trails: Recreating song lines: The transgenerational effects of trauma in indigenous Australia.* Spinifex Press.

Australian Constitution. (1900). https://www.aph.gov.au/About_Parliament/Senate/Powers_practice_n_procedures/Constitution

Butler, J. (2002). *Antigone's claim*. Columbia University Press.
Butler, J. (2003). Afterword: After loss what then? In D. L. Eng & D. Kazanjian (Eds.), *Loss: The politics of mourning*. University of California Press.
Butler, J. (2004). *Precarious life: The powers of mourning and violence*. Verso.
Butler, J. (2005). *Giving an account of oneself*. Fordham University Press.
Butler, J. (2009). *Frames of war: When is life grievable?* Verso.
Clarke, M. (1896). "Holiday peak". In *Australian Tales* http://whitewolf.newcastle.edu.au/words/authors/C/ClarkeMarcus/prose/AustalianTales/holidaypeak.html
Deadly Story. (2017). *The 1988 bicentenary protest*. https://deadlystory.com/page/culture/history/The_1988_Bicentenary_Protest
Derrida, J. (1994). *Specters of Marx: The state of the debt, the work of mourning, and the new international* (P. Kamuf, Trans.). Routledge.
Gibson, R. (2002). *Seven versions of an Australian badland*. University of Queensland.
Glynn-McDonald, R. (2019, May 27). Death and sorry business. *Common Ground*. https://www.commonground.org.au/articles/death-and-sorry-business
Harris, L. C. (2018, August 7). The riots history erased: Reckoning with the racism of lambing flats. *The Guardian*. https://www.theguardian.com/artanddesign/2018/aug/07/the-riots-history-erased-reckoning-with-the-racism-of-lambing-flat
Honig, B. (2001). *Democracy and the foreigner*. Princeton University Press.
Honig, B. (2009). Antigone's laments, Creon's grief: Mourning, membership, and the politics of exception. *Political Theory, 37*(5), 5–43.
Keating, P. (1992, December 10). *Australian launch of the international year for the world's indigenous people, Redfern*. [Redfern Speech]. PM transcripts: Transcripts from the Prime Ministers of Australia. Department of the Prime Minister and Cabinet. https://pmtranscripts.pmc.gov.au/release/transcript-8765
Kociumbas, J. (2004) In A. Dirk Moses (Ed.), *Genocide and settler society: Frontier violence and stolen indigenous children in Australian history* (pp. 77–102). Berghahn Books.
Korff, J. (2020a). The 1963 Yirrkala bark petitions. *Creative Spirits*. https://www.creativespirits.info/aboriginalculture/land/the-1963-yirrkala-bark-petitions
Korff, J. (2020b). Australian 1967 referendum. *Creative Spirits*. https://www.creativespirits.info/aboriginalculture/history/australian-1967-referendum

Lydon, J. (1996). 'No moral doubt…': Aboriginal evidence and the Kangaroo Creek poisoning, 1847–1849. *Aboriginal History, 20*, 151–175. http://www.jstor.org/stable/24046133

Marcus, J. (1988). Bicentenary follies: Australians in search of themselves. *Anthropology Today, 4*(3), 4–6. https://www.jstor.org/stable/3032638

McKeon, N. (2016, March 2). Vincent Lingiari & Gough Whitlam: The story behind the image. *NITV.* https://www.sbs.com.au/nitv/article/vincent-lingiari-gough-whitlam-the-story-behind-the-image/t0m0ejh6i

McKinnon, C. (2020). Enduring indigeneity and solidarity in response to Australia's Carceral colonialism. *Biography, 43*(4), 691–704. https://doi.org/10.1353/bio.2020.0101

McLean, I. (1998). *White aborigines: Identity politics in Australian art.* Cambridge University Press. Print.

Miller, R., Ruru, J., Behrendt, L., & Lindberg, T. (2012). *Discovering indigenous lands.* Oxford University Press.

Moreton-Robinson (Ed.). (2015). *Whitening race: Essays in social and cultural criticism* (pp. 208–221). Aboriginal Studies Press.

Moreton-Robinson, A. (2021). Incommensurable sovereignties: Indigenous ontology matters. In *Routledge handbook of critical indigenous studies* (1st ed., Vol. 1). Routledge (pp. 257–268). Web.

National Inquiry into the Separation of Aboriginal and Torres Strait Islander Children from their Families. (1997). *Bringing them home.* (Sir Ronald Wilson, president). Equal Opportunity Commission, Sydney. https://bth.humanrights.gov.au/the-report/bringing-them-home-report

National Mental Health Commission. (2013). A contributing life: The 2013 national report card on mental health and suicide prevention. *NMHC.* https://www.mentalhealthcommission.gov.au/getmedia/62e98949-980b-4791-a90a-4ae92adbf2a3/2013-National-Report-Card-on-Mental-Health-and-Suicide-Prevention.pdf

Perkins, C. (1975). *A bastard like me.* Ure Smith.

Peters-Little, F., McGrath, A., & Macfarlane, I. (2006). Preface: On 'exchanging histories'. *Aboriginal History,* 30 [special edition: Exchanging Histories].

Pierce, P. (1999). *The country of lost children: An Australian anxiety.* Cambridge University Press.

Rutherford, J. (2010). Homo nullius: The politics of pessimism in Patrick white's the tree of man. *Cross / Cultures, Suppl. Remembering Patrick White,* (128), 47–64,213. Retrieved from http://ezproxy.uws.edu.au/login?url=https://www.proquest.com/scholarly-journals/homo-nullius-politics-pessimism-patrick-whites/docview/757064681/se-2

Stanner, W. E. H. (2009). *The dreaming and other essays*. Black Inc. Agenda.
Stow, S. (2011). Agonistic homegoing: Frederick Douglas, Joseph lowery, and the democratic value of African American public mourning. *American Political Science Review, 104*(4), 681–697.
Uluru Statement from the Heart. (2017). https://ulurustatement.org/the-statement
Whitlam, E. G. (1972, November 13). *It's time: Australian labor party policy speech*. Blacktown Civic Centre, Sydney. https://whitlamdismissal.com/1972/11/13/whitlam-1972-election-policy-speech.html
Wolfe, P. (2006). Settler colonialism and the elimination of the native. *Journal of Genocide Research, 8*(4), 387–409. https://doi.org/10.1080/14623520601056240
Zizek, S. (2000). Melancholy and the act. *Critical Inquiry, 26*(4), 657–681.

4

Waiting with Baseball Bats (1972–1996)

Mourning is hard work. It hurts. It is disorienting and, as observed by Sigmund Freud, can lead to (but hopefully through) psychosis and instability. As noted earlier, periods of mourning and psychological growth—despite being periods of integrating the Other and becoming whole—are phases of fragility and uncertainty. In Melanie Klein's reckoning of psychological development, an infant (nation) needs the containing safety of the ever-vigilant—or at least good enough—mother to keep the fear of disintegration at bay. But if enough pressure and fear is brought to bear on the infant (nation), psychological splitting will (re)occur and the wholeness that made it possible to have love and affection for the (m)Other will shatter.

For those in power and with resources these were exciting times of potentially enormous growth. For others they were times of fear and uncertainty. Many people felt a sense of being largely irrelevant and no longer special. Jennifer Rutherford (2000) examines this moment in *The Gauche Intruder* as she interrogates the rise of One Nation and the defensive position maintained by many of its supporters:

> One Nation's fantasy of defending a beleaguered moral universe – a good nation peopled by a good and neighbourly people – serves as camouflage for aggression ... What remains invisible, and yet essential, is the shared discourse of One Nation and its critics, is this belief in a good and fair nation. (p. 9)

After twenty-odd years of a new national narrative and mourning guided by Labor under the leadership of Whitlam, Hawke and Keating, many Australians were anxious, uncertain and angry. Anthropologist Ghassan Hage observed that a large demographic of 'paranoid nationalists' were finding the going hard in Keating's Australia:

> [T]he newly marginalised are not used to their state of marginality. They are not used to being denied a share of hope by society ... They live in a state of denial, still expecting that somehow, their nation and their 'national identity' will be a passport to hope for them ... but like a child whose mother has stopped feeding her, the very idea of such a reality is too hard to accept and to think ... Increasingly their attachment to such a non-feeding nation generates a specific paranoid form of nationalism. They become vindictive and bigoted always ready 'to defend the nation' in the hope of re-accessing their lost hope. (2003, p. 21)

Many of Australia's citizens were waiting for the 'good-enough' (Klein, 1946) parent to contain, support and feed them. Instead, they were witnessing implementation of a series of national policies and developments that shook the ground beneath their feet.

Financially, a lot was changing domestically and internationally. Responding to restless industrial action, the Prices and Income Accord struck by Prime Minister Bob Hawke in 1983 was an agreement between the Australian Council of Trades Unions (ACTU) and the government wherein unions agreed to restrict wage demands and the government pledged to minimise inflation. This Accord saw an end to wage growth. Then, neoliberal deregulation of the finance sector involved removing tariffs and floating the Australian dollar, with devastating consequences for the fashion and manufacturing industries. Results included high anxiety and unemployment. Hawke's Treasurer, Paul Keating, also championed the emerging logic of neoliberal ideology as he set about privatising

4 Waiting with Baseball Bats (1972–1996) 61

iconic Australian businesses such as Qantas Airways and the Commonwealth Bank. In November 1990, Keating announced to a packed press conference that the country was in 'a recession that Australia had to have'. Interest rates rose to 18 per cent and Australia experienced its worst recession since the Great Depression.

This financial turbulence created an atmosphere of agitation as people tried to adjust to the new conditions. For those with power and resources, these were exciting times of potentially enormous growth but for others they were times of fear and uncertainty. When the High Court ruled in favour of the Mabo decision, the Coalition used that moment to amplify fear of displacement, dispossession and a possibility of being abandoned by the state. Farmers were told that their farms could be reclaimed and mining companies that they might be denied access to coal and gold. Opposition rhetoric reached absurd levels of paranoia when in 1992 the Liberal premier of Victoria, Jeff Kennett, declared that no one's backyard was safe under the current federal government—not even the Melbourne Cricket Ground!

A combination of all these factors left many—in fact, a majority—of Australians feeling excluded from Keating's vision for Australia. Perhaps this upheaval could have been soothed by a different kind of national leadership more attuned to containing or assuaging paranoia. However, Keating was not that kind of leader, and as he took the reins from Hawke he failed to notice, or at least take seriously, rising anxiety about who and what was important to Australia. When opposition leader John Howard delivered a confrontational 'Headland Speech on National Identity' (1995b) that claimed that the colonial 'past is a legitimate source of pride', that Australians should resist 'attempts to rewrite our past or reposition our history by people with axes to grind who aren't all that interested in the truth' and that '[e]ndless bouts of introspection and navel gazing are unhealthy', Prime Minister Keating's (1995) response was characteristically scathing:

> Mr Howard's 'reflection' on Australia's national identity will go down in history as one of the most vapid statements about Australia ever delivered by an Australian political leader. It was ultra conservative ideology thinly and soporifically disguised as thoughtfulness and moderation.

'Vapid', 'shallow' and 'thin' are all words that have been used to describe the tonal quality of the lifelessness inherent in melancholia—in the persistent denial of proven reality, the vitality and depth of the real also drains away.

An Unlikely Leader

Recent history has valorised John Howard's prime ministership, but in 1995 when he became opposition leader for the third time, few would have imagined he would govern for eleven years. At the time he described himself as 'Lazarus with a triple by-pass'. He was a suburban solicitor from Wollstonecraft, a monarchist, a conservative who continued to challenge the global boycotts imposed on White South Africa, a man with no tolerance for a 'black armband' version of Australia's colonial heritage. Anyone who thought his two previous electoral losses might have updated his demeanour or values was proven wrong when in 1996 he gave veteran journalist Liz Jackson a pre-election interview on the Australian Broadcasting Corporation (ABC) *Four Corners* programme. In this interview, he told Jackson that his greatest ambition was 'to be an average Australian'. When asked what his vision was for the Australia of 2000, Howard said he would 'like to see an Australia that was comfortable and relaxed about three things. Comfortable and relaxed about their history, comfortable relaxed about their present and comfortable and relaxed about their future'. He then explained that a 'comfortable and relaxed' state meant 'that as a nation we don't spend our lives apologising for our past' (Jackson, 1996).

National identity and who 'owned' it was a central debate in the 1996 federal election, which Howard won with a 45-seat majority in an historic defeat for Keating's Labor. There was a sense of fury in the electorate's repudiation of Keating. Queensland Premier Wayne Goss said at the time that it felt like Australians were sitting on their verandas waiting for Keating 'with baseball bats'.

Every election is won and lost on myriad issues and this one was no exception. Nevertheless, the size of the win made it clear that the majority of Australians disagreed with any commentariat and media who thought a vapid Howard offered nothing by way of national vision. Though Howard had not changed in his conservative values since his first or second failed attempt at the leadership, by 1996 Australia had changed, and he had also become far more strategic about how he framed those values. His lifelong objections to Medicare, industrial relations and foreign investment were now minimised or waived in the interests of electability.

Of course, there were in fact real policy differences and, post-election, Howard created the idea of core and non-core promises as he broke faith with numerous election commitments. He never broke faith with this implicit promise not to look back or apologise however. When the electorate voted overwhelmingly for John Howard, he knew he had a mandate to end the years of questioning and imagining. It was his time to close the book on mourning with its complexity and interdependency, its moments of not knowing and the constant incursion of equity and voice for those who had never had either. In electing Howard with his ambition to be average, his hope for a comfortable and relaxed country and his foreclosure on mourning the death of White Australia's foundational myth, the electorate left mourning still born and heralded in its darker twin, melancholia.

It is worth noting that during the two decades of mourning the machinery of government and the public service were still largely in public ownership. This meant that public performances of mourning played out in communal spaces like parks, courtrooms, Parliament House, the lawns of Parliament House, the streets, and the city's foreshores and town halls. The neoliberal notions that would justify the privatisation of Australia's detention regime (discussed in detail in Chap. 7) had yet to become fact. Media ownership was more diverse and the era of campaigning media and 'fake news' was still decades into the future. The courts were still accessible to those seeking Australia's protection. The artefacts produced by this time of mourning often intersected with, and were supported by, the public service via the Royal Commission, Inquiries, human rights reports, High Court decisions, the Aboriginal and Torres Strait Islander Commission (ATSIC) and the Land Councils. Mourning as a nation had been what British economist Guy Standing (2019) refers to as an experience of 'commoning', an effective and affective reclamation of our shared work, leisure, space and, critically, entitlement. In contrast, the descent into melancholia and the paranoid-schizoid phase of splitting is reflected in an acceleration of the sale of almost everything held in common. Neoliberalism's atomisation of work, workplaces and workers, and its privatising of public spaces, places and utilities epitomise this malevolent psychological state.

The End of the Symbolic

Disavowal, denial and an abhorrence of the symbolic followed on the footsteps of the new Howard government. His prime ministership was characterised by his consistent refusal to countenance the symbolic: in reconciliation with First Nations, climate change and the Iraq war. He spent much of his political capital denying the need to mourn for the loss of the White Australian phantasie. This denial was revealed in his belligerent insistence that his generation could not be expected to say sorry for the work of a previous generation, and his repudiation of the idea that Australia's history since 1788 is 'little more than a disgraceful record of imperialism' (Howard, 1997a). While refusing to lay claim to any sense of responsibility for past acts of dispossession on these grounds, he nevertheless insisted Australia remember and honour the ANZAC legend of 1915.

But if the death of the phantasie of the peaceful settler was to be avoided, how was the nation to deny and disavow the recently revealed violent history and dispossession at its heart? How does the nation unknown what is known? If there was to be no further public performance of mourning and no 'looking back' in this comfortable and relaxed nation, what was to be done with the pain and knowledge of harm done by White Australia? Where would this shameful cargo go and who would carry it?

At the 1997 Australian Reconciliation Convention, Aboriginal and Torres Strait Islander Elders made it clear that they would no longer carry the melancholic phantasie of Howard's White Australia. When Howard attempted to reduce Australia's acts of colonial violence to 'blemishes in its past history', Elders across the audience, not averse to symbolism in the least, stood up and turned their backs to him. They literally and metaphorically turned their back on his message and the projection of his whitewashed history where the horror of invasion, frontier wars and torture was reduced to a blemish. If Aboriginal and Torres Strait Islander people refused to carry it, where was the state to relocate the unresolved mourning with its attendant elements of guilt and shame and remorse?

With melancholia tightening its grip, the nation was pitched back into a primitive stage of psychological development. Ghassan Hage captures this infantile moment by suggesting the worry and anxiety of White Australia circled the fear of being abandoned by the 'motherland'—a situation that, along with the nation's xenophobia, may have contributed to the nation's willingness to believe that women and men were throwing their babies overboard. Hage argues only a people in fear of being thrown over by their own motherland could imagine such a reality. There is something deeply sad about a people so adrift and abandoned that the nation's dreams are haunted by such a creeping unworthiness.

Splits Appear as Melancholia Tightens Its Grip

At least a year before his election in 1996, Howard was framing his new Australia and the aspirations of his 'Australian mainstream'. In 1995 he raised the idea of the privileged and powerful Other, a 'new class' he portrayed as bullying and selfish, riding roughshod over the genuine concerns of the legitimate community. A thinly veiled attack on Aboriginal and Torres Strait Islander organisations and multicultural communities and their supporters, this claim deftly pulls together the narcissism and the victimhood of the melancholic while splitting off and Othering the 'new' threat.

> There is a frustrated mainstream in Australia today which sees government decisions increasingly driven by the noisy, self-interested clamour of powerful vested interest with scant regard for national interest ... This bureaucracy of the new class is a world apart from the myriad of spontaneous community-based organisations which have been part and parcel of the Australian mainstream for decades. (Howard, 1995a)

Six days after being sworn in as prime minister in 1996, Howard demoted the Office of Multicultural Affairs from its high-profile position within the Department of the Prime Minister and Cabinet to a marginal position in the Department of Immigration and Multicultural Affairs (DIMA).[1] Multiculturalism as social policy was further enfeebled when it was drained of funding in the August 1996 Budget. An ally to Howard in this respect, who gave voice to basic social splintering via the categorising of 'us' and 'them', was newcomer politician Pauline Hanson. In her maiden speech to federal parliament in September 1996, Hanson declared:

> I and most Australians want our immigration policy radically reviewed and that of multiculturalism abolished. I believe we are in danger of being swamped by Asians ... a truly multicultural society can never be strong or united.

Between 1996 and 2000, both Howard and Hanson were loud and busy pitting 'good Australians' against people from Asia and, more generally, 'bad' non-Anglo-Celtic Australians.

By January 1997, Howard was articulating a further split between ordinary, worthy Australians and a devious 'cultural elite'. His first Australia Day address claimed that

> the symbols we hold dear as Australians and the beliefs that we have about what it is to be an Australian are not things that can ever be imposed from above by political leaders of any persuasion. They are not things that can be generated by a self-appointed cultural elite who seek to tell us what our identity ought to be. Rather they are feelings and attitudes that grow out of the spirit of the people. (Howard, 1997b)

In this address Howard is creating a class of people that Hage (1998) refers to as 'refugees of the interior'. Hage argues that until the late 1960s, just being of Anglo-Celtic heritage in Australia was enough to ensure a sense of belonging and access to political capital, but that privileged position was undermined in the following decades by the emergence of the

---

[1] Superseded in 2001 by the Department of Immigration and Multicultural Affairs and Indigenous Affairs (DIMIA).

cosmopolitan multiculturalist. Hage then describes a process of the internal 'global reject'—the White Australian who ironically perceives that *they* have been dispossessed—turning against the external 'global reject'—any culturally different person living in Australia upon whom this fear is projected. Ron Hoenig of the University of South Australia describes how

> the cultural ascendancy of the white cosmopolitan multiculturalists in the 1980s meant that social capital, and even the fantasy of governmental belonging, was being taken away from the rural and working-class poor who identified with the assimilationist paradigm of the 1950s. (Hoenig, 2011)

Anglo-Celtic Australians' sense of being rightfully, unchallengeably 'at home' in their society was being depleted through 'a devaluing of Angloness in the field of Whiteness in favour of a wider cosmopolitan Whiteness', according to Hage (1998, p. 183).

Control is a central concern for the melancholic. Splitting is the way control is enforced. From 1996 to 2001, borders and boundaries assumed a totemic power in the Howard government as he bolstered 'us' by finding a 'them'. Under Howard there would be no symbolic apology and no Treaty, just 'practical reconciliation'. Australia would become an all-powerful nation that would make decisions for non-Australians and deny, if it wished, the validity of the real-world circumstances of those seeking help. This is delusional and belligerent narcissism, identified by psychiatrist Jacques Lacan in the infant who, like Narcissus, assumes the illusion of autonomy, imposing an imaginary unity and self-sufficiency upon its own irredeemable internal divisions and fractures.

The Opposite of Love Is Not Hate, It's Indifference

The Australian Government's abuse and, in some instances, torture of those who seek refuge here is supported by a growing indifference to the pain of the Other on the part of the electorate, akin to Freud's listing some of the symptoms of melancholia as 'cessation of interest in the outside world [and] loss of the capacity to love' (1917/1957, p. 243).

While it is possible to now look back and see a psychoanalytic terrain emerge, at the time there was a sense in which the federal government was testing each incursion into the newly emerged territory. For instance, when the idea of providing merely temporary protection visas to those fleeing persecution was first pushed by Pauline Hanson's One Nation party in the lead-up to the 1998 federal election, Howard's immigration minister Philip Ruddock criticised it, saying quite rightly that asylum seekers were 'likely to have been tortured, traumatised, and in need of support for rebuilding a new life' and that protection classified as temporary was 'highly unconscionable in a way that most thinking people would clearly reject'.

> It would mean that people would never know whether they were able to remain here. There would be uncertainty, particularly in terms of the attention given to learning English, and in addressing the torture and trauma so they are healed from some of the tremendous physical and psychological wounds they have suffered. (Miller, 1998)

Health Minister Michael Woolridge labelled the One Nation policy proposal 'deeply flawed and dangerous', arguing that the uncertainty and insecurity of temporary protection would 'continue the suffering of refugees who have been tortured and could well complete the insidious work that torture began'. Australia, he insisted,

> must and will remain true to its traditions of welcoming people who have fled to this country fearing persecution in their original homeland. We must not and will not turn our backs on those who come here for refuge. To do so would be to betray our moral obligation as a community and to betray that great Australian tradition of helping out those in need. (Woolridge, 1998)

However, a year later, in October 1999, the Howard government adopted the policy of temporary protection visas (TPVs) as an expedient measure to facilitate Kosovar refugees in need of an immediate safe haven. Having introduced it conditionally and event-specifically, Howard made the TPV policy a permanent fixture when public outrage failed to materialise.[2]

---

[2] The policy was removed in 2023 by the Albanese Labor government.

4 Waiting with Baseball Bats (1972–1996)

The *Tampa* crisis is often cited as the event that transformed Australia's treatment of asylum seekers. But with Pauline Hanson's One Nation party taking votes from the Howard government, Howard had been tightening the numbers and nature of Australia's humanitarian intake since 1997. Four years before the MV *Tampa* came into view, the Howard government made changes to Australia's immigration and family reunion policies that had the effect of transforming the protection of asylum seekers into an issue of national security and laid the groundwork for criminalising the act of seeking protection. Michelle Peterie, Research Fellow at University of Sydney's School of Social and Political Sciences, explains that during this time the government—first the Coalition and subsequently Labor—was able to subvert the discourses of compassion itself, discourse that now 'functioned not as expressions of equality or solidarity, but as demonstrations of power. Discourses of compassion for refugees and asylum seekers have worked to reconcile Australia's self-conception as a good and "decent" country, with its overarching desire for power and control' (Peterie, 2017).

Peterie explains how the Australian Government was able to rhetorically split the 'good' refugees, those who queued patiently in camps across the world, from the 'bad' refugees who did not or could not wait and came to Australia by boat. The resulting indifference to the plight of boat arrivals typifies this paranoid-schizoid phase of national underdevelopment. The sociopathic attitude particularly towards people who arrive by boat is underscored by the fact that never, in the last twenty years, has the number of unauthorised sea arrivals exceeded the number of unauthorised air arrivals, nor the number of people who over-stay authorised Australian visas. The latter group has sometimes run to over eighty thousand people per year but has never attracted media or public attention (Phillips, 2015). In a classic case of Freudian projection, it is boats that present a psychosocial threat to White Australia because that is how White Australia arrived and took possession of the country.

When the merchant ship, MV *Tampa* hoved into view in August 2001 and rescued over 400 asylum seekers, Howard saw an opportunity to take control and begin to criminalise Australia's borders. What followed on the heels of the Howard government's refusal to allow the ship entry was an extraordinary roll-out of new public policy that led to the creation of the Pacific Solution, a decision to push back boats to Indonesia and the use of offshore detention centres on Nauru and Papua New Guinea's (PNG's) Manus Island.

When the names of people seeking Australia's protection were removed, replaced by numbers, the work of demonising these people was well under way. The process was given energy and focus after the attacks on the US mainland on 11 September 2001. Both Nauru and Manus Island became increasingly inaccessible, enabling the Howard government to tell the story of the asylum seekers and refugees warehoused in these centres. Ensuring the camps were off-limits to the media also guaranteed the face of the Other would not be seen, there would be no relationship, imaginative or empathetic connection between those fleeing persecution and the Australian community (see Chap. 7).

Australians working to alter the development of this punitive policy, and any hoping that the end of the Howard era would be the end of the policy as well, were to be disappointed over the next fourteen years. The Rudd Labor government did close the offshore detention camps in 2008, but four years later Prime Minister Kevin Rudd signalled his intention to reopen them and then the newly instated Prime Minister Julia Gillard did so. The camps in Nauru and Manus Island reopened in 2012. In returning to this now infamous remedy, the Gillard government displayed the compulsive repetition that is part of the melancholic psychic makeup. On 13 August 2012, framing her response as the 'can-do' attitude of an able government concerned with the arrivals' welfare, Gillard announced that she had accepted the recommendations of an expert panel she had convened to find a political solution to the 'problem' of an increase in asylum seekers arriving by boat:

> What this report is calling on parliamentarians to do is to compromise and to act. This report is telling us not to stay in our fixed positions but to act and get things done. When our nation looks at what is happening at sea, too many lives have been lost. (Gillard, 2012)

The government was quickly informed that the decision to repel refugee boats to processing offshore would put Australia in breach of the nation's international treaty obligations. 'Penalising people based on their mode of arrival is clearly in breach of obligations', Graham Thom of Amnesty International told ABC television.

> We are only talking about people who come by boat, we're not talking about the thousands of people who come by plane and seek asylum in this country. What we are doing is penalising one particular group and actually taking them to a very remote place where we know they've been damaged in the past and holding them hostage to stop other people from coming. (Rourke, 2012)

The refugee advocacy sector also met Gillard's announcement with appalled recriminations. Pamela Curr of the Asylum Seeker Resource Centre told *The Guardian that* the report was 'a comprehensive package of harm. … People will still drown. What this [report] is making sure is that people drown elsewhere and don't drown right in front of us' (Rourke, 2012). But that was the point of the policy. If Australia had real and primary concerns about people drowning *en route* to Australia, other available options would better address them. These options include having the Australian navy rescue boats in trouble rather than pushing them back out to sea, and/or increasing funds and capacity to process asylum seekers in Indonesia and then take them to their destination by airplane. But by now the securitisation of borders had become the grim obsession of successive governments, and the capacity to imagine a different response was nowhere evident.

During the following years the Manus Island and Nauru detention camps became sites of extraordinary suffering and death. Twelve people would lose their lives through murder, suicide and medical neglect. Conditions grew to be appalling. Nauru became a site of systemic rape and humiliation of women (Bacon et al., 2016). The nation was now submerged in its melancholia. The splitting that managed the fear of being overwhelmed and maintained the *phantasie* of the 'good Australian' had become the dominant frame. The above process of politically grooming the electorate to accept behaviour that would have been unthinkable a few years previously was cemented by a bipartisanship between both major political parties. The Australian community was informed about some of the abuses in the camps by newspapers and broadcasts, but the electorate was given sufficient deniability to ensure that the practice of blatant cruelty remained in the realm of known/not known. This led to the curious situation wherein opinion polls continued to track widespread approval for the government's refugee policy, even while media coverage, Senate Inquiries, non-government organisations and overseas watchdogs reported evidence of human rights abuses.

Freud detected a 'belligerent narcissism' at the heart of the melancholic—a belief both that the melancholic is not accorded sufficient attention and that their unease is always someone else's fault. On the morning of 25 August 2001, social researcher Hugh Mackay wrote presciently to Melbourne's newspaper *The Age*:

> When there is a lack of inspirational leadership, two things always happen. The community's focus narrows and turns inwards as people disengage from the national agenda and become almost exclusively concerned with local issues, and the vacuum created by the lack of social vision sucks a flood of vicious prejudice to fill the space.

Asylum seekers have been contaminated by White Australia's psychic projections of the split-off national traits, creating the opportunity for cruel, degrading and inhumane treatment. Othering of refugees through political practices such as the isolation and privatisation of detention centres, driving them away to places where they would not be seen or heard, enable those in control of refugees to act in belligerent ways that ultimately produce torture. Though we would like to say that most Australians would say they were opposed to the use of torture, especially on children, nevertheless ongoing reports of torture from a number of credible sources failed to change the situation or the number of Australians voting in support of these policies.

Media commentator Waleed Aly wrote in *The New York Times in* 2016 that the reductive, repetitive chant '*stop the boats*' acts like a cultish mantra, enabling Australians to condone even torture as long as they themselves are safe.

> This is the great sedative of Australian politics: dulling our attention, rendering all else some indecipherable white noise we only vaguely register

before we fall asleep. Then we can snooze through any bombshell. Even Amnesty's language isn't arresting anymore. Merely a year and a half ago a United Nations special rapporteur found systematic violations of the Convention Against Torture. None of it registers because as long as boats carrying asylum seekers aren't making it to Australia, all is justified.

Though the processing centre in Papua New Guinea was closed at the end of 2021, the centre in Nauru is still operating, and Aly's comments are still valid today.

Australia's movement from mourning to melancholia and into the paranoid-schizoid phase is particular to its own history. Nevertheless, comparisons abound with other nations travelling a similar route. In a recent study of Polish attitudes towards Syrian refugees, researchers found that 'collective narcissism predicts prejudice and retaliatory hostility in response to past, present, actual and imagined offenses toward the in-group' (Dyduch-Hazar et al., 2019). The study revealed that a greater sense of social connectedness and gratitude correlated with less collective narcissism within some groups. Inversely, participants with lower self-esteem and heightened self-criticism were proportionately more vulnerable to individual narcissism, that is antagonistic self-entitlement manifesting in a distrustful and neurotic interpersonal style. An example of this belligerent narcissism on a national scale in Australia was seen in a viciously provocative yet passively aggressive motion put to the Australian Senate in 2018 by Senator Pauline Hanson, and only voted down by a narrow margin of three, that 'It's OK to be White'—as if that were ever in doubt.

References

Aly, W. (2016, October 26). Australia's poisonous refugee policy. *The New York Times*. https://www.nytimes.com/2016/10/27/opinion/australias-poisonous-refugee-policy.html

Bacon, W., Curr, P., Lawrence, C., Macken, J., & O'Connor, C. (2016). *Protection Denied, Abuse Condoned: Women on Nauru at Risk*. Australian Women in Support of Women on Nauru. http://www.awswn.org/the-report

Dyduch-Hazar, K., Mrozinski, B., & Golec de Zavala, A. (2019). Collective narcissism and in-group satisfaction predict opposite attitudes toward refugees via attribution of hostility. *Frontiers in Psychology, 10*(1901). https://doi.org/10.3389/fpsyg.2019.01901

Freud, S. (1957). Mourning and Melancholia. In J. Strachey (Ed.), *The Standard Edition of the Complete Psychological Works of Sigmund Freud* (Vol. XIV, pp. 237–258). Hogarth Press. (Original work published 1917).

Gillard, J. (2012, August 13). *Houston Expert Panel on Asylum Seekers. Joint press conference* [transcript]. https://web.archive.org/web/20130420080533/. http://www.minister.immi.gov.au/media/cb/2012/cb189223.htm

Hage, G. (1998). *White nation: Fantasies of white supremacy in a multicultural society*. Pluto Press.

Hage, G. (2003). *Against paranoid nationalism*. Pluto Press.

Hanson, P. (1996, September 10). *Maiden Speech in the House of Representatives*. Australian politics.com. https://australianpolitics.com/1996/09/10/pauline-hanson-maiden-speech.html

Hoenig, R. (2011). *The borderscape of detention: Media depictions of the denizens of Woomera* [PDF]. MnM Working Paper No 7, International Centre for Muslim and non-Muslim 260 Understanding. University of South Australia. https://www.unisa.edu.au/siteassets/episerver-6-files/documents/eass/mnm/working-papers/hoenig-borderscape-of-detention.pdf

Howard, J. (1995a, June 6). *The role of government: John Howard Headland Speech*. Australian Politics.com. https://australianpolitics.com/1995/06/06/john-howard-headland-speech-role-of-govt.html

Howard, J. (1995b, December 13). *National identity: John Howard Headland Speech*. Australian Politics.com. https://australianpolitics.com/1995/12/13/national-identity-howard-headland-speech.html

Howard, J. (1997a, January 24). *Address by the Prime Minister to Australia Day Council*. Sydney. (Transcript) https://pmtranscripts.pmc.gov.au/release/transcript-10217

Howard, J. (1997b, May 26). *Opening address to the Australian Reconciliation Convention Melbourne*. PM Transcripts: Transcripts from the Prime Ministers of Australia. Department of the Prime Minister and Cabinet. https://pmtranscripts.pmc.gov.au/release/transcript-10361

Jackson, L. (Reporter). (1996, February 19). An Average Australian Bloke [TV series episode]. *Four Corners*. ABC. https://trakt.tv/shows/four-corners/seasons/1996/episodes/2

Keating, P. (1995, December 13). *Vague is best – John Howard's view of national identity*. Statement by the Prime Minister The Hon. PJ Keating, MP. PM Transcripts: Transcripts from the Prime Ministers of Australia. Department of the Prime Minister and Cabinet.
Klein, M. (1946). Notes on some schizoid mechanisms. *The International Journal of Psycho-Analysis*, 99–110.
Mackay, H. (2001, August 25). Politics fans the flames of ugly prejudice. *The Age*.
Miller, S. (1998). *Welcoming the stranger*. Southern Cross Online. http://web.archive.org/web/20010425201827/http://www.anglicanmediasydney.asn.au/September/features1.html
Peterie, M. (2017). Docility and desert: Government discourses of compassion in Australia's asylum seeker debate. *Journal of Sociology*, 53(2), 351–366. https://doi.org/10.1177/1440783317690926
Phillips, J. (2015, March 2). *Asylum seekers and refuges: What are the facts?* Research Paper, Parliamentary Library. https://www.aph.gov.au/about_parliament/parliamentary_departments/parliamentary_library/pubs/rp/rp1415/asylumfacts#_ftn32
Rourke, A. (2012, August 13). Australian refugee plan criticised by human rights groups. *The Guardian*. https://www.theguardian.com/world/2012/aug/13/australian-refugee-plan-criticised
Rutherford, J. (2000). *The gauche intruder: Freud, Lacan and the white Australian fantasy*. Melbourne University Press.
Standing, G. (2019). *Plunder of the commons: A manifesto for sharing public wealth*. Penguin.
Woolridge, M. (1998, August 20). *Speech at the Launch of GP's Manual on Refugee Health and General Practice*. Department of Health and Family Services. https://web.archive.org/web/20080813072038/http://health.gov.au/internet/main/publishing.nsf/Content/health-archive-mediarel-1998-mwsp980820.htm

5

Is It Torture?

Leaving Omelas

In 1973 Ursula K. Le Guin (1975) wrote a short story called 'The Ones Who Walk Away from Omelas'. Omelas is,

> in my words like a city in a fairy tale, long ago and far away, once upon a time. Perhaps it would be best if you imagined it as your own fancy bids, assuming it will rise to the occasion, for certainly I cannot suit you all.

Omelas is a wonderful, peaceful, happy place where there is no sorrow—except one, a singular atrocity. The city's peace, prosperity and security depend on a child being held in mandatory detention where the little one is kept in filth, darkness, helplessness and despair. No act of mercy, kindness or care towards this child is allowed, or the entire easy life of the city will be destroyed. There are no exceptions. Once citizens are old enough to know this truth, they are told. Most, although initially shocked and disgusted, ultimately acquiesce to this injustice against one that enables the flourishing of the rest. However, a few citizens, young and old, silently walk away from the city, and no one knows where they go. Le Guin suggests that they may be going towards a place even less imaginable to most of us than the city of happiness. I cannot describe it at all. It is possible it does not exist. But they seem to know where they are going, the ones who walk away from Omelas.

Few stories better capture the critical elements of Australia's immigration detention regime: the abuse that remains out of sight, the almost-obliviousness of the population and the logically challenged argument that brutalising a child keeps the state secure. And of course, there are the handful of people who refuse to accept that deal.

In this chapter I seek to answer the question: does Australia's treatment of asylum seekers amount to torture? I begin with Le Guin because, unbeknownst to each other, a number of the medical professionals I interviewed for this research referred to this particular story of Omelas as a way of explaining what they believe is happening in Australia. The population exhibits a capacity to know and yet to not-know about the abuse of innocence at the heart of Australia's national security calculus. The Omelas story is a way of revealing and trying to understand the logic of the bystander, because the least examined element in the three-legged stool of institutional abuse is neither the victim nor the perpetrator: it is the silent bystander. The reader of Le Guin's story must decide whether they stay or walk away from Omelas, but it is the job of all of us to know about the child living in darkness and despair at the centre of Omelas.

The chapter explores the accusation that many Australians would contest and that Australia is guilty of cruel, inhumane and degrading treatment of asylum seekers; treatment that stems from structurally violent systems within the detention regime and that constitutes torture for many detainees. It introduces those who advocate and care for those caught in this pernicious regime.

To begin I will outline the definition and nature of the alleged torture and examine the public record, which includes articles, reports and legal processes undertaken to try to hold the Australian state to account and include the opinion of the International Criminal Court (ICC). I will then view the allegation through the lens of medical professionals who have treated asylum seekers—children and adults—for over a decade, in some cases two decades. Each has published their research and experience widely, having made the decision to speak publicly about this regime despite potential impacts on their professional lives.

I interviewed five medical professionals between December 2020 and June 2021. Interviews were conducted in-person and online via Zoom. I structured my questions in two parts. In the first part of each interview I asked the practitioner to reflect on how their patients were treated by detention centre guards, by corporations that provide services and by government policy itself. I also asked for their clinical assessment of the detention centre environment and their ethical assessment of privatised immigration management. The second part of the interview creatively addressed the affective and psychiatric dimensions of the issue. I asked participants to engage in an imaginary exercise of having the Australian state as a patient and thinking through treatment options for such a patient who was compulsively inflicting cruel and inhumane treatment on vulnerable people. After posing my questions, I followed the discussion wherever the participants took it, remaining open to new discoveries. This openness led me along with my research participants to consider the therapeutic quality inherent in physical acts of radical political resistance (even if that action takes the form of hunger strike or self-mutilation).

I chose to interview medical professionals rather than refugees for this chapter because I believe detainees could be re-traumatised by being questioned about their trauma and obliged to retell it. Nevertheless, I, and my interviewees, recognise that the real authority of what constitutes torture is the person upon whom it is inflicted.

Particularities of Torture

State-sanctioned torture of asylum seekers and refugees is an extraordinary accusation. Like genocide, slavery and piracy, torture carries an absolute prohibition—there is never any excuse for it. The prohibition against torture is a *jus cogens*—a norm from which no derogation is permitted. On the map of shared humanity, the line of torture is delineated with the legend: *beyond this point there be dragons*. It is increasingly unclear whether Australia has learnt to swim with dragons or has become one.

The idea that a Western democracy would deploy torture in peace time, against women, children and men who have committed no crime is shocking. So much so, that the accusation that Australia tortures refugees is most often summarily dismissed. The very idea is preposterous. Coaxing the reality of the existence of torture into consciousness, therefore, does not yield to a head-on assault. The term 'torture' is slippery. Commonly held ideas of it conjure darkened rooms, battered victims, blood-stained walls. Torture is the hooded man standing on a chair, electrodes dangling from his fingers. It is deafening music and constant light and terrifying dogs, waterboarding and sleep deprivation in far-flung prisons. It is the ultimate aberrant behaviour, taking place in the liminal known/unknown spaces of international intelligence operations and desperate, failed states. Torture is perceived as discrete action, not public policy. The United Nations Convention Against Torture does not draw any distinction between physical and mental torture. The definition of torture is established internationally by Article 1 of the Convention against Torture and Other Cruel, Inhumane and Degrading Treatment or Punishment (1987). Article 1.1 of the Convention defines torture as

> any act by which severe pain or suffering, whether physical or mental, is intentionally inflicted on a person for such purposes as obtaining from him, or a third person, information or a confession, punishing him for an act he or a third person has committed or is suspected of having committed, or intimidating or coercing him or a third person, or for any reason based on discrimination of any kind, when such pain or suffering is inflicted by or at the instigation of or with the consent or acquiescence of a public official or other person acting in an official capacity. It does not include pain or suffering arising only from, inherent in, or incidental to, lawful sanctions.

The nature of the torture discussed in this book is largely centred on the mind. Some may find the idea of psychological torture less confronting than removing fingernails and smashing bones but for those suffering it, it is no more endurable. This form of torture destroys the internal psychic scaffolding that holds and protects the 'sacred core' of the self, and the ties that bind us to our own humanity. It is often inflicted through the violent removal of markers and tools that constitute personhood.

Names are replaced by numbers; people become 'illegals' and 'queue jumpers'; documents are removed; the cohesion of families is shattered as they are separated and disregarded; future plans are unsecured; goalposts are constantly moved; and arbitrary and capricious processes dominate life within the immigration detention camps. People's stories are denied and young women live with the endless terror of the night, and the ongoing threat of assault and rape, a threat that grows in the bright Pacific sunshine.

Psychological torture enacts daily humiliations: of showering as a performance for the guards in return for more time and space; of watching mums and dads fail to give their kids protection, health and food; of having guards whisper how much Australia hates you, how you will never leave this camp, how you will never see your mum, or dad, kids or husband again; of destroying hope. As the weeks become months and the months years, as hope drains through the dead coral carapace, a lethal form of resignation takes hold of many detainees.

A Contested Accusation

I want death, I need death (Farrell, 2016).

The allegation of torture within Australia's detention system is highly contested, but it is not contested that the policy and its practice are intentionally harsh. Asylum seekers, refugees, teachers, doctors, lawyers, advocates and the Australian Greens political party allege torture. Prime Ministers John Howard (Liberal), Kevin Rudd (Labor), Julia Gillard (Labor), Tony Abbott (Liberal), Malcolm Turnbull (Liberal) and Scott Morrison (Liberal) have all conceded the treatment is harsh: 'We do have a tough border policy, you could say it's a harsh policy, but it has worked' (Turnbull in Doherty, 2016).[1] It has been compared to 'a hanging in the

---

[1] The narrative has taken a turn in recent years with politicians from both major parties now insisting Australian border policy is in fact compassionate, because it discourages and therefore prevents drownings. Of course, rescuing those at risk would also prevent such deaths. The aim 'to end drownings at sea' by repelling boats as a matter of principle is glib longhand for not letting people drown in sight of Australian land; there was no attempt to pretend that anyone landed elsewhere safely.

public square' (Global Legal Action Network, 2017), designed to intimidate future asylum seekers and deter them from attempting the journey to Australia. It is a policy deliberately calculated to inflict pain and suffering, physical and mental, that sends a message of dominance and intolerance to the wider world for the sole purpose of deterrence. When Prime Minister Howard sent Australia's most elite fighters in the form of the Special Air Service (SAS) to deter the rescue ship MV *Tampa* (see Chap. 4), he was reframing refugees as a national security threat rather than vulnerable people caught up in a global crisis (Devetak, 2004), and the frame of security crisis rather than humanitarian response has continued to inform public policy more broadly in Australia. National security demands a 'hard-hearted' response, unlike a humanitarian crisis that demands compassion and empathy.

At the national level, torture is defined by the Attorney-General's Department (2021):

> For an act to be prohibited as torture, it must involve severe pain and suffering, it must be intentionally inflicted, and it must be inflicted for a purpose referred to in the definition in the Convention against Torture and Other Cruel, Inhuman or Degrading Treatment or Punishment (CAT). Conduct not meeting the threshold of torture may be regarded as cruel, inhuman or degrading treatment or punishment ('ill treatment') … no legislation, policy or program should permit the infliction of torture or cruel, inhuman or degrading treatment or punishment.

In August 2014, Dr. Peter Young accused the Immigration Department of deliberately inflicting harm on refugees in a way that could only be described as torture. Young, an Australian chief psychiatrist, was Director of Mental Health Services for International Health and Medical Services (IHMS)—the body contracted by the Australian Government to provide health services to detainees in immigration detention centres—from 2011 to 2014. He says the system is deliberately harsh, breaks people's health, compromises the ethics of doctors and is intended to place asylum seekers under 'strong coercive pressure' to abandon plans to live in

Australia. 'Suffering is the way that is achieved'. He told *The Guardian*, this process is akin to torture: 'If we take the definition of torture to be the deliberate harming of people in order to coerce them into a desired outcome, I think it does fulfil that definition' (Marr & Laughland, 2014).

From the beginning, advocates, medical professionals and lawyers have raised concerns about establishing immigration camps in isolated desert locations far from any support services. The logic of these locations soon became clear as stories of abuse, neglect and torture emerged from them. Over many years the United Nations, the Australian Human Rights Commission and the Palmer Inquiry would attempt to shine a light on these dark places.

The torture experienced in Australia's detention regime is not the 'spectacular' torture of Abu Ghraib or the US Black Sites of Extraordinary Rendition; it is primarily what Danielle Celermajer (2018), Professor of Sociology at the University of Sydney, refers to as 'banal torture'. This is where the basic conditions of incarceration are so abhorrent and structurally violent that they themselves constitute cruel, degrading and inhumane treatment. However, within this banality there are indeed moments of 'spectacular' torture: refugees in Australian-run camps have been tied to metal bed frames, or physically thrown around rooms (Senate Select Committee, 2015), or raped or sexually humiliated (Bacon et al., 2016). As scholars John-Paul Sanggaran and Deborah Zion (2016, p. 402) note:

> The use of force-feeding during hunger strikes, restraints used for deportation and the incarceration of children are examples of these phenomena. The indefinite nature of the detention, the use of numbers to refer to human beings and the harsh physical conditions of the camps add further to this picture.

American psychoanalyst Lisa C. Beritzhoff (2021) describes these kind of places as 'the Meantime'. They are places of 'interminable incertitude filled with existential terror as a result of death encounters and repeated assaults, past and present, enforced helplessness, meaninglessness and an excess of unmourned loss'.

The Camps

In April 2001, ordinary Australians got to see for the first time the impact of camp life on the most vulnerable people: children. Debbie Whitmont reported the plight of Iranian refugee Shayan Badrai in a Walkley award-winning episode of ABC's *Four Corners* titled 'The Inside Story'. Shayan was a six-year-old child who had witnessed so much trauma in the urban Villawood detention complex in Sydney that he had retreated into a state of withdrawal where he had stopped speaking and eating. His days were spent drawing the same picture over and over again: his parents, his little sister and himself standing behind razor wire crying, as a stick-man in the corner of the picture cut his own wrist and blood flowed out. The child was drawing a scene he had witnessed at Villawood of another asylum seeker who had cut his wrist and collapsed into a pool of his own blood. Shayan's parents were given three choices: to return to Iran voluntarily, to stay together as a family in Villawood Immigration Detention Centre until they were deported at an unspecified time, or to send their son away to live outside detention without them.

The 'Inside Story' episode interviewed clinical psychologist Dr. Zachary Steel, Professorial Chair of Trauma and Mental Health at the School of Psychiatry at the University of New South Wales, who described the Villawood centre as populated by 'the most traumatised people on the face of the planet' (Whitmont, 2001). In 2003, Steel gave a keynote address about the psychiatric harm of long-term detention, drawing on such authoritative sources as the Human Rights and Equal Opportunity Commission (HREOC), the Commonwealth Ombudsman, the UN High Commissioner for Human Rights, and the federal parliament's Joint Standing Committee on Foreign Affairs, Defence and Trade, as well as statements from psychiatric specialists who were members of the Immigration Detention Advisory Group. He stressed that it is important to remember that these isolated—and later offshore—camps housed thousands of people who came to Australia for protection—people who were deeply traumatised before they arrived.

The remote desert camps of South Australia and Western Australia were also places of violence, despair and child abuse. Between July 1999 and December 2002, the Woomera, Port Hedland and Curtin detention centres collectively held close to four thousand people. They became sites of hunger strikes, riots and fires. Hundreds of people held demonstrations; some detainees would sew their lips together in silent protest. The razor wire that surrounded the camps caught the bodies of those who tried to jump clear of the fences. Water cannons and tear gas were used on populations of adults and children with nowhere to run (HREOC, 2004). An excerpt from a February 2001 HREOC report on a visit to the centre at Woomera says that statistics provided to HREOC officers by Australasian Correctional Management (ACM), the company then managing the centre, cited the following incidents of self-harm over one two-week period: attempted hanging—one child; lip-sewing—five children; slashing—three children (one slashed the word 'freedom' into his forearm); ingestion of shampoo—two children; threats of self-harm—thirteen children.

Woomera Immigration Reception and Processing Centre was opened in November 1999 near the South Australian village of Woomera. It had capacity for 1200 people, but within a year the total population was 1442, including over 450 children comprising both accompanied and unaccompanied minors. In 2004, the HREOC conducted a national inquiry into children in immigration detention, publishing a report called *A Last Resort?*. In it, an unaccompanied child refugee in Woomera is quoted as saying:

> I believe you [Australians] are nice people, peace seekers, you support unity. If you come to see us behind the fence, think about how you would feel. Are you aware of what happens here? Come and see our life. I wonder whether if the Government of Iran created camp like Woomera and Australians had seen pictures of it, if they would have given people a visa to come to Australia then. (HREOC, 2004)

The next year, in 2005, the Australian Council of Heads of Schools of Social Work also auspiced a People's Inquiry into immigration detention. The inquiry heard almost two hundred verbal accounts and received two hundred written submissions from former detainees, detention centre employees, nurses, doctors, lawyers, educators and former Department of Immigration officials. The following is an example of evidence given at the Inquiry:

The worst thing, I will never forget it, was people cutting themselves. It was horrible. I remember one time a person was harming himself up a tree and his children were crying under the tree. His wife was crying and yelling under the tree. His blood was dropping from the tree. (Briskman et al., 2008, p. 25)

Those are the images that made it over the wire, but for people tasked with the care of this incarcerated community, there was an escalating sense of frustration and bewilderment. Harold Bilboe, former psychologist at Woomera Immigration Reception and Processing Centre, put it like this:

No matter how much I worked with the clients, I couldn't change the cause of the behaviour, the cause of their stress. It's like having a patient coming into the hospital with a nail through the hand and you are giving them pethidine injections for the pain, but you can't remove the nail. That's exactly what is happening in Woomera ... We're not treating it; we're just containing it. Eventually when those people return to their homelands if they don't get temporary visas, they are going to carry that with them. (Macken, 2002)

Anatomy of a Death in Custody

Later in this chapter I present the viewpoints of other psychiatric professionals who have personally seen the atrocities in the camps. One of these eyewitnesses observed, 'there is an obvious horror and trauma about the place itself. But I think it is the de-legitimisation of the people caught there and the bureaucratic cruelty that was probably worse and an even more disabling force'. Jon Jureidini witnessed a weaponised bureaucracy wherein forms were required for the simplest of tasks and nobody could, or would, take responsibility to rectify problems: 'if you asked Immigration they would tell you to ask ACM, and ACM would tell you to ask Immigration, and that could happen three or four times a day, every day'.

As a journalist for the *Australian Financial Review* (*AFR*) who began covering this emerging crisis in 1999, I sat in the HREOC's 2004 Inquiry for many days listening to the evidence. In many ways what I found most disturbing were the answers given by the Department of Immigration and Multicultural and Indigenous Affairs (DIMIA) employees. On 7 December 2002, I published an article in the *AFR* that described in detail just one day of this inquiry. Below I include an extended passage from this article as, in a way, my own testimony.

> Wednesday, the commission spent the entire day observing the life of a family of three asylum seekers mother, father and 12-year-old boy who had spent 20 months in Australian detention centres. The trio came to Woomera in April 2001. This was the time of mass breakouts, riots, and the desperation of detainees sewing their lips together. Nonetheless, they were considered a fully functioning family when they arrived.
>
> By late August 2001, despite his own loneliness, the father had encouraged his wife and son to move to the residential-style housing program, as life in the camp closed in around him.
>
> The woman and their son remained in that program until late May 2002. By the time they were moved back into the camp, the father had gone from being suicidal to psychotic, the mother was only barely coping, and the son was confused and suicidal. In the words of one mental health worker: 'The boy presents as angry, worried; he is trying to assert his inner strength, but he can no longer cope'.
>
> Over the next five months the family totally disintegrated. By October, a senior psychiatrist had admitted the father to an intensive care unit in a psychiatric hospital, telling a teleconference that after numerous suicide attempts, 'he is now psychotic and completely disassociated'.
>
> At this stage of the evidence, Christine McPaul, an assistant secretary with DIMIA, told the commission: 'The family could have returned to their country of origin'.
>
> Commissioner Sev Ozdowski asked McPaul where choice came into it, given the father was now psychotic. To which Douglas Walker, assistant secretary, Visa Framework Branch, replied: 'Ill health doesn't affect his capacity to make a choice'.
>
> At this point, counsel for the commission, Michael Wigney, produced one of two documents that went off like bombs.
>
> The first, from Ann Dutney, executive general manager of ACM, was a letter dated November 5, 2002 addressed to McPaul. It said, in part: 'ACM has sought external assessments [of the family] and numerous reports have been written. All reports say the family should stay together away from

Woomera, as the son is at high risk of suicide and self-harm. ACM options and management strategies are insufficient. The company does not have the capacity to deal with this. Intrusive observation and control has the potential to exacerbate the issues. We understand our contractual obligations to DIMIA but ACM also has responsibilities to raise serious concerns such [as] these with the department'. As of December 5, McPaul had not responded in writing to the letter.

The second document was more specific. It was written by ACM's psychologist at Woomera and addressed to the South Australian Department of Family and Youth Services.

'I accuse DIMIA and the federal government of the emotional abuse of children at Woomera and the residential housing project,' the psychologist wrote. 'They have continued to ignore all the reports from the experts that continual detention further harms children'. She then lists a number of children, one of whom is the 12-year-old boy under discussion and says: 'These children are now completely dysfunctional and we cannot treat them in a detention environment. What is happening in Woomera is a medical and psychiatric emergency.'

It is these two letters that led a number of people to believe that ACM was addressing two audiences. One was the commission, the other a future coronial inquiry after a successful suicide attempt.

'This is the anatomy of a death in custody except we're still waiting for the death to take place,' says Charandev Singh, human rights activist at the Brimbank Community Legal Centre.

Finally, there is the issue of money. ACM is a private company and a subsidiary of Wackenhut, a US private prison company. On the last day of evidence, the case study concerned a family of four: a mother and her three sons, one of whom is profoundly disabled.

This family came to the commission's attention when Ozdowski witnessed the diminutive woman pushing her 15-year-old son across the desert terrain of Woomera in an old pram. In March 2001, the Kimberley Health Service had approached DIMIA with a request for a wheelchair. The chair finally arrived 14 months later, in May 2002.

However, it seems the issue of who was responsible for the cost of the care of the child was a bone of contention between ACM and DIMIA. Frustrated with DIMIA's response to its demands, in June 2002 ACM sent the department an email saying: 'ACM will be dumping this child on DIMIA's doorstep tomorrow morning if payment is not forthcoming. (Macken, 2002)

The Inquiry made the following major findings: that Australia's immigration detention laws create a detention system that is fundamentally inconsistent with the Convention on the Rights of the Child; that children in immigration detention for long periods of time are at high risk of serious mental harm; and that the Commonwealth's failure to implement the repeated recommendations by mental health professionals that certain children be removed from the detention environment with their parents amounted to cruel, inhumane and degrading treatment of those children in detention.

Moving the Camps Out of Site/Sight: A Timeline

When Prime Minister John Howard began his Pacific Solution by building detention camps offshore on Manus Island (PNG) and in Nauru, even constraints that had been in place in Australia began to unravel. Australia signed an Administrative Agreement with Nauru on 10 September 2001 for Nauru to accommodate asylum seekers for Australian processing. A Memorandum of Understanding was signed with Papua New Guinea on 11 October 2001. By April 2002, the combined population in the centres in Nauru and PNG was 1511 people: 125 women, 213 children and 30 unaccompanied minors in Nauru; 65 women and 125 children on PNG's Manus Island. There were nineteen babies born in the Nauru Regional Processing Centre between 2001 and 2004, and three babies born in Manus Island Regional Processing Centre between 2001 and 2003. The Nauru caseload also included the majority of the 433 asylum seekers rescued during the *Tampa* incident.

In July 2002, the United Nations Report on Mandatory Detention was released. Former Indian Supreme Court Chief Justice Rajendra Bhagwati wrote this report after visiting Australia's immigration detention facilities in 2002 as a personal envoy of the UN Human Rights Commissioner. The report stated that the Australia's immigration detention policy contravened the International Covenant on Civil and Political Rights, which outlaws arbitrary detention and the denial of access to legal review of incarceration, and the UN Convention on the Rights of the

Child, which prohibits detention of children except as a last resort. Bhagwati reported that children were suffering mentally and physically and that many were 'traumatised and led to harm themselves in utter despair' (2002, p. 16). This report did not alter the course of Australian immigration policy.

The two offshore camps operated at varying levels of capacity—and over-capacity—for the next seven years. During that time, information from them became almost completely inaccessible in Australia, with next to no transparency about how detainees on these two distant islands were treated or about whether they were processed or sent back to their countries of origin. When the Rudd government dismantled the Pacific Solution in February 2008, closing both the camps, Kevin Rudd said in his capacity as prime minister: 'Labor will end the Pacific Solution, the so-called Pacific Solution, the processing and detaining of asylum seekers on Pacific islands, because it is costly, unsustainable and wrong as a matter of principle'.

The Gillard government reopened Manus Island Regional Processing Centre in 2012 and Nauru Regional Processing Centre in 2013. By 2015, the principal contracted service provider, Broadspectrum (formerly Transfield) had mandatorily reported thirty formal allegations against its staff of child abuse, fifteen allegations of sexual assault or rape, and four allegations of receiving sexual favours in exchange for contraband. Wilson Security provided details of eleven cases in which staff were terminated for misconduct including inappropriate relationships, alleged sexual assault, sexual harassment, excessive use of force towards an asylum seeker, trading in contraband including for sexual favours and throwing a rock at an asylum seeker (No Business in Abuse, 2015).

On 6 March 2015, the UN Special Rapporteur released a report on torture and other cruel, inhumane or degrading treatment or punishment. The report found Australian border officials to be in breach of the Convention against Torture for, among other things, tying refugees to chairs and threatening 'physical violence, rape, and prosecution for "becoming aggressive"' (Méndez, 2015), and that Australia had violated the right of the asylum seekers, including children, to be free from torture.

In May 2016, I co-authored the report '*Protection Denied, Abuse Condoned: Women on Nauru at Risk*' (Bacon et al., 2016) documenting the sexual assault and routine humiliation of women refugees living in Nauru and the plight of their children. Rapes in and around Australia's centre in Nauru, where single women and families have been detained since 2013, regularly resulted in pregnancies that became a source of further anxiety, humiliation and pain for the women raped. A young woman who had been given refugee status to live in Nauru but not allowed to go to the Australian mainland told her story to Australia's *The Saturday Paper*:

> In April 2015 she was waiting at a bus stop [in Nauru] when a car pulled up beside her. The bus wasn't coming, the men said, and if she waited at the stop she would fall prey to 'dogs that eat humans'. They offered her a lift. 'So I told myself that the driver might say truth, so I said OK. But when they arrived where they want, they said "get out of the car". I understand what they want. It was one man who wants to rape me, that is why they told me to get out of the car. The other man – I don't know where he has gone. Only one man left with me. I tried to beg him but that was impossible. What he want he got it from me'. (McKenzie-Murray, 2015)

A story emerged about another woman who was twenty-four years old when she decided to use her day release from the processing centre to visit a refugee friend who was living in the community in Nauru. Her mother and brother became concerned when she failed to return to the centre by the evening curfew and her brother began a frantic search for her, assisted by some guards. She was not found until 9 pm that night. The local police discovered her slumped beside the road outside the detention centre. She was deeply traumatised and bruised, with bite marks all over her body. She had been the victim of serious sexual assault. The Minister for Immigration, Scott Morrison, sent Philip Moss, a former Commonwealth Integrity Commissioner, to investigate. The subsequent Moss' report confirmed that assaults and rapes were regularly occurring but not being reported for fear of reprisal (Moss, 2015).

On 10 August 2016, *The Guardian* released 'The Nauru Files', documents totalling more than eight hundred pages detailing more than two thousand leaked incident reports from Australia's detention arrangement in Nauru. The files allege seven reports of the sexual assault of children, fifty-nine other reports of assaults on children, thirty reports of self-harm involving children and numerous serious threats of self-harm. Allegations of sexual assault against children and young single women living in the camps feature largely. In one of the reports, a young asylum seeker described being told she was 'on a list' complied by local Nauruan guards who named the women they would be 'waiting for' when they were released into the community in Nauru. She said she had received offers to get her pregnant when she got out of detention. The files allege serious misconduct by Wilson Security guards. One reported a 'cultural adviser' employed by Wilson Security telling a woman who had been sexually assaulted in the camp that 'rape in Australia is common and people don't get punished' (Evershed et al., 2016).

On 17 October 2016, Amnesty International launched its report *'Island of Despair: Australia's "Processing" of Refugees on Nauru'*.

> Mental illness and incidents of self-harm among refugees and asylum-seekers in Nauru are shockingly commonplace. Nearly all of the people who Amnesty International's researcher met on Nauru in July 2016 reported mental health issues of some kind: high levels of anxiety, trouble sleeping, and mood swings were frequently mentioned. One man told Amnesty International that he had tried to kill himself twice in the previous ten weeks. An Iranian refugee has tried to kill herself many times, sometimes two or more times a week. Eventually she set the family dwelling on fire and is now confined to a medical ward in a Refugee Processing Centre. Another man described how his pregnant wife tried to hang herself – he found her in the bathroom with rope marks on her neck. (Amnesty International, 2016, p. 5)

All of Amnesty's findings, and more, were conveyed in the Communiqué to the Office of the Prosecutor of the International Criminal Court Under Article 15 of the Rome Statute by the Global Legal Action Network in February 2017. On 13 February 2020, the Prosecutor of the International Criminal Court (ICC) wrote to Independent Australian MP Andrew Wilkie, concluding that Australia's policy of mandatory offshore detention for asylum seekers constituted cruel, inhuman or degrading treatment but declining to open a preliminary examination.

The Court's preliminary opinion found:

These conditions of detention appear to have constituted cruel, inhuman, or degrading treatment ('CIDT'), and the gravity of the alleged conduct thus appears to have been such that it was in violation of fundamental rules of international law. This conclusion – including regarding the relevance of victims being subjected to CIDT – is consistent with jurisprudence from other international courts and tribunals and human rights supervisory bodies regarding the level of severity required to establish a deprivation of liberty that falls within the intended scope of the crime provided under article 7(1)(e). ()

Dr. Sarah Williams Professor at UNSW Law offered an analysis of the prosecutors' response finding in part:

The Prosecutor highlighted the degrading, overcrowded and primitive conditions in the Regional Processing Centres, the limited access to medical care, and the physical and sexual violence committed by staff and members of the local population. And found these conditions caused asylum seekers severe mental suffering, culminating in suicide, suicide attempts, and other forms of self-harm. She did not accept that the Government's policies were *deliberately* designed to lead to cruel, inhuman or degrading treatment. As the ICC requires that there be a link between the criminal conduct and a state policy, the crime against humanity of severe deprivation of liberty had not been committed and no Australian politicians could be prosecuted. She also found in her opinion the conditions they were held in did not constitute torture (as the mistreatment of asylum seekers was not sufficiently severe), and the Government's targeting of asylum seekers was not persecution (as the crime was not committed on discriminatory grounds).

The Prosecutor's opinion did not clearly address all the legal questions about Australia's policy. For example, the Prosecutor determined that the detention of asylum seekers was not committed on discriminatory grounds. She did not respond to the argument that a policy directed against asylum seekers *is* discriminatory. She concluded by noting she may reconsider her position based on new facts or information. This occurred in the case of UK soldiers in Iraq—the Prosecutor initially declined to open an examination but did so after lawyers for victims sent further information. Thus, a future prosecution of Australian politicians before the ICC is not impossible, but unlikely. (UNSW news 2020)

Over these years the death toll in both Nauru and Manus Island grew. The Australian Border Deaths Database maintains a record of all known deaths associated with Australia's borders since 1 January 2000. Of all these over two thousand deaths, seventeen occurred in Manus Island and Nauru and forty-one occurred in Australia's onshore detention regime.[2] The sheer volume of deaths doesn't detract from the agony of each. I remember watching a live stream video of Omid Masoumali killing himself, on my mobile phone, and seeing him try to yell to a United Nations team who were leaving the Nauru camp; he was crying out in despair and utterly exhausted as he self-immolated. Though he suffered burns to more than 57 per cent of his body, an inquest heard that he had been given an initial trivial 'diagnosis of a scald' and was treated on a baby's cot in a dirty, old hospital with mould on the walls. It took two days for Omid to die.

What the Doctors Found

Resistance to Australia's detention policies has existed for the duration of the policies. One of the first groups to advocate for those seeking protection was the medical profession—nurses and physicians who work with asylum seekers to try to find healing for the body and mind. Approaching five of these committed individuals who excel in the mental health sphere, I asked them to describe psychiatric conditions in Australia's detention centres, short- and long-term impacts on asylum seekers and families, and, more abstractedly, how they would 'treat' the nation of Australia if it were a person and their patient.

Interview 1: Professor Louise Newman

Louise Newman is Professor of Developmental Psychiatry and Director of the Monash University Centre for Developmental Psychiatry and Psychology. She comes to questions of torture as a psychiatrist working in the areas of gendered violence and refugee abuse. I first interviewed her

---

[2] The database was established by Professor Sharon Pickering and Associate Professor Leanne Weber as part of Bob's Deaths at the Global Frontier project, which culminated in the 2011 publication of the book *Globalization and Borders: Death at the Global Frontier*

in 2004 for an article for the *AFR*. I asked her to describe the psychiatric impact on those subject to Australia's detention regime. The following is excerpted from that article:

> Any human could become suicidal in this situation,' says Newman. 'People become blind, mute, develop conversion disorders, becoming unable to walk, paralysed … it's the extreme response to trauma. Children regress and relationships break down, families fragment and people can't trust each other it's a meltdown.
>
> This 'meltdown' is hard for the average person to understand, particularly in Australia where life for most is so safe. But try to imagine being constantly observed, being identified by a number, and not being able to protect your children from the abuse of guards or other detainees. Put yourself in the place of parents unable to tell children why they are locked up, or when they will be getting out. Worst of all, imagine what it's like for children whose mum or dad have stopped speaking, eating or caring, or are trying to kill themselves. One of Newman's patients was a 14-year-old girl who said the guards kept telling her, 'Don't get your hopes up. You're never going to be released. You're going to die in here'.
>
> People deal with the mounting stress in different ways. The conversion disorders Newman refers to are very unusual in the broader community, but in the detention centres they became common. 'There's a man I see in Baxter (immigration detention centre) who is blind,' Newman explains. 'He has a conversion disorder which has made him go blind. He understands it's caused by stress. He says: 'My eyes are normal, but my brain tells them not to see,' which is a very good explanation. He's from Iraq. He has made inquiries and he knows that he will never see his daughter again. So he's blind and has been for nearly two years.' (Macken, 2004)

Eighteen years later, on 12 January 2020, I asked Newman her thoughts on the same topic: the mental health impacts of Australia's immigration detention.

> The use of solitary confinement in Australian's detention centres, being treated with contempt, being potentially sexually assaulted by the guards, these sorts of things; there's a long and inglorious tradition of acting out on

the body of the enemy and that's what is going on here. ... We are very good at driving people to suicide in these camps. Being told you will be imprisoned forever, that there is no hope. That's a common tactic. When you look at it in totality, they're all things that destroy people's sense of psychological safety and security and identity. Who can I be in the face of what I'm told? How do I come to accept that I am nothing, that I am powerless, that I'm a number? I have no friends. I don't have a name. We can unpack the building blocks of that, but the net result is destruction of hope and of any sense of being safe in the world. That's psychological torture. Physical pain, in a sense, transcends that. Torture survivors often speak about physical pain as a bit of a relief because it proves to you that your body is still alive.

Professor Newman described what she witnessed walking through the Woomera and Baxter detention camps:

People were openly slashing themselves. I saw men digging their own graves and people burying themselves in the sand to try and die. We saw people on the roofs. We saw people attempting to strangle themselves and hang themselves on a mass scale. Nothing prepares you for that. It was a mass breakdown of the human will to live or cope.

Newman's reflection on how she would treat Australia if the state were her psychiatric patient begins with the need to reassert reality for the patient.

I think it's a combination of first working out how people can start the process of coming to terms with what reality is. I think our national psyche needs to have a moral discussion. We're in the midst of the collapse of collective values. The fact that we are psychologically torturing people; the fact that we locked children up from birth until they're two and a half years of age and they're damaged for life: this is a form of collective madness. I think we need to be able to name that, but also help people survive the naming of it. I don't think it's easy, but that's what I'd engage in, a moral discussion. A reconstruction of core values. And maybe as we face calamity from climate change or this COVID virus it may be something we are more likely to have discussions about.

5 Is It Torture?   97

This suggestion is akin to what Freud (1917) described as 'reality testing', an integral part of the mourning process. Klein (1946) saw it as the stricken infant moving beyond terror into what she called the depressive position. Both describe the point at which the infant's anxiety for itself begins to morph into a concern for the (m)Other, and eventually resolve into a sadness and deepening love as the infant understands the harm it has willed and/or done. It is the beginning of both love and psychological maturity.

Interview 2: Professor David Isaacs

Medical professionals who have spoken out about abuses of refugees and asylum seekers know that, at the very least, it will affect their professional careers. David Isaacs came into the national spotlight in June 2015 when he risked two years' jail to convey what he described as conditions of torture in Nauru. A highly regarded paediatrician, on a trip to Nauru he witnessed these conditions first-hand:

> 'I saw a six-year-old child who tried to hang herself with a fence tie. I saw a 15-year-old lad who'd sewed his lips up and his parents were cross with him for doing it, and he was cross with them because when he collapsed they let the medical staff cut the ties on his lips,' he recalled. 'I just saw endless trauma … I saw 20 or 30 children and the trauma they were going through, over a year in prison really without knowing what their fate was going to be, it was appalling.' (Shoebridge, 2015)

Five years later, when I interviewed him on 3 December 2020, he remained convinced.

> I think it's torture and it meets the criteria, that it is deliberately damaging people's mental health, knowing that what you're doing is going to damage their mental health. They've seen the evidence. We've all talked about. And it is intentional. They are abusing people to make sure they go back and that's also why they are not processing any claims. No matter how much you tell the people in power: "This is damaging people. Don't do this. Bring them to Australia in community detention, process them that way" – they won't do it.

When asked how he would hypothetically treat an anthropomorphised Australia, his approach also began with the need to reassert reality and establish some degree of trust.

> This is all about trust. So, I would be trying to win the trust of the Australian state while helping the state reflect on the way they're treating people. So, I would be saying: "You're talking about these people as if they're not humans, but they are humans. Here they are. I see them every day and you can meet them if you want." Then I would suggest that this is not what Australia is about. We need you to reflect on that because it's in danger of damaging our image. I would appeal to both their conscience and self-interest. But if I thought they were going to damage a child – their child – then I may say: "I know you love your child, but I disagree with you so strongly I'm prepared to involve legal measures over your treatment."

Of course, that's the problem in Australia, there is no police force or judge or jury to protect asylum seekers. There are no boundaries around the state to impose a containing safety for either its victims or its 'self' in its drive to abuse the Other. The state is in the grip of melancholia that remains dangerous to both itself and Others. There is no good-enough mother/police/court that can contain this damage.

Interview 3: Dr Jon Jureidini

Child psychiatrist Dr. Jureidini works with ill and disabled children and their families at the Women's and Children's Hospital in Adelaide, South Australia. He first went to the Woomera detention centre in 2003, and clearly remembers the first day he walked into the camp. On 9 March 2020 he described it to me. 'It was June and a beautiful sunny day; the UN had just visited so everything had been tidied up … and I love desert landscapes … but it was just horrifying walking into Woomera. Just terrible. It was a life-changing experience for me'.

Reflecting on that time in his interview with me on 14 March 2020, he outlined the stages of disintegration many asylum seekers tended to undergo:

> The first thing that seemed to go was parenting capacity. In the first cohort of people that we saw in Woomera – about six to ten families – in every case there were significant child protection issues within the family because

the parents had lost their capacity to care for their children. One florid example was a young mother with an infant. The other people in the compound were complaining about the baby crying, and so she taped the baby's mouth [shut].

I saw people who were good enough parents in their own environments failing in the camp environment. And often you'd have the children adopting more of a parental role. One little boy whose father had become more or less catatonic and whose mother was very severely depressed and suicidal … was eating coffee to keep himself awake at night to keep an eye on his parents. Another father asked to have his children taken [away] and given to an Australian family, clearly so he could take his own life.

So, there was the parental failure. Then there were three stages that people, particularly single men, went through. First, they came in with hope and optimism and engaged in any activities around the place that they could. And as time went on and nothing changed, they got angry and tried to protest, and that would attract mental health attention, who would be saying it is a manifestation of madness rather than legitimate protest. And it was a messy, ugly process: sewing lips together and burying themselves alive and throwing themselves on the razor wire, that kind of thing. And then: what the centre considered recovery but what was in fact giving up and going to bed. Those that get out [of detention] during the protesting, angry phase get well, but those who don't get out until they reach the given-up stage rarely get well.

On the question of recovery for the state, how would Jureidini begin to treat Australia?

First, I think it would be important for Australia to be weaned off the moral antidepressant it's on, because it is numbing the state's capacity to take responsibility for this behaviour. It's making Australia feel comfortable and relaxed, but it is diminishing the nation. There is no comfortable way to recover from this. Australia is going to have to face up to the bad things it's done and that's going to be a painful process. The nation can't just say sorry and bring flowers, it is going to have to earn the right to apologise for what has been done. Australia is so sanctimonious and self-righteous, but perhaps that is compensatory. This system is so destructive that every asylum seeker I have asked has said they would prefer to be in jail than in this detention. I know I would.

Interview 4: Dr Peter Young

Peter Young came into the detention complex at the peak of his career in mental health services, at a time when a wave of optimism flooded the sector after the Palmer Inquiry (2005). However, as Young described his years within the immigration system in his interview with me on 29 June 2020, I began to wonder if the detention centres functioned as psychotic pockets where everyone—workers, asylum seekers and guards—went mad. 'We certainly encountered some very bizarre sort of phenomenology in them', Young said about observing neurotic levels of denial within the Canberra bureaucracy.

> I would be sitting in meetings with very senior health bureaucrats and say how I was concerned with the way people were referred to by a number. They would deny that was happening and then within a few minutes they would be referring to people by their number.

On the question of conditions within the Nauru detention centre, Young described the chosen landscape for the camp in Nauru as helping to drain hope.

> [Nauru] is a place ruined by colonisation – a failed state with stray dogs and rubbish everywhere. The Kafkaesque element is that [the Nauru camp environment] is a place full of rules that change every day; people are given arbitrary, contradictory messages and no one has any agency at all. That's a key element of the abuse.

But is it torture or just harsh treatment?

> It's torture. If you're trying to coerce people, through suffering, to make a decision which is against their interests, and you're causing deliberate suffering in order to try and achieve your outcome – that's the definition of torture. You can't get around that. That's your intention and why you are imposing this intentional suffering. The government knows this: they even made a series of cartoons and sent them to Pakistan and Afghanistan to try and stop people coming. The series shows the story of someone coming to Australia through a people smuggler and the last image in the series is a broken man sitting in a green tent sobbing with an anguished face. They advertised what they were doing in these cartoons.

The whole thrust of the detention is to put people into a hopeless state with the aim that if they do that, it will make them willing to return to where they came from. And the others will take that [hint], you know, or see what they're suffering and decide not to come. Inevitably, that means some people will die – they will kill themselves. So, I guess, in terms of torture it is efficient. It is so bad that people would choose to take their own life rather than continue.

Rather than discussing how he would treat Australia as a patient, Dr. Young spoke about the need for mental health professionals to consider their own position in this system and boycott detention. Psychiatrists are still acutely aware of role played by their profession during the Nazi regime. With that history it is unsurprising how many mental health professionals have struggled with the question of working within this abusive system to care for their patients when they can, or whether their very involvement implicates them in the abuse. This is an ongoing issue for doctors, social workers and nurses within this regime.

Dr. Young also agreed with Dr. Newman and Dr. Juredini that political action within the camps could be a mental health strategy that preserves an essential part of one's selfhood.

Interview 5: Dr Michael Dudley

Michael Dudley is Chair of Suicide Prevention Australia, senior lecturer in psychiatry at the University of New South Wales, psychiatrist at Prince of Wales Hospital and Sydney Children's Hospital, and a founding member (2001) of Mental Health Alliance for Refugees. On 12 May 2020, I asked him to describe the conditions of detention in Australia's offshore immigration processing camps.

The conditions of detention are diabolical. They are places of terror interspersed with extreme boredom in extreme conditions. People witness violent acts, they witness terrible self-harm; they are brutalised, racially vilified and dehumanised in a range of ways. Pain is pain, whether it is physical or psychological. It is torture in those places. The harms have been proven and the government knows this.

Much of Dudley's work has been in the field of suicide prevention in adolescents, so I asked about the role of safety in contributing to mental health or illness.

Safety is absolutely fundamental to the construction of our sense of self. Safety and security of attachment, and a sense of justice, are absolutely essential. There is no safety in these places, nor security. At an absolute minimum the neglect constitutes abuse. The government does nothing to remediate the injuries or abuse because they are persecuting people in order to force them back to where they came from.

Dudley is not new to the heat of this debate: in February 2016 he came under fire after publishing a paper condemning 'public numbing and indifference' towards state abuses in Australia's immigration detention centres. He also likened public complicity and its enabling effects on a torturing government to both the White Australia policy and Nazi Germany. I asked Dudley how he would treat the nation if it were his patient.

> Because of the violence I would be getting the police involved and warning the next of kin. So, the first step would be containment. Then they would have to own what they have done and for that we would need to give the state support to do that. Particularly so they don't keep passing it along.

Activism and 'lifestyle choices'

On the issue of detainees physically resisting the dehumanisation imposed by the guards, the poverty of the environment and the wanton capriciousness of Australia's immigration policy itself, Newman, Jureidini and Young all argued that political action could be a mental health strategy that preserves an essential part of one's selfhood. 'I think that's why the government hated it when people began hunger strikes', Dr. Young said: 'because hunger strikes are a political act over which they had little control. But that's also why the force-feeding is so destructive [to people's free will]'. In the murk of melancholia, the act of political resistance represents a vitality and reality that is absent otherwise. The act of taking a stand, for instance, in the form of hunger strikes and/or sewing the lips together, is a way of clearly and loudly signalling transgression and desperation in a language understood across cultures and time.

Given the narcissistic and victimistic nature of melancholia, it should come as no surprise that these actions have been framed by the Australian cabinet and mainstream media as attacks on the goodness of Australians.

The attempted suicides and escapes, the self-harm, are villainised while the perpetrator, a violent and abusive detention system, remains hidden from view. Such is the power of this melancholic denial and the bizarre situations it creates within the state and its ministers that in 2003 the immigration minister, Philip Ruddock, tried to deny the existence of mental health damage by denying mental illness itself, saying, 'I'm not sure that everybody would regard depression as a mental illness' (Special Broadcasting Service, 2003). A few weeks later, challenged about the level of distress and mental illness in the Woomera centre, he told host Kerry O'Brien on the ABC's *7.30 Report* that he blamed those detained for their distressed reactions.

> There were perceptions in the centres themselves that, by action of self-harm, people had achieved outcomes. And it led to a belief amongst a proportion of the Afghan population that the only way in which they were going to obtain visas was to be involved in the same sort of conduct.

This form of gaslighting is endemic in Australia's immigration detention regime.[3] Here the immigration minister denies the existence of mental illness and when pressured to explain, he dismisses the distress and pain as a tactic used to achieve an outcome (a visa). In so doing, he exemplifies the reversal of power characteristic of the melancholic paranoid-schizoid phase (Klein, 1946), as an authoritative government minister frames defenceless asylum seekers as powerful and the dominant state as the underdog, a plucky defender of flailing national interests. Speaking to *Los Angeles Times,* Ruddock reduced the trauma of fleeing persecution—the primary reason asylum seekers arrive in Australia—to a 'lifestyle choice':

> The Australian Government does not 'lock up' refugees, nor does it detain people for seeking asylum. We do, however, place in detention people who arrive unlawfully until their asylum claims are determined and we find out who they are [and] where they are from … They make a lifestyle choice to travel to Australia, breaking the laws of many countries along the way. (Crosweller & Saunders, 2002)

---

[3] I am using the term 'gaslighting' to describe an emotionally abusive strategy that causes someone to question their feelings, thoughts and sanity. The purpose of gaslighting is to convince a person or group that they can't trust their experience, thoughts or instincts, even when there is direct evidence supporting them.

I would contend that remaining to live in Omelas is in fact the 'lifestyle choice'. But at some point it should become unbearable to live in complacency while people are tortured nearby. This leads me to my next questions: How is this abuse operationalised, and how can abuse on this scale, and with this intensity, occur with consent from the electorate?

References

Amnesty International. (2016). *Island of despair: Australia's 'processing' of refugees on Nauru.* https://www.amnesty.org.au/island-of-despair-nauru-refugee-report-2016/

Attorney-General's Department. (2021). Prohibition on torture and cruel, inhuman or degrading treatment or punishment, public sector guidance sheet. *Australian Government.* https://www.ag.gov.au/rights-and-protections/human-rights-and-anti-discrimination/human-rights-scrutiny/public-sector-guidance-sheets/prohibition-torture-and-cruel-inhuman-or-degrading-treatment-or-punishment

Bacon, W., Curr, P., Lawrence, C., Macken, J., & O'Connor, C. (2016). *Protection Denied, Abuse Condoned: Women on Nauru at Risk.* Australian Women in Support of Women on Nauru. https://www.awswn.org/the-report

Beritzhoff, L. C. (2021). Psychoanalysis in the meantime. *Psychoanalytic Dialogues, 31*(1), 81–99. https://doi.org/10.1080/10481885.2020.1863075

Briskman, L., Latham, S., & Goddard, C. (2008). *Human rights overboard: Seeking asylum in Australia.* Scribe.

Celermajer, D. (2018). *The prevention of torture: An ecological approach.* Cambridge University Press.

Convention against Torture and Other Cruel, Inhuman or Degrading Treatment or Punishment, opened for signature 10 December 1984, 1465 UNTS 85 (entered into force 26 June 1987).

Crosweller, A., & Saunders, M. (2002, January 8). Refugees' plight a 'lifestyle choice'. *The Australian,* p. 2.

Devetak, R. (2004). In fear of refugees: The politics of border protection in Australia. *The International Journal of Human Rights, 8*(1), 101–109. https://doi.org/10.1080/1364298042000212565

Doherty, B. (2016, October 17). Australian immigration regime on Nauru an 'open-air prison' and akin to torture, says Amnesty. *The Guardian.* https://www.theguardian.com/australia-news/2016/oct/17/australian-immigra(on-regime-on-nauru-an-open-air-prison-and-akin-to-torture-says-amnesty

Evershed, N., Liu, R., Farrell, P., & Davidson, H. (2016). The Nauru files. *The Guardian*. https://www.theguardian.com/news/series/nauru-files.

Farrell, P. (2016, August 10). 'I want death': Nauru files chronicle despair of asylum seeker children. *The Guardian*. https://www.theguardian.com/news/2016/aug/10/i-want-death-nauru-files-chronicle-despair-of-asylum-seeker-children

Global Legal Action Network. (2017). Communiqué to the Office of the Prosecutor of the International Criminal Court Under Article 15 of the Rome Statute. https://docs.wixstatic.com/ugd/b743d9_e4413cb72e1646d8bd3e8a8c9a466950.pdf

Human Rights and Equal Opportunity Commission. (2004). *A last resort? National inquiry into children in immigration detention*. HREOC. https://humanrights.gov.au/our-work/asylum-seekers-and-refugees/publications/last-resort-national-inquiry-children-immigration

International Criminal Court. (2020, February, 12). OTP-CR-322/14/001. Letter from the Office of the Prosecutor to the Office of Andrew Wilkie MP [PDF]. https://andrewwilkie.org/wp-content/uploads/2020/02/200213-Andrew-Wilkie-Response-from-International-Criminal-Court-Australian-Government-treatment-of-asylum-seekers.pdf

Klein, M. (1946). Notes on some schizoid mechanisms. *The International Journal of Psycho-Analysis*, 99–110.

Le Guin, U. K. (1975). *The wind's twelve quarters*. Harper & Row.

Macken, J. (2002, December 7). The face of the refugee, in focus. AFR perspective. *Australian Financial Review*.

Macken, J. (2004, May 14). On citizenship and the care of other people's children. AFR Perspective. *The Australian Financial Review*.

Marr, D., & Laughland, O. (2014, August 5). Australia's detention regime sets out to make asylum seekers suffer, says chief immigration psychiatrist. *The Guardian*. https://www.theguardian.com/world/2014/aug/05/-sp-australias-detention-regime-sets-out-to-make-asylum-seekers-suffer-says-chief-immigration-psychiatrist

McKenzie-Murray, M. (2015, August 22). Nauru rapes: 'There is a war on women'. *The Saturday Paper*. https://thesaturdaypaper.com.au/news/immigration/2015/08/22/nauru-rapes-there-war-women/14401656002263

Méndez, J. E. (2015). *Report of the Special Rapporteur on torture and other cruel, inhuman or degrading treatment or punishment. Addendum: Observations on communications 146 transmitted to governments and replies received*. Office of the United Nations High Commissioner for Human Rights. https://ap.ohchr.org/documents/dpage_e.aspx?si=A/HRC/28/68/Add.1

Moss, P. (2015). *Review into recent allegations relating to conditions and circumstance at the regional processing Centre in Nauru: Final report*. Department of Immigration and Border Protection [PDF]. https://apo.org.au/sites/default/files/resource-files/2015-03/apo-nid53915.pdf

O'Brien, K. (presenter) (2003, May 20). Interview with Philip Ruddock. *7.30 Report* [TV series]. ABC.

Palmer, M. J. (2005). *Inquiry into the circumstances of the immigration detention of Cornelia Rau: Report* [PDF]. Department of Immigration and Multicultural and Indigenous Affairs. https://www.homeaffairs.gov.au/reports-and-pubs/files/palmer-report.pdf

Sanggaran, J.-P., & Zion, D. (2016). Is Australia engaged in torturing asylum seekers? A cautionary tale for Europe. *Journal of Medical Ethics, 42*(7), 420–423. https://www.jstor.org/stable/44014403

Senate. Select Committee on the Recent Allegations Relating to the Conditions and Circumstances at the Regional Processing Centre in Nauru. (2015). Submission 95. https://www.aph.gov.au/Parliamentary_Business/Committees/Senate/Regional_processing_Nauru/Regional_processing_Nauru/Submissions

Shoebridge, J. (2015, June 19). Paediatrician may face prison for speaking out about Nauru. *ABC North Coast*. ABC Local website. https://www.abc.net.au/local/stories/2015/06/19/4258214.htm

Special Broadcasting Service. (2003, May 8). *Insight* [TV series]. SBS.

Whitmont, D. (Reporter). (2001, August 8). The Inside Story [TV series episode]. *Four Corners*. ABC. www.abc.net.au/4corners/theinside-story—2001/2844922.

6

Words Make Worlds

I write this chapter in August 2021, having just returned from a cold and windswept inner-city campus of the University of Technology Sydney (UTS), where the National Justice Project and Amnesty International co-hosted a press conference to reveal the coroner's findings into the death of Omid Masoumali. A young Iranian refugee, Masoumali died after setting himself on fire in Nauru. Melissa Iaria reported for news. com on 1 November 2021:

> Omid started his journey [seeking asylum] in 2013 as an optimistic and perhaps naïve 22-year-old. Within three years he had died a painful death in a Brisbane hospital after struggling to come to terms with the reality of an indefinite period in Nauru.

Brisbane Coroner Terry Ryan found that the uncertainty of endless detention had become unendurable for Omid, despite his initial hope and resilience, and that therefore he had found a way to end his own life.

At the press conference, I looked across the small crowd of activists and recognised all their faces even if I didn't know all their names. We have been turning up to these grim performances for decades. We know where to stand, what to bring and how to manage the microphone and the

© The Author(s), under exclusive license to Springer Nature Switzerland AG 2025
J. Macken, *Australia's Schism in the Soul*, Studies in the Psychosocial,
https://doi.org/10.1007/978-3-031-93813-9_6

banners. For some reason, the weather for these events is almost always cold. There are banks of media cameras while just one senior reporter from *The Guardian* asks all the questions. He asks all the questions because he knows the territory—he has been reporting on this subject for close to a decade. A large number of the media need to be told about the inadequate condition of the hospital in Nauru; they need to be told about the nation of Nauru itself and its status as an almost failed state despite a drip-feed of funds from the Australian Government for running our detention camps.[1] It's not the younger media personnel's fault that they don't know all the details. This is a long story, and they were still school students when it started. But the very fact that they don't know the history is a reminder, should one be needed, that coverage of the state-sanctioned Australian abuse of asylum seekers is now lengthy and complicated. The story lives on—and asylum seekers die—at the intersection of government discourse, media practice and the carceral complex.

Because of its complexity, it is not enough to rely on a media analysis of the coverage of Australia's treatment of asylum seekers or a review of government discourse. Sociologist Ignacio Mendiola (2014) describes how dehumanising narratives and the transformation of a human being into Other create the conditions for the exercise of torture, turning the disempowered Other into a torturable subject. To make sense of how asylum seekers are made into torturable subjects, I investigate a number of interlocking narratives and key words, examine the elevation of certain voices and disappearance of others. Finally I question how the absence of asylum seekers themselves generated sufficient centrifugal force to stabilise the state's narrative concerning the 'illegality', 'threat' and 'danger' posed by those fleeing persecution. This powerful absence, the inaccessibility of asylum seekers locked away in the detention camps and the introduction of tactics such as 'on water matters' gave the state unprecedented control of the narrative. But for all the invisibility or because of the invisibility, the state was able to co-opt asylum seekers to create entire federal election campaigns around the threat of their presence. The

---

[1] Nauru, once rich, has acquired most of the characteristics of a failed state, in large part because of the consequences of an extreme 'resource curse' scenario. The Australian Government funding of the offshore immigration camp comprised almost two-thirds of the local economy.

mainstream media played a vital role in all these developments. To investigate that I will look at particular moments of reporting in the mainstream media because as Australian linguist Mary Macken-Horarik (2003, p. 1) has pointed out, 'Multisemiotic texts such as newspapers should be subject to rigorous discourse analysis not least because such texts have real civic and political effects. They are important sites for the (re)production of nationalist and racist discourses' (Macken-Horarik, 2003).

Yet while words create worlds, on their own they are not capable of doing the heavy lifting necessary to reconceptualise a child as a potential terrorist. To make this melancholic, victimising leap the state requires an ecology of communication made up of simplified narratives, disappearances and a powerful negative space redolent of the half-life of narcissism (Freud, 1917). Facilitating the cruel, inhumane and degrading treatment of a child, a pregnant mother or an old woman is not easy. This is particularly true when the state has previously been capable of humane, legal and compassionate management of a national refugee policy.

Meet the Media

Foremost, it is important to say two things about media in Australia. The first is that Australia's media market is one of the most concentrated in the world. The industry's four largest commercial players, News Australia, Nine Media (formerly Fairfax Media), Seven West Media and APN News and Media were estimated in 2015–2016 to account for over 90 per cent of industry revenue. The two largest companies, News Australia and Nine Media, publish content that reaches most Australians.

Second, the majority of journalists in Australia are White. In 2020, Media Diversity Australia commissioned the first in-depth study of cultural diversity in Australian television news. The study found that during the survey period June 2019 to June 2020, people from an Anglo-Celtic background made up almost 76 per cent of appearances on Australian screens. Only 6 per cent were from an Indigenous or non-European background despite the fact that these groups account for about a quarter of the Australian population. The other 18 per cent had European backgrounds other than Anglo-Celtic. Only one board member across the whole television news industry was Indigenous.

The media, news gathering, news production, news reporting, what gets reported, what doesn't, are cultural constructs. Given the Whiteness of Australian media and ownership, what is and what is not considered news are viewed through a White lens, usually unconsciously so. The media reflects the dominant White worldview, constructing a political, social, economic and cultural reality. This is not an issue of personal racism per se; it is an issue of the cache of privilege and cultural capital.

White privilege bestows institutional power on people who physically look like people that (have) dominate(d) the country by occupying powerful positions in administration, workplaces, churches and so on. How this privilege manifests is often invisible to the White journalist. For instance, White journalists might discuss ethnic diasporas living within Australia, without recognising that they themselves could fall under discussion, being of Irish, Scottish, Welsh and/or English descent. (In the present day, the category of diaspora is rarely, if ever, used for White Australians.) Another vivid example is the routine description of the Port Arthur massacre as 'the worst massacre in Australian history', completely ignoring the massacres of Aboriginal and Torres Strait Islander people in the colonial frontier wars, events which have been submerged under settler/nationalist White mythology.[2]

The often-unconscious privilege of Whiteness goes unexamined even as it determines the national narrative. The journalism field implicitly defines a news reporter and an ideal news reader, as representing the category of 'not-Other'—and this happens even if they outwardly 'belong' to an Othered category. Jay Rosen, press critic, writer and Professor of Journalism at New York University, noted in his 2011 keynote address at New News in the Melbourne Writers Festival that being 'not-Other' eventually means being an insider.

> How did we get to the point where it seems entirely natural for the Australian Broadcasting Corporation to describe political journalists

---

[2] The Port Arthur massacre was a mass shooting that occurred on 28 April 1996 at Port Arthur in Tasmania. The (White) perpetrator Martin Bryant killed thirty-five people and wounded twenty-three others.

appearing on its air as 'The Insiders'? ... Promoting journalists as insiders in front of the outsiders, the viewers, the electorate ... this is a clue to what's broken about political coverage in the US and Australia. ... Journalists are identifying with the wrong people. Therefore, the kind of work they are doing is not as useful as we need it to be.

Media scholar Ron Hoenig (2011) has argued that the 'objective' stance of the journalist implicitly constructs the same 'we/they' binary that Prime Minister John Howard famously used in the pronouncement, 'we will decide who comes to this country and the circumstances in which they come'. The binary is well explicated in the essay 'Whiteness in Constructions of Australian Nationhood: Indigenes, Immigrants and Governmentality':

> 'we' are representatives of the mainstream, the protectors of the national interest that is threatened by 'them' (the external other). The effect of discursively positioning non-white people in this way is that 'their' inclusion in the nation – in both real and metaphorical terms – is then restricted by the parameters of the white 'national will'; that is, they are included but only in the dominant group's terms. (Elder et al., 2004, p. 210)

This can be a problem when the largely White media are covering the largely non-white 'Other' asylum seeker. But even before we get to the question of who is reporting on who, there is the problem of asylum seekers as people with agency, voice and legitimacy.

Disappearing the Asylum Seeker

Who is heard and who is not is also significant. The absence of asylum seekers in these narratives generated sufficient centrifugal force to stabilise the state's assertions concerning the 'illegality', 'threat' and 'danger' posed by those fleeing persecution.

The state has been able to co-opt asylum seekers to create entire election campaigns promising vigilance against the threat of their presence, even while (or because) they have been practically invisible. In a sense, asylum seekers have been the dominating absence—the hole that makes the political doughnut—for two decades. This absence has powered much of the state's authorisation of abuse. In 'Theorising Unknowability and Jane Crow' (2017), Black American feminist scholar Kristie Dotson (2017) traces the steps that make it possible to disappear whole communities while holding them in plain sight, a process of making them 'unknowable' in a way which leads to Othering and then total exclusion. Her work helps to unpack an ongoing contradiction in the Australian media: asylum seekers and refugees possess a powerful political presence—front and centre in each federal election campaign—all the while being rationally unknowable by the electorate and also invisible.

Dotson presents three overlapping conditions that go to the creation of invisibility and therefore unknowability: it happens via 'firstly occupying negative socio-epistemic space, secondly persisting with reduced epistemic confidence, and thirdly, heightened epistemic backgrounding' (2017, section 4.1). She explains these abstract states as follows: we all choose to attend to and let go of shared resources in order to produce knowledge. These resources include language, habits and cultural ways of perceiving, conceptualising, knowing and experiencing. The decision—however unaware we are of having made it—of relegating any resource to irrelevance creates a negative socio-epistemic space. When people, or a whole population of people, are rendered irrelevant and uninteresting to the civic narrative and theme, they gradually fade from collective knowledge; it is no longer possible to know someone who has been disappeared or submerged in this way. The person—or population—becomes unknowable and endangered.

In making asylum seekers unknowable and invisible, they become suspect. From Australia's melancholic, paranoid-schizoid position, being suspect is enough to be hated, feared and expelled. Asylum seekers held in Australia's detention regime—both onshore and offshore—are among the most unknowable people on Earth. They no longer have names but numbers. Often they cannot use their real names even when trying to communicate their stories, because their families may be targeted if they do. They have no history, as usually their documentation is destroyed at the outset of their voyages to Australia. They have no citizenship they can safely claim and no inherited resources—indeed almost no resources at all. They don't even have their face as a shared way of knowing who they are because access to them is close to impossible. They have been made invisible and therefore unknowable. They become vague outlines of human, spectres waiting to be filled with the content of others more powerful, more detailed and embodied.

The second element is what Dotson calls reduced epistemic confidence. Having reduced a person or group to a state of unknowability, the state and mainstream media's ubiquitous use of pejorative terms (such as 'illegals' and 'queue-jumpers') makes their targets appear suspect and deceptive. In this way they become unbelievable. Asylum seekers are rarely believed or even believed in. For example, in late September 2014, detailed allegations emerged of sexual and physical abuse of children being detained in Nauru. A week later, the immigration minister, Scott Morrison, held a media conference in which he claimed to have received reliable intelligence that the allegations 'may have been fabricated as part of an orchestrated campaign, involving service provider staff, to undermine the government's border protection policies'. Morrison doubled down and attacked the workers who had disclosed the abuse, saying that '[m]aking false claims and allegedly coaching self-harm and using children in protests is completely unacceptable' (Feik, 2014). The service provider was the reputable Save the Children International. The so-called intelligence report Morrison was relying on to denounce and discredit Save the Children came from Transfield, the company whose employees were accused of assault. On the strength of this internal 'intelligence', ten Save the Children workers were suspended from duty and removed from the island.

The final component of being processed into unknowability, says Dotson, is 'backgrounding': when 'the economy of disregard and disbelief is protected against detection with a robust structure of disavowal … [E]pistemic backgrounding refers to being relegated as a means of framing some other domain without ever becoming the "point" of inquiry' (2017, section 4.2). Since 1999, those seeking Australia's protection have rarely been the main point of the refugee story for the state, even as they have been reduced to political strategy and used as fodder for Australia in asserting the need to protect itself. They have been unable to live as protagonists in their own stories. Their immense needs have been submerged in the interest of the state and its demand for control of its borders. They have been interesting only for the framing of a power struggle with a spectral enemy, which has accorded the government reason to develop an ever more tough-on-borders rhetoric.

Having been created as an unknowable, unbelievable, shadow population, it is extraordinary the story of any asylum seekers could be known as a singular issue of concern. Media revelations of the appalling treatment and conditions of Australia's detention regime have appeared at times over the last two decades like a lightning strike on a darkened landscape. Their story is briefly illuminated before the darkness closes in and the whole population is again submerged under the unknowability, disbelief and marginal nature they occupy in Australia's political and psychological landscape.

Dotson's structure helps make sense of why the revelations of abuse and humiliation have failed to create lasting change, or enduring knowability, believability and foregrounding of asylum seekers within this system. It helps explain why their stories don't stick in a 'news' sense—despite being extraordinary stories—and why they so easily slip from view without finding purchase in the public imagination or politics.

We Weren't Always This Fragile

La Capra (2001) has argued that mourning can be seen as a form of psychologically working through while melancholia is a form of acting out. Australia's discursive engagement with the issue of asylum seekers embodies both the working through of mourning and the acting out of melancholia. Despite an ambivalence and anxiety about asylum seekers, prior to 1996 the nation was occasionally able to grapple with the issue and its complexity. An example of this 'working through' can be seen in a joint media statement from November 1977, issued by the foreign minister Andrew Peacock and the immigration minister Michael MacKellar.

> This government will not indiscriminately 'make examples' of boat refugees by turning some of them back. Our controls are designed to prevent the

entry of people falsely posing as refugees, but we will not engage in risk taking action against genuine refugees just to get a message across. That would be an utterly inhuman course of action. (Peacock & MacKellar, 1977)

This statement demonstrated a nation's ability to balance the tension between humanitarian demands and the electorate's anxiety and prejudice, and to handle a legal, humane and sustainable engagement with those seeking protection. Guy Goodwin-Gill, the United Nations High Commissioner for Refugees representative in Australia, reported that Australia had undergone 'extensive national soul-searching' on the issue of asylum seekers and refugees but that the government fundamentally took 'a benign interest' towards them (Goodwin-Gill, 1977). This is what is required when psychologically working through a complex, high-stake issue like how a nation manages a legal, humane and sustainable engagement with those seeking protection. It is what is required when a nation remains in contact with reality which is a central element of mourning. Another instance of this 'working through' can be seen in the response of former prime minister, Malcom Fraser, when I asked him September 2002 how he managed to bring so many Vietnamese refugees to Australia—more than sixty thousand people—without provoking an electoral backlash.

> Firstly, I didn't ask the electorate for permission. I was the leader, so after consulting my colleagues and others in the field, I did it because it was the right thing to do – it was part of our international treaty obligations. Secondly, we made sure we funded all the support services necessary: education, housing, health and counselling. This also eased people's anxiety.

Journalist Margaret Simons, referring to mandatory detention, explains that:

> Fraser remembers the idea of the immigration reception centre coming before cabinet. He says that [Michael] MacKellar did not push it. It originated within the Department of Immigration and Ethnic Affairs. 'We disposed of it in about thirty seconds. I thought it was a piece of racist barbarism.' (Fraser & Simons, 2010, p. 419)

The Subtle Art of Criminalising Movement

No comparable process of painstakingly working through the complexity of the issue can be seen during the melancholic phase post-1996, in which all contact with reality has been lost. Asylum seekers, including their children, were politically reframed as 'queue-jumpers' or 'illegals', or as potential terrorists—a possibility that Dennis Richardson, head of the Australian Security Intelligence Organisation (ASIO) and the Prime Minister's most senior security adviser, described as 'extremely remote'. As the Refugee Council of Australia has been arguing since 2000, people seeking asylum are not 'queue jumpers' partly because there is no queue for resettlement. In practice, the resettlement system works more like a lottery than a queue. Likewise, it has never been illegal to seek protection in Australia regardless of the mode of arrival and whether the person arrives with valid documents. All levels of government and the mainstream media were aware of these facts. Nevertheless, the pejorative term 'illegals' denoting those seeking protection was used extensively by mainstream media. There was nothing accidental or careless about this usage. As a communications officer in the Immigration Department anonymously explained to The Reuters Institute, soon after the Liberal/National Coalition won government in 2013 a Department directive changed its terminology from 'irregular maritime arrival' to 'illegal maritime arrival'.

> [T]his also carried through to other terms – such as the directive not to use 'clients' but 'detainees'. ... The overall effect of this is one of framing: framing the department's approach, framing the media's attitudes, framing the public's understanding ... Asylum seekers became an amorphous group and I think this language merely reinforced the 'otherness'. (Doherty, 2015, pp. 47–48)

These instructions were issued by the new immigration minister, Scott Morrison, who would later (when he rose to prime minister) become known in the media as Scotty from Marketing, in recognition of his capacity for political spin (Tingle, 2021).

In an interview with *The Guardian's* Ben Doherty in 2015, former immigration minister Chris Evans argued that the language of government has been profoundly influential on media reportage and consequently on public understanding of the issue of seeking and providing asylum.

> The media tend to use that language, journalists will use the lines out of a press release, young journos in particular are just trying to file their story, and if the government pushes the border security context, if the issue is presented in that way, you report it in that context. It's not just the particular words, it's the whole structure and context. The government can announce: *'as part of Operation Sovereign Borders, the minister for Border Protection announced the border force had caught 40 more illegals,'* or it can say, *'today, the minister for immigration and citizenship reported customs had rescued 40 asylum seekers'.* It's a different story. (Doherty, 2015, p. 48, emphasis in original)

At this juncture, government discourse becomes problematic for journalists. As Evans points out, reporters are forced to use the language of the media release or the politician in the first instance, whether that language is truthful or dissembling. The Australian Broadcasting Corporation (ABC) has a publicly available style guide that all its reporters and news makers are expected to follow. The guide makes it clear that news makers must:

> Use *asylum seeker* to describe people who arrive in Australia (including Australian waters) without travel documents, claiming (or apparently claiming) refugee status. If authorities recognise a valid claim for protection, such people could be referred to as *refugees*. Avoid inaccurate modifiers with the term *asylum seeker*, e.g. *unlawful asylum seeker, illegal asylum seeker*. Under international law, anyone can apply for asylum.[3]

The problem is that a journalist interviewing or reporting on a government minister who chooses to describe asylum seekers as 'illegals' is forced to use the term in their reporting, despite its inaccuracy and characteristic as propaganda (Klocker & Dunn, 2003). Doherty argues the

---

[3] This guide is intended for anyone who writes or edits ABC content. Accordingly, much of its guidance is geared towards the preparation and editing of digital news: for platform-specific guidance.

government's new rhetorical insistence that boat-borne asylum seekers had arrived improperly and were 'illegal' was not an additional element intended to smooth the passage of a potentially controversial policy; rather, the rhetorical campaign was a keystone in policy outcomes being achieved. Asylum seekers being no longer 'refugees' but 'illegals' did more than simply allow the government to act against those people, it compelled the government to do so, explained Doherty in an interview with me in December 2020.

> The government constructed the action of seeking asylum as something threatening and illegal and then said, "I am the only one who can protect you". Because asylum seekers are now framed as 'illegal' the government must act to protect the nation from such illegality ... By changing the language, you changed people's understanding of what was going on and changed the very nature of what seeking asylum is. And finally, seeking asylum is presented as an injury to Australia's sovereignty. Even though obviously being able to grant someone asylum is an expression and demonstration of national sovereignty. By changing these words, the government was reconstructing what is meant by seeking asylum. These were structural changes.

In 2015 Doherty interviewed Arja Keski-Nummi, who was an officer in the Immigration Department for thirty-two years from 1979 and First Assistant Secretary of the Refugee, Humanitarian and International Division between 2007 and 2010. Keski-Nummi argued that using the word 'illegal' to refer to asylum seekers was

> crucial to the government achieving its policy outcome. The government's rhetorical insistence that asylum seekers who arrived by boat were acting illegally – at the very least, behaving wrongly – enabled it to justify policies condemned by human rights lawyers and refugee advocates as illegal and draconian. Implied by, and in alliance to, this argument was the government's converse position: that the government was acting to uphold the law and due process, to protect its sovereign mandate, and to defend the nation from a possibly malign external influence. (Doherty, 2015, p. 32)

This faux inversion of power, wherein asylum seekers are framed as powerful criminals and the state as plucky defender of its people, is in keeping with the narcissist victim-profile of the melancholic. Its language—part of what Freud's nephew, public relations pioneer and theorist Edward Bernays (1947), would consider the 'engineering of consent'—needs to be read as more than just rhetoric in service of a political opportunity to wedge Labor, because this 'consent' was being orchestrated from a melancholic and paranoid-schizoid position of shallow anxiety. Splitting is perhaps the most critical strategic outcome of this phase. It follows that borders and border anxieties would be central to discussions of refugees/asylum seekers and the defence of White privilege.

The nation's psychological splitting becomes clearer to see in content analyses of government media releases between 2001 and 2002 by academics Natascha Klocker and Kevin Dunn (2003), which sketch out the role played by mainstream media in reporting on issues concerning refugees and asylum seekers. Finding the releases to accord with the typology of propaganda, Klocker and Dunn reveal that '[w]hile the government's negative tenor was constant during the study period, the specific terms of reference altered, from "threat" through "other", to "illegality" and to "burden"' (2003, p. 71). 'The most frequently used terms of reference by the federal government portrayed asylum seekers as "illegitimate" (36 per cent), "illegal" (11 per cent) and "threatening" (16 per cent)' (2003, p. 77). Klocker and Dunn consider Australia's media to be captive to the negative narrative promulgated by government: 'Analysis of newspaper reporting during the same period indicates that the media largely adopted the negativity and specific references of the government. The media dependence upon government statements and spokespersons in part explains this relation' (2003, p. 71). This amplification, reverberating ever further from the reality of the situation, may go some way towards explaining why the national discourse moved so quickly and easily from the humanitarian frame to the Othering embodied in the national security frame; it may explain how children could be so persuasively framed as manipulative terrorists.

Criminalising movement is an increasingly global practice. As scholars Rimple Mehta and Monish Bhatia argue, the mainstream media of each nation has a particular frame for migration and seeking protection—and these framings tend to be negative.

For instance, in United States, the media uses a range of framings techniques – 'illegal' (which criminalises the very existence), amnesty (that shows the benevolence or mercy of the supreme power), border protection (linked to the war on terror and war on drugs which by default casts doubt on the motives of border crossers), undocumented worker (a less accusatory frame when compared to 'illegal', and yet racialised and degrading), and temporary worker (that serves capitalist interests and treats humans beings as disposable and discardable). (Bhatia & Mehta, 2022, p. 34)

It is chilling to note the part played by the Australian Government and the political leadership of both major parties in developing the international criminalisation of asylum seekers.

Wounded Sovereignty

As a senior writer with the *AFR* from 1995 to 2006, I covered the rise in numbers of people in Australia's immigration detention system and was involved in a number of investigative stories that examined the deployment of national security resources, particularly the Australian Security Intelligence Organisation (ASIO), in the initial assessment of refugee status. I was privy to ongoing internal debates in news conferences about how to cover this emerging national story and what kind of language to use. Many colleagues at *The Sydney Morning Herald* and the ABC were engaging in similar debates. It was a fast-moving story, and we sensed that the Howard government was testing how far it could go in reframing refugees as a national security risk. Discussed in Chap. 2, the *MV Tampa* stand-off was a critical moment in the testing of such powers. When Howard sent elite Australian fighters to board the Norwegian cargo ship in 2001, it created the visual tableau of a nation forced to defend its borders through military intervention. This was an intervention that worked for Howard's electoral ambitions, and he backed it up with intense sloganeering. According to Geoff Walsh, a former journalist, diplomat and National Secretary of the Australian Labor Party from 2000 to 2003,

> *Tampa* restored a massive 10 per cent to the Liberal Party primary vote. And the great bulk of these votes came from One Nation and right-wing independents ... *Tampa* effectively knee-capped One Nation and anointed John Howard. Three quarters of the One Nation vote loss went straight to the Coalition. (Walsh, 2001)

The *Tampa* crisis was able to harness a banal form of nationalism to legitimise an action that would have previously been unthinkable—the boarding of a civilian ship by armed soldiers. Moreover, it did the heavy lifting in reframing asylum seekers as aggressors and criminals that only the state could protect the nation from. The media played critical roles in the exploitation of these opportunities.

Two scholars from the University of Adelaide, Kieran O'Doherty and Martha Augoustinos, have analysed the national discourse around the stand-off between the *Tampa* and the Howard government. They tracked how military action against a group of civilians was justified in the public discourse by arguments relying on nationhood and national identity. Their findings list three portentous outcomes:

> First, by emphasizing the (alleged) well-being of the nation above the individuals comprising that nation, a precedent is set for future infringements of individual freedom and rights ... Secondly, by emphasizing the autonomous rights of the nation, beyond the rights of individual human beings who are not Australian, a kind of siege mentality is evoked, which seems to reverse traditional notions of victims and perpetrators (Burke, 2001). That is, through anthropomorphizing the category 'nation', and portraying it as a vulnerable entity, refugees fleeing from violence and persecution are made to seem like aggressors. Thirdly, by drawing on the category of nation as a primary referent of association, differences between nations are foregrounded. (O'Doherty & Augoustinos, 2008, p. 579)

O'Doherty and Augoustinos highlight the split between the reality of those seeking asylum and those denying them safety. On one side, more than four hundred vulnerable people sit on the deck of a cargo ship in the blistering sun surrounded by heavily armed soldiers, having just survived the trauma of the sinking of their boat. On the other side of the split, the 'nationally empowered group' who determine the framework of the national interest discuss these people's fate in cool, air-conditioned conference rooms and political offices.

Just weeks after the *Tampa* stand-off, before the dust from the September 11 terrorist attacks in the United States had settled, ministers within the Howard government had overtly linked asylum seekers to terrorism. The defence minister, Peter Reith, warned that unauthorised arrival of boats 'can be a pipeline for terrorists to come in and use your country as a staging post for terrorist activities' (Pain of one world, 2001). Peter Slipper, Liberal MP and Parliamentary Secretary to Minister for Finance and Administration, stated that there was 'an undeniable link' between illegal immigrants and terrorism (Clennell & Murdoch, 2001).

When a Picture Lies

Concentrated media ownership, the dominance of the White gaze, criminalising and framing the need for protection as an issue of national security rather than a humanitarian crisis are not the only complicating issues in the coverage of asylum seekers. In Australia, it happens in conjunction with the splintering of the mediascape as the national broadcaster comes under sustained political attack and the megalith News Corp appears to walk away from even the semblance of impartial news coverage (Muller, 2019). The lack of access to Australia's immigration camps not only cut off the voice of asylum seekers, it also removed their face. In this loss I am reminded of the missing traces 'where God passes' as the ethic of French philosopher Emmanuel Levinas outlines. For him the face-to-face encounter with the Other was of primary importance. The time Lévinas spent in a labour camp under Nazi Germany gave him a visceral understanding of the power of our face and the face of the Other in holding each other accountable to mutual humane treatment. In his essay 'A Name of a Dog', Lévinas describes the dehumanising and silencing brutality of his captors to whom Jews had never been more than 'animals', as he glimpses himself through their voracious eyes,

eyes that stripped us of our human skin: We were subhuman, a gang of apes. A small inner murmur, the strength and wretchedness of persecuted people, reminded us of our essence as thinking creatures, but we were no longer part of the world … We were … beings without language. (Lévinas, 1997)

What breaks the force of his humiliation is a stray dog named Bobby who wanders into the camp and 'unwittingly' bears witness to the humanity of Lévinas and the other prisoners.

He would appear at morning assembly and was waiting for us as we returned, jumping up and down and barking in delight. For him, there was no doubt that we were men … This dog was the last Kantian in Nazi Germany. (1997, p. 153)

Specifically, Lévinas says that the human face 'orders and ordains' us. It calls us into 'giving and serving' the Other. Before we had words, we knew the face of the (m)Other that called us beyond our solitary, lonely world.

The face, in its nudity and defencelessness, signifies: "Do not kill me". … Any exemplification of the face's expression, moreover, carries with it this combination of resistance and defencelessness: Lévinas speaks of the face of the other who is "widow, orphan, or stranger". (Bergo, 2019)

I remember the beautiful photographic image of the face of young Omid Masoumali (see also Chap. 5) grinning up at the photographer as he was finally rescued from the sea, before being taken to a camp in Nauru where his life would end.

It's true that the visual encounter with the vulnerable Other can have a galvanising effect on the viewer. The publication of photographs of the drowned body of two-year-old Alan Kurdi on the shore of the Mediterranean in September 2015 showed the profound impact visual representations can have in humanising an otherwise securitised story. This impact is often referred to as the 'CNN effect'. It reverses facelessness. In Australia, 'distance, facelessness and mass sea migration remain the dominant representations of refugees in Australian media, despite such arrivals accounting for less than half of asylum-seeking statistics' (Lenette & Miskovic, 2018).

Perhaps the most notorious example of this inversion of compassion and empathy is an event that became known in Australia as the 'children overboard' affair. The incident demonstrates what can happen when the state is almost exclusively in control of narrative, and the face of the Other can thus be hidden. Reporters confronted immense difficulties in trying to get to the facts and what we now know illuminates how important the pre-existing pyscho-affective state can be in preparing and filtering information.

In a sense, the 'children overboard' affair emerged out of an airy nothing (Macken-Horarik, 2003). It began in a hurried phone call between naval officers trying to prevent a small boat carrying asylum seekers from landing on Australian soil on 7 October 2001. During the exchange, the Commander of the HMAS *Adelaide*, Norman Banks, told Brigadier Mike Silverstone that someone aboard was threatening to throw a child overboard. This message was relayed to Air Vice Marshall Titheridge, who phoned it through to a People Smuggling Task Force meeting that morning in Canberra. Within four hours of this report, Immigration Minister Phillip Ruddock announced to the media that children had been thrown overboard from an illegal entry vessel just intercepted by the Australian Defence Force. This was not true, but politically it was 'too good to not be true'.[4]

The story was on the front pages of every Australian newspaper the following day. The totemic power of this socially significant moment cannot be understated: it occurred four weeks after the 9/11 attack on the United States, seven weeks after the *Tampa* affair and in the first week of the 2001 federal election campaign. Over the course of four days the government would find itself telling and retelling a big lie. The reporting

---

[4] The phrase 'too good to not be true' captures the opportunistic features of the stories told by conservative political figures intent on capturing the electorate's support for stronger border protection, the war on terror and national security. It highlights the politics of 'truth' distorting the issues. The phrase became the title of an investigative ABC *Four Corners* programme produced in March 2003.

context that both produced and failed to correct the details of the incident has been noted by political commentator Patrick Weller:

> The problem began 'with a series of miscommunications'; what the commander thought was 'threatening to throw a child overboard' became 'throwing a child overboard', which metamorphosed into 'children overboard' and hence a high-profile story that would be embarrassing to correct. Whether the problems were caused by the 'fog of war' or just a muddle, a false story became a fact that then had to be disproved, not merely checked. This is the worrying factor of this case: the mindset. (2002, p. 65)

This event had many troubling aspects, starting from the first announcement by Ruddock that asylum seekers *had thrown* children overboard. I remember the unease of my colleagues in the Federal Parliamentary Press Gallery the following day; many concerns were expressed about the veracity of the statement, and frustration grew as it became apparent that the state was restricting information on this extraordinary situation. Over the following days our unease heightened as Howard's, Ruddock's and Defence Minister Peter Reith's tone changed. Australian linguist Mary Macken-Horarik (2003) points out several semiotic features unique to this presentation. They include the use of photographs as 'visual news' in support of non-factual political claims, the use of third-person voicing to reproduce slurs on asylum seekers in quotations in newspaper reports, and the effects on audience interpretation of the interplay of story, image and headlines in frontpage news texts.

Attribution is an important aspect of journalistic practice. Knowing who said what can determine whether something is newsworthy in the first place. This 'children overboard' story had no attribution except Ruddock, Reith and Howard stating as fact that children had been thrown, presumably by their parents, into the Indian Ocean. On Sunday 7 October 2001, Ruddock said:

> Disturbingly a number of children have been thrown overboard, again with the intention of putting us under duress. [It was] clearly planned and premeditated. People wouldn't have come wearing life jackets unless they intended some action of this sort.

Again, emanating from the paranoid-schizoid position, the state is under 'duress' and vulnerable while the asylum seekers on the sinking vessel are framed as powerful agents. The victim's anger is thus justified. The following day Howard said, 'I express my anger at the behaviour of those people and I repeat it. I can't comprehend how genuine refugees would throw their children overboard'.

Journalists demanded proof of the government's allegations, and three days later this 'proof' was delivered in the form of two tightly cropped photographs without any captions. The navy had a dossier of one hundred and thirty photos entitled 'Sinking', but the media received but two. They were tight shots of people in dark seawater, indeed wearing lifejackets. The faces are obscured. We now know that the shots are cropped so that it is not possible to see the sinking boat in the background—this larger context only became visible when more photos were attained, years later. It is fitting and emblematic that while the larger lie obsessed about the borders of the nation, the 'proof' provided of their trespass was images whose borders had been artificially cropped. It was not possible to discern the identities of the objectified human beings, substitutes for the paranoias of the state, semi-invisible and silenced, floundering in grey and menacing sea. The wild claims about who they were, and how they got there, were presented as iron clad. Such is the semiotic power of the state that was deployed against their faceless bodies.

What the images actually show is a rescue taking place because the boat carrying asylum seekers had broken up as it was being towed by the navy. This was twisted into Howard's 'evidence' that asylum seekers had 'thrown' their children into the water. But not all photos are equal, and as Jonathan Bignell (1997), Professor of Television and Film at the University of Reading, has observed:

> Since photographs bring with them the assumption that they simply record something which 'naturally' happened, the meanings which the text loads onto the photograph are themselves 'naturalised', rendered innocent and apparently self-evident. The photograph functions as 'proof' that the text's message is true. (p. 99)

In this instance, with no written captions provided by the photographic source, it was conveniently left to the cabinet to tell journalists what the photos 'meant'.

Within weeks of the 'children overboard' claims, Howard had placed a media blackout on anyone not directly connected to holding the government's line that children had been thrown into the water as a manipulative strategy. Eminent journalists David Marr and Marian Wilkinson (2004) remember that there were no press briefings from the military on operational detail, no maps, no contextual photographs, nor any Q&As. The only photos or videos released were those purporting to show children being thrown overboard. The media had no other sources through which to confirm or refute the government's reports. The issue of the reports' veracity continued to be raised throughout the federal election campaign, but in the absence of disproof, at worst Howard was able to deny he knew anything to the contrary on the matter of children overboard.

The inscrutability eventually resulted in the Federal Parliamentary Press Gallery taking unprecedented collective action. In 2002, nine federal gallery journalists representing commercial and public sector mainstream bureaus (News Limited, Fairfax Media, Special Broadcasting Service [SBS] and ABC) put a joint, strongly worded submission to the Senate Select Committee on a Certain Maritime Incident (commonly known as the 'children overboard' affair). In it they alleged a sustained campaign of obfuscation orchestrated at the highest levels of government. The introduction to the journalists' submission said:

> A government campaign of censorship and misinformation, which peaked during the *Tampa* incident and continued through the HMAS *Adelaide* 'children overboard' affair, is unprecedented in recent times. It involved the Ministries of Defence and Immigration as well as the office of the Prime Minister. However, the high level of deliberate deception – which came clearly to light in Senate Estimates committee hearings – could not have been perpetrated without the involvement of senior and junior public servants. As well as fostering feelings of distrust and resentment in the Federal Parliamentary Press Gallery, this affair has underscored an urgent requirement for safeguards and guidelines to avoid a repeat of such blatant political manipulation of the bureaucracy. (Parliamentary Press Gallery Committee, 2002)

Those 'safeguards and guidelines' never appeared, and that brief moment of collective action ended. Its failure to hold power to account established a corrosive pattern for the following decades, during which the Coalition in particular has had an evolving, oligarchical strategy for dealing with those arriving at Australia's borders. With each new reach for control, there is a sense that it is testing not only the electorate's tolerance of cruelty but also the media's tolerance of propaganda and lies. The 'children overboard' affair tested such limits for the Australian media, who were covering events upon which the only source available was the state while also being aware that the state was lying. Unfortunately, this is an ongoing dilemma.

It is worth imagining for a moment what the outcome for Australia could have been if that moment of collective action had developed into a political strategy to hold the state to account. This would have required more powerful leadership from either senior journalists or their union, the Media Entertainment and Arts Alliance (MEAA), because journalism is a solitary trade and journalists rarely consider themselves part of a collective, except perhaps when enterprise bargaining is underway with their employers.

The consecutive political leaderships of John Howard, Kevin Rudd, Julia Gillard, Tony Abbott, Malcolm Turnbull and Scott Morrison have taken extraordinary and historic steps to control the media management of asylum seekers, their treatment, their numbers and their fate. Pertinent among these was the edict by the Department of Immigration in 2002 that no humanising images of asylum seekers were to be used in national media (Transcript of Evidence, CMI 1152).[5] And finally, the creation of the bastard-child of the national security frames 'on water matters'.

---

[5] A Select Committee on a Certain Maritime Incident had been appointed to inquire into and report on the following matters: (a) the so-called 'children overboard' incident, where an Indonesian vessel was intercepted by HMAS Adelaide within Australian waters reportedly 120 nautical miles off Christmas Island, on or about 6 October 2001.

Secrecy and Disclosure

When Scott Morrison was Liberal immigration minister, he began using boat turnbacks to try to ensure no asylum seekers arrived in Australia by boat, and he also introduced the idea of 'on water matters'. From 2013 onwards, any questions about the fate of those who attempted to come by boat were blocked by Morrison on grounds that these incidents happened on the water rather than on Australian soil. By 2014, 'on water matters' included off-water matters such as what training navy personnel received, whether naval vessels had GPS devices and even the public statements of Morrison himself. Eventually, the secrecy extended to the safety of Australian navy equipment. Labor Senator Pat Conroy discovered this when he asked the Immigration and Border Protection portfolio in a Budget Estimates Hearing on 25 February 2014 the following question:

> Have you done a Health and Safety risk assessment of each piece of equipment issued to Australian personnel? a. Can you please provide copies of the risk assessments those to the committee?

> Answer: Yes. Where applicable, the equipment issued to Australian personnel to conduct operations has been part of a health and safety risk assessment completed either at an equipment or system level. a. No. The disclosure of risk assessments of the equipment and systems issued to Australian personnel would require detailed descriptions of their characteristics and operation. Disclosure would prejudice the safety of personnel conducting on-water operations and cannot be released.

The flat refusal to disclose any information surrounding the operations was supported by policy and tolerated by much of the media.

Yet despite difficulties reporting on the conditions of interception, detention and related abuses, a small number of journalists let the Australian electorate know what was going on. There is always a risk of leaving someone out when naming who broke news about whichever event, but those who did in connection with Australia's detention regime have three things in common. First, most of them are senior journalists with experience, agency and the trust of others. Second, they had established contacts within the asylum seeker community and/or advocacy networks, so they were not reliant on the government for all their information. Third, they cared about the issue and often the people. 'These stories only happen because a journalist won't stop pushing for it', Ginny Stein, a senior journalist with SBS and the ABC covering South Africa, Asia and conflict zones, told me via Zoom on 21 August 2021. 'The media organisation has a huge role to play, but it always gets back to how hard the journalists push for it'.

Having a face (ideally, a beautiful face) can help make a difference to one's personal outcome. Two Tamil asylum seekers who had fled Sri Lanka in 2012 were living in the small country town of Biloela in Queensland, Australia, with their two little Australian-born girls, Kopika and Tharnicaa. The Murugappan family, known to the public as the Biloela family, had been integral members of this community for four years when they were woken by a dawn raid on their house by Border Force in 2018. So began four years of fighting to stay in Australia that saw the family removed to Christmas Island, and in and out of the federal and supreme courts as the Biloela community fought to bring them back to 'Bilo'. Those doing the fighting were their friends in the Biloela community.

Despite legal support and a community that was working day and night to bring their friends back, the Turnbull and Morrison governments remained committed to sending the family to Sri Lanka. That was until Tharnicaa, the youngest girl, became critically sick on Christmas Island and the only treatments offered were the over-the-counter painkillers Panadol and Nurofen. Veteran journalist Paul Bongiorno took up the story in *The Saturday Paper*.

> This weekend, Morrison would be hoping pictures of him rubbing shoulders with United States President Joe Biden and the world's major democratic leaders at the G7 summit in Britain would speak volumes about his importance and worth to Australian voters. But he will be vying for screen time with the heart-wrenching pictures of two distressed children kissing before they are separated so that the younger of them might be evacuated to mainland Australia, an emergency caused by a failure of medical treatment.
>
> That one image has thrown into bold relief the human toll of Australia's so-called border protection policies. The jury is out on what sort of toll it

may take politically on Morrison and his government, but few agree it is a positive. Some Labor old hands fear every moment the national conversation is about refugees and borders is a plus for the Liberals, yet there are plenty of Liberals who aren't so sure in this case. 'If the little girl dies, it would be a disaster for the government,' is the assessment of one. Not to be forgotten, the community behind the Home to Bilo campaign is not in some inner-city electorate but in the vast, Nationals-held seat of Flynn. (Bongiorno, 2021)

Twelve months later, one of the first decisions made by the incoming Albanese Labor government was to return the Murugappan family to the rural Queensland town. The interim home affairs minister, Jim Chalmers, said on Friday afternoon, 27 May 2022, five days after his party had won, that he was exercising his powers under the *Migration Act 1958* to give them bridging visas, fulfilling a pre-election promise to let them go home. The family's homecoming was covered live by the ABC almost as a national celebration. Upon arrival, an exhausted and happy Pryia Murugappan said,

> I cannot believe it. My prayer is that this government will make a change to the lives of every single refugee who comes here. All refugees are survivors. They need hope. I had the support of Nades and we had the support of the people of Bilo. But many others don't have that support. So I want to help. (Shepherd, 2022)

Had the Biloela community not mobilised, had the two little girls not been photographed in such distress and concern for each other, and had the media not had access to those photographs, it is highly probable that the family would have been deported back to Sri Lanka and certain danger.

Access to Facts

Disclosures of the reality of life in the newly erected tent cities of detention were initially hard to grasp for many journalists. When I interviewed multi-award-winning journalist Margot O'Neill, who covered the issue of asylum seekers under the Howard government, she remembered her initial shock at discovering what had been hidden from the public.[6]

> My first inquiries began after a lawyer told me she'd been dealing with unaccompanied asylum seeker children in detention who'd been given numbers instead of names, adults as well. I didn't believe her at first, especially in relation to children being so labelled and left alone in detention, but soon realised she was right. Then I started hearing from sources about how brutal the detention regime was – with children, with families, with adults, with visitors; the shocking propaganda from the government about them being first-class hotel facilities when infants couldn't learn to walk in Woomera because the sand was too hot; the listlessness of detained children still wetting their beds at 10 or older; constant suicide attempts. I was shocked that we didn't care that it sent children and adults mad or that medical bodies unanimously tried to intervene; that the government was willing to sacrifice all detainees to make ministers look tough as they pursued deterrence to stop the boats. I was genuinely shocked at how little regard was shown for vulnerable people's welfare. The deporting of people to danger was another shock; the deporting of an Australian citizen with mental health issues was another surprising low point. (1 February 2022)

Personally, the first news report I wrote on asylum seekers was for the *AFR* on 31 August 2001. The headline was: 'Support wavering for Howard's hard-line stand REFUGEE CRISIS'. It detailed the fall in support for Howard's stand-off with the *Tampa* according to analysis by media monitor Rehame Australia. In three hundred and thirty words it describes why the Australian Government decided that no faces were to be seen, no names recorded and no stories told about those being held in its detention regime.

> Support for the Government's refusal to allow the freighter to enter Australian waters peaked at 78 per cent of talkback callers on Monday, with those arguing for a more humane response at a low of 12 per cent. But that support had dropped to just 50 per cent yesterday afternoon, with 27

---

[6] O'Neill has worked for several decades in television, radio and print journalism, in Australia and overseas, covering politics, national security and social justice issues, as well as a variety of ABC programmes including the investigative flagship programme *Four Corners*.

per cent of callers demanding the Government allow the freighter and its human cargo be allowed to dock in Australia and processed as refugees.

'The tide of public opinion really began to turn when the SAS boarded the ship and people started to see photos of men, women and children on board,' Rehame senior analyst Ms Nicole Tomlinson said.

Ms Tomlinson has noted a change in the tone of callers.

'At first there was a strong racial element, with people frightened about Muslims over-running the country,' she said. 'That seems to be disappearing as people see the photos and realise they're just human beings like themselves.'

While the Prime Minister, Mr John Howard, can take comfort that his initial response was seen as strong and decisive, Ms Tomlinson said callers were growing increasingly impatient about his apparent inability to end the crisis.

'The mood of the public is changing and things could go horribly wrong if the Government doesn't take that change into account,' she said. 'Also, if people were to start seeing body bags coming off the boat, the Government would lose support even more quickly.' (Macken, 2001)

More than twenty years later, I believe that a good way to assess the role played by the mainstream media in the creation of asylum seekers as torturable subjects is by employing wild imagination, in the vein of Paul Keating's famous Redfern Speech. Imagine if every time the government used the term 'illegal' in relation to an asylum seeker, they were corrected and reminded in print media/online publication that seeking asylum is not illegal and all people have a right to ask for political protection. Imagine if reporters refused to report on the issue unless they were given access to asylum seekers or their representatives to assess the veracity of government claims and put their side of their story forward. Imagine if the Australian media insisted on showing the faces of children and the elderly being held in the camps. Imagine if stories of fleeing persecution were foregrounded, believed and made relevant. Imagine if the Federal Parliamentary Press Gallery had failed to get 'safeguards and guidelines to avoid a repeat of such blatant political manipulation of the bureaucracy' when they asked, but instead boycotted covering parliament until those commitments had been made and implemented. Imagine the media using their industry's enormous power to build transparency and refuse to be co-opted into the state's propaganda.

The media played a critical role in the creation of torturable subjects; however, without the privatised camps, the abuse would not have happened at the scale that it did.

References

Bergo, B. (2019, Fall edition). Emmanuel Levinas. In E. N. Zalta (Ed.), *The Stanford encyclopedia of philosophy*. https://plato.stanford.edu/archives/fall2019/entries/levins/

Bernays, E. (1947). The engineering of consent. *250 annals of the American Academy of Political and Social Science*. 250, 114.

Bhatia, M., & Mehta, R. (2022). Representations of Bangladeshis and internal 'others' in the Indian press: The cases of Felani Khatun, Zohra Bibi and the 'woman in red sari'. *From the European South: A Transdisciplinary Journal of Postcolonial Humanities.*, 9, 31–46. https://eprints.bbk.ac.uk/id/eprint/46784/

Bignell, J. (1997). *Media semiotics: An introduction*. Manchester University Press.

Bongiorno, P. (2021, June 21). Tehe human toll of border protection. *The Saturday Paper*. https://www.thesaturdaypaper.com.au/opinion/topic/2021/06/12/the-human-toll-border-protection/162342000011861

Burke, A. (2001). *In fear of security: Australia's invasion anxiety*. Pluto Press.

Clennell, A., & Murdoch L. (2001, September 20). Bad apples could barely make a cricket team. *The Sydney Morning Herald*.

Doherty, B. (2015). *Call me illegal: The semantic struggle over seeking asylum in Australia* [PDF]. Reuters Institute for the Study of Journalism, University of Oxford. https://reutersinstitute.politics.ox.ac.uk/sites/default/files/2017-10/Call_me_illegal_The_semantic_struggle_over_seeking_asylum_in_Australia_0.pdf

Dotson, K. (2017). Theorising Jane Crow, theorising unknowability. *Social Epistemology*, 31(5), 417–430. https://doi.org/10.1080/02691728.2017.1346721

Elder, C., Ellis, C., & Praatt, A. (2004). Whiteness in constructions of Australian nationhood: Indigenes, immigrants and governmentality. In A. Moreton-Robinson (Ed.), *Whitening race: Essays in social and cultural criticism* (pp. 208–221). Aboriginal Studies Press.

Feik, N. (2014, November 20). Scott Morrison's response to claims of refugees' molestation, self-harm is immoral, unjust. *The Sydney Morning Herald*.

https://www.smh.com.au/opinion/scott-morrisons-response-to-claims-of-refugees-molestation-selfharm-is-immoral-unjust-20141120-11q8bo.html
Fraser, M., & Simons, M. (2010). *Malcolm Fraser: The political memoirs.* Melbourne University Press.
Freud, S. (1957). Mourning and melancholia. In J. Strachey (Ed.), *The standard edition of the complete psychological works of Sigmund Freud* (Vol. XIV, pp. 237–258). Hogarth Press. (Original work published 1917).
Goodwin-Gill, G. (1977). *Report for 1977: End of year report from UNHCR Sydney Branch to United Nations High Commissioner for Refugees.* Guy Goodwin-Gill Collection, Refugee Studies Centre Collection, Bodleian Social Science Library, University of Oxford.
Hoenig, R. (2011). *The borderscape of detention: Media depictions of the denizens of Woomera* [PDF]. MnM Working Paper No 7, International Centre for Muslim and non-Muslim understanding. University of South Australia. https://www.unisa.edu.au/siteassets/episerver-6-files/documents/eass/mnm/working-papers/hoenig-borderscape-of-detention.pdf
Iaria, M. (2021, November 1). *Omid Masoumali: Refugee who died after setting himself alight on Nauru received 'below standard' care, coroner finds.* news.com.au. https://www.news.com.au/national/courts-law/omid-masoumali-refugee-who-died-after-setting-himself-alight-on-nauru-received-below-standard-care-coroner-finds/news-story/2dcabd1e7a670a73416f90b5215cd796
Klocker, N., & Dunn, K. M. (2003). Who's driving the asylum debate? Newspaper and government representations of asylum seekers. *Media International Australia Incorporating Culture and Policy, 109*(1), 71–92. https://doi.org/10.1177/1329878X0310900109
La Capra, D. (2001). *Writing history, writing trauma.* Johns Hopkins University Press.
Lenette, C., & Miskovic, N. (2018). 'Some viewers may find the following images disturbing': Visual representations of refugee deaths at border crossings. *Crime Media Culture, 14*(1), 111–120.
Lévinas, E. (1997). *Difficult Freedom. Essays on Judaism.* (S. Hand. Trans.). The Johns Hopkins University Press. (Original work published 1990).
Macken, J. (2001, August 31). Support wavering for Howard's hard-line stand Refugee Crisis. *The Australian financial Review.*
Macken-Horarik, M. (2003). A telling symbiosis in the discourse of hatred: Multimodal news texts about the 'children overboard' affair. *Australian Review of Applied Linguistics, 26*, 1–16.

Media Diversity Australia. (2020). *Who gets to tell Australian stories. Cultural diversity and leadership in Australia's media*. https://mediadiversityaustralia. org/wp-content/uploads/2020/08/Who-Gets-to-Tell-Australian-Stories-Report.pdf

Mendiola, I. (2014). *Habitar lo inhabitable: la práctica político-punitiva de la tortura [Inhabiting the uninhabitable: The political-punitive practice of torture]*. Edicions Bellaterra.

Muller, D. (2019, May 13). Mounting evidence the tide is turning on news Corp, and its owner. *The Conversation*. https://theconversation.com/mounting-evidence-the-tide-is-turning-on-news-corp-and-its-owner-116892

O'Doherty, K., & Augoustinos, M. (2008). Protecting the nation: Nationalist rhetoric on asylum seekers and the Tampa. *Journal of Community and Applied Social Psychology, 18*(6), 576–592.

Parliamentary Press Gallery Committee. (2002). Submission to senate inquiry into a certain maritime incident. Senate. Select Committee for an Inquiry into a Certain Maritime Incident. Submission 13.

Peacock, A., & Mackellar, M. (1977, November 29). *Refugees: Joint statement by Minister for Foreign Affairs, Hon. Andrew Peacock, MP and Minister for Immigration and Ethnic Affairs, Hon. Michael Mackellar, MP*. [Press release].

Rosen, J. (2011, August 30). *Why political coverage is broken*. [Transcript of keynote address at New News 2011]. ABC Opinion. https://www.abc.net.au/news/2011-08-30/rosen%2D%2D-why-political-coverage-is-broken/2862328

Shepherd, T. (2022, May 27). Murugappan family to return to Biloela on bridging visas. *The Guardian*. https://www.theguardian.com/australia-news/2022/may/27/murugappan-family-to-return-to-biloela-on-bridging-visas

Tingle, L. (2021, March 19). Morrison bamboozled by his own spin. *The Australian Financial Review*. https://www.afr.com/politics/federal/morrison-bamboozled-by-his-own-spin-20210318-p57btu

Walsh, G. (2001, December 3). Federal election analysis: Address to the National Press Club, Canberra [transcript]. https://australianpolitics.com/2001/12/03/geoff-walsh-alp-election-analysis.html

Weller, P. (2002). *Don't tell the prime minister*. Scribe Short Books.

7

Privatising Abuse

Australia's immigration detention network is the world's largest privatised network of carceral sites. Yet its immigration camps have been described as 'a space where the "national" is placed in suspension: it is "not-Australia"' (Perera, 2002). The 'not-Australia' liminality of immigration detention has been made possible by its isolated location—both onshore and offshore—and a process of privatisation that began a few months after the Howard government won the 1996 federal election. Disavowal and denial of reality, so emblematic of the melancholic state, are realised by creation of camps that are both part and not part of Australia. They facilitate the denial of their own existence even as they erect the barriers so necessary to the splitting of the paranoid-schizoid phase; they entomb the 'ghosts' to keep 'us' safe.

Privatising the immigration detention regime in 1998 has created lucrative centres of suffering. It has also created legal, political and psychological complications. This chapter examines the role played by a privatised regime. Was it the act of privatising detention that enabled the Howard government and all successive Australian Governments to operationalise cruel, inhumane and degrading treatment of those held within? Given the inherent violence of mandatory detention, what, if any, difference would it make if camps were controlled by the public service—would the same level of abuse have been possible had immigration detention remained in public administration, staffed by public servants governed by the *Public Service Act 1999*? Could a public administration of camps, or other facilities and solutions, have produced less damaging treatment, and could it have provided a political context in which to understand the state's overreach and strategic manipulation?

Let me say that from the outset any form of mandatory detention of innocent people whose only 'crime' is to seek protection from persecution is ethically wrong, and wrong in international human rights law. It is in contravention of numerous treaties signed by Australian Governments previous to Howard's. Simply put, under international law, immigration detention must only ever be used as a last resort. States must first seek to implement alternatives to detention which allow individuals to live in non-custodial, community-based settings while their immigration status is being resolved. There are effective, economic and humane alternatives to detention that are currently used. The International Detention Coalition (2022) has an extensive Alternatives to Detention Database that collates examples from around the world. The idea of a non-transparent, frontline detention regime was an anathema in Australia prior to 1992.

The privatised system has delivered cruel, degrading and humiliating treatment of asylum seekers that has often devolved into torture. The Albanese Labor government, elected in 2022, has committed to bringing the system back into public administration. Unfortunately, it appears to have recanted that commitment by granting MTC, a private US prison company, the contract to run the Nauru camp and by allocating a further 150 million dollars to run the offshore camps in their first Budget. Furthermore, the commercial-in-confidence contracts used by this privatised system make the camps essentially black sites—though Albanese's immigration minister Andrew Giles refutes this description: he informed me in person that he knows exactly what occurs within them. There is, however, a steady stream of media revelations regarding home affairs overseeing corrupt payments in both Nauru and Manus Island.

Before Privatisation

Prior to December 1997, Australian immigration detention facilities were operated by the Department of Immigration and Multicultural and Indigenous Affairs (DIMIA). Security at detention centres was provided by the public service through the Australian Protective Service, an agency within the Attorney-General's portfolio, while other services such as food, health, education and welfare were provided either by DIMIA directly or by individual sub-contractors. This meant anyone employed by the Commonwealth to work at or manage immigration detention camps was covered by the Public Service Act and related Commonwealth statutes. The Community Public Sector Union (CPSU) covered the highly unionised workplace. The operations and the people who staffed the services were subject to oversight by the Australian Parliament and could be called before the Senate and the Human Rights and Equal Opportunity Commission (HREOC). Public servants could be subject to judicial review of acts and decisions taken in detention camps and were governed by the Australian Public Service (APS) Code of Conduct and five APS Values. Moreover, on ordinary principles, the Commonwealth would be liable for any unlawful acts and acts of omission by public servants.

Changing the Nation: Less Heart Less Soul

In August 1996, six months after winning the federal election, the Howard government announced its intention to privatise the operations of Australia's immigration detention centres as a means of cost saving and improving efficiency. At the time, the move to privatise immigration detention appeared in context of a long list of already privatised government services begun under the Hawke Labor government during the 1980s. Labor's privatisation goals had focused on making the Australian economy more globally competitive: a 'tactical privatisation' (Aulich & O'Flynn, 2007). For Howard, the drive to privatise and divest was concerned with the devolution of power from the public service—and the

CPSU—to the individual: 'systemic privatisation' (Aulich & O'Flynn, 2007). It was a drive that began long before he became prime minister. In August 1985, he addressed the National Press Club as shadow treasurer and opposition leader:

Privatisation not only entails the transfer of public assets to individual Australians, it also makes possible the provision of incentives and opportunities for individual Australians to obtain services in the private sector as an alternative to those available in the public sector. (Cited in Aulich & O'Flynn, 2007)

Howard understood well what British Prime Minister Margaret Thatcher had meant when she declared, 'economics are the method; the object is to change the heart and soul' (Butt, 1981). As economist Richard Denniss has argued, the cache of neoliberalism is not just economic tools of outsourcing and privatising provision of public services but also cultural tools used to change our values. 'Children in Australia die in the custody of our governments, but our public debate focuses on our fiscal deficits, not our moral deficits. That's quite a feat' (Denniss, 2018, p. 12). Our detention camps were privatised while neoliberal ideology, embraced by the Hawke and Keating governments, became the dominant ideology globally. Alarmingly, our camps may offer the most powerful example of a nation whose 'heart and soul' was transformed utterly.

Was it neoliberalism that made the camps palatable, or did privatising the camps stabilise the neoliberal hegemony? It is clear, at least, that the ideology made sense of what would have previously been considered implausible. Neoliberalism created the possibility that privatising immigration detention would be accepted electorally—one of its most potent effects is how it changes the way we view ourselves and others, our Commonwealth, environment, work and communities. Making a profit from detaining adults, let alone toddlers, would have been unacceptable to the Australia of the 1970s, 1980s and early 1990s.

In *Undoing the Demos*, Wendy Brown puts forward 'a theoretical consideration of the ways that neoliberalism, a peculiar form of reason that configures all aspects of existence in economic terms, is quietly undoing basic elements of democracy' (2015, p. 17). Brown contends that one of the many outcomes of the neoliberal agenda has been to transform and empty the dynamic, energetic political spheres into the economic sphere and in the process to re-define *homo politicus* as *homo oeconomicus*:

> When the domain of the political itself is rendered in economic terms, the foundation vanishes for citizenship concerned with public things and the common good. Here, the problem is not just that public goods are defunded and common ends are devalued by neoliberal reason, although this is so, but that citizenship itself loses its *political* valence and venue. Valence: *homo oeconomicus* approaches everything as a market and knows only market conduct; it cannot think public purposes or common problems in a distinctly political way. Venue: Political life, and the state in particular … are remade by neoliberal rationality. (2015, p. 39, Brown's emphasis)

There is a slipperiness around this privatisation. The lines of accountability are blurred as neoliberalism not only ensures transfer of what was once public into private ownership but also plays a critical role in determining what is thinkable and what is unthinkable. In context of our situation in Australia, who is responsible for what in purely contractual terms has been an ongoing struggle between the state, courts and companies that ran the immigration camps. Who can be held responsible for abuse, riots, the destruction of two camps by fire? Who is responsible for ensuring the safety of babies born in detention, and the wellbeing and education of toddlers and youngsters detained there?

An example of how radically this ideology recalibrated the political calculus in Australia can be glimpsed in a disclosure by Neal Blewett, former Minister for Social Services in the Keating government, of a late-night conversation he had in May 1992 with Gerry Hand, then Minister for Immigration, Local Government and Ethnic Affairs. Hand suggested, 'interning all who sought refugee status in camps, mostly at Port Hedland, where they would be fed and looked after'. Blewett's response (according to his own account) resonates powerfully with the state of the nation in those pre-neoliberal days: 'This is a nonsensical proposal—politically unsellable to the liberal constituency, impossible in practice (if any significant number of refugees took up the option [Hand's] department would collapse) and financially irresponsible—if it worked it would cost more than the other options' (Blewett, 1999, p. 83). Just five years later, this 'nonsensical proposal' was on its way to becoming orthodoxy. As Brown argues, 'neoliberalism transmogrifies every human domain and endeavor, along with humans themselves, according to a specific image of the economic. All conduct is economic conduct' (2015, p. 10). Certainly, while both Thatcher and Howard may have been pursuing a change of our 'heart and soul', divestment of public goods was sold to the Australian public on the grounds that the private sector could deliver better value for money and greater efficiencies.

But how are those efficiencies and cost savings to be made when the stock in trade are children, women and men held in mandatory immigration detention? Is it possible that the systemic violence practised in Australia's detention regime could have been prevented, or limited, if immigration detention had remained in public administration? If so, what are the characteristics of the privatised regime that facilitates the cruel, inhumane and degrading treatment of those held within? Finally, could it be that the two real attractions of privatisation is its potential to provide distance and deniability for the state and that it drains the camps of political power for asylum seekers and advocates alike?

Before investigating this question, it is important to understand the extraordinary and historic advent of the privatised immigration camps. While Howard had already introduced punitive measures such as the temporary protection visa before the attack on the United States on 9/11 (see Chap. 4), those attacks emboldened him to introduce privatised camps as 'state[s] of exception' (Briskman & Dimasi, 2010). To philosopher Giorgio Agamben (1998) a camp is a 'piece of land placed outside the normal juridical order', a 'zone of indistinction'. Agamben has primarily analysed the role of concentration camps under the Nazi regime. While I make no suggestion that Australian immigration camps are comparable with the camps of Nazi Germany, it is clear that Australia's immigration regime has also created zones of indistinction as Agamben defines them. They hold shadowlike people who are

> [b]oth excluded from Australia and held in camps in the very interior of the nation, both abandoned and utterly subjected to the violence of Australian sovereignty, both external to the political community and constitutive of the

nature of this political community and of its ability to continue to regulate the composition of its population. (Whyte, 2008, p. 80)

The detention centres became places neither here nor there, a limbo to store people, none of whom had done anything wrong. And because the people held there were 'not us', their presence helped to constitute an 'us'.

Meet the Detainers

Ambiguity and a lack of legal clarity concerning the accountability, administration, staffing and objective of the detention camps became apparent as the numbers of asylum seekers sent to them grew. It was unclear—and remains unclear—how the contracts operated in the interests of the taxpayer. I first started reporting on these places two months after 9/11, and even by this time there was a palpable sense of chaos and slippage as the government struggled to control the camps' security, communications, contracts and the companies in charge. On the following pages I reprint a news article I wrote, published on 15 December 2001, in which the problems surrounding the still relatively new sites of detention are laid out plainly. The problems themselves are not contested. Yet, despite none of the issues raised here being resolved—indeed many were to become chronic and lethal—the privatised camps remain an integral part of the state's immigration policy to the present day. Reading the article now I am freshly taken aback by how problematic the privatised regime was after just three years of operation and a little embarrassed because I had honestly thought these published revelations could lead to a change of practice if not policy. Unbeknownst to me and the general public, with a brief respite from 2008 to 2012 the camps would continue as sites of international scandal and abuse for thousands of people right up to the time of this writing.

The Detainers
They're making money for a US-owned company but Australia's detention centres have become a PR nightmare for the Government.

Before September 11, shares in companies running private prisons were dropping. Even in the United States, investors felt the market had reached saturation point. Post September 11, companies with interests in private detention centres as opposed to private prisons are experiencing renewed interest. Private detention centres are now considered hot stock.

Nevertheless, the experience of Australasian Correctional Management (ACM) in Australia offers some useful tips for young players.

On March 6, 1997, the Department of Immigration and Multicultural Affairs sent out a pro forma letter. The letter advised a number of companies that the department was putting the function and management of its detention centres out for tender. Were the companies interested in making a bid?

You bet they were. The two main contenders were Corrections Corporation of Australia and ACM, a wholly owned subsidiary of US giant Wackenhut. Four years later, the rest would appear to be history. ACM won the contract and went on to provide its parent, Wackenhut, with $110 million a year, a growing and captive market and unique positioning in what is tipped to become the growth segment in private prisons worldwide and the detention of asylum seekers. DIMA in turn became Wackenhut's third-biggest client and contributed 11 per cent to its earnings for 2000.

However, if the federal government was hoping for a quick, cost-effective solution to the issue of detainees in Australia, it was in for an awful shock. While the tendering process attracted little public interest or scrutiny, the service delivery has become a public relations nightmare for both the Coalition and ACM. So much so that four years later the question of prisons and detention centres for profit is back on the agenda of the ALP, the Democrats and the Greens.

CCA pursued DIMA through the Federal Court over the tendering process in 1997, which it believed favoured ACM. It settled out of court for an undisclosed amount two months ago. And finally, the Coalition has exercised its right to put the contract out for tender again, after only four years of the 10-year contract have elapsed.

When ACM won the contract in 1997, no-one outside the negotiations was aware that it had also won 'approved provider provisions'. That is, it had won the contracts for the first four centres and would automatically get the contract for any other centres established by DIMA. ACM was positioned to take all new business generated by people smugglers.

While ACM had been in the business of private prisons since 1995, the first the general public knew of its existence or the fact that it ran DIMA detention centres was when 17 people escaped from the Villawood detention centre in Sydney in May 1999. In June 2000, 500 people broke out of the Woomera detention centre in South Australia and 250 more escaped from the Port Hedland and Curtin detention centres in Western Australia. There were four more breakouts over the subsequent 12 months.

During their brief periods of freedom, the detainees spoke to the media. Tales of verbal and physical abuse, neglect, sexual assault, self-harm and mental distress emerged. Advocacy groups demanded answers, the media wanted calls returned and the Government, through the Minister for Immigration, Philip Ruddock, became the surrogate mouthpiece for ACM.

Privatising public services has always involved resolving questions of accountability and access to information, however the privatisation of detention centres has taken these issues to a new level. When a whistle-blower reported the suspected sexual assault of a 12-year-old child in one of ACM's centres, the minister's first response was to say that it didn't happen. The whistle-blower knew her job was on the line for what she believed was fulfilling her duty of care. Why, interest groups were asking, is the privacy surrounding this company so intense?

According to Amanda George, a solicitor with the Brimbank Community Legal Centre, any investigation should begin with the contract between ACM and DIMA. 'The contract raises two key issues,' she says. 'The first concerns the profit-sharing arrangement between DIMA and ACM. The second concerns the ways in which the Government has achieved cost savings by outsourcing this public service.'

According to information posted on the department's website, the Immigration Detention Agreement includes a clause that states:

'3.2 Sharing of Cost Savings

'(a) In acknowledgment of the co-operative relationship necessary for cost reductions, the Contractor agrees to share with the Commonwealth any Savings achieved at a proportion to be agreed between the Parties in each Service Contract.

'(b) Savings will be identified as follows or as specified in the Service Contract: [Details deleted for commercial reasons]'

No-one outside the contract negotiations knows what the percentage breakdown is for this profit-sharing arrangement. However, according to Charandev Singh, an advocate with Brimbank Community Legal Centre, whatever the division of profit, the problem remains the same. 'The Department [of Immigration] is supposed to be the regulator of this private American company', Singh says. 'But that clause in the contract means it has now entered into a perverse commercial relationship with ACM that encourages the maximising of profits to the advantage of both parties. That clause has destroyed the integrity the department may have had as a regulator.'

A spokesman for Philip Ruddock sees no problem with the clause. 'The amount of money paid to ACM depends on how many detainees it has to deal with', the spokesman says. 'If they get past a certain number then economies of scale kick in and they can provide the same service for less. They're not paid a flat fee per person. And the department doesn't get a rebate or anything'.

This issue becomes more sensitive because of the secrecy surrounding the amount of taxpayers' money paid to ACM. However, the same spokesman says the secrecy is to protect the taxpayer, not the company or the department: 'We're testing the value in the market-place at the moment and we need to ensure we get value for money so we must maintain the confidentiality of these negotiations'.

Value for money has become a vexed issue. Eighty per cent of the budget for these detention centres goes on wages for wardens, health-care professionals, educators, cleaners, translators and administrators. While George Wackenhut, founder and chairman of Wackenhut Corrections Corporation, has boasted that he has been able to get food prices down to $1 a day for prisoners in his US facilities, the area of staffing provides the most scope for savings.

In August, the AWU's Occupational Health and Safety director, Yossi Berger, reported that guards at the Port Hedland centre were 'fatigued, poorly trained, at times distressed and sometimes abused'. 'Officers ... are exploited by ACM and opportunistically managed,' he said, and ACM was seeking to save money by limiting training. 'It is a calculated, delinquent and offensive failure under the simple requirements of duty of care.' His surveys showed 95 per cent of Port Hedland officers believed their training was inadequate.

The question of cost saving was raised during the week when The Australian Financial Review revealed that typhoid had been discovered among detainees being held on Christmas Island. Health-care workers were appalled at what they described as 'Third World conditions'.

7 Privatising Abuse 147

When private companies are expected to make a profit out of public services that straddle complex constituencies, a fundamental conflict exists. Australia has experience in this area. The First Fleet came to Australia as part of a public service. The Second Fleet was a private enterprise. As the founding fathers dragged the corpses off the coffin barges of the Second Fleet, even they could see the sense in keeping some services within the public sector. (Macken, 2001)

Three years after the privatisation of the camps, lack of transparency regarding the perverse incentives to grow the detention population had allowed critical issues to fester. It is important to note the role the state was already beginning to assume with this private company. All media inquiries directed to ACM were redirected to either the minister, Philip Ruddock, or the spokesperson of DIMIA. I know of no other corporations that had that kind of political cover and protection.

The government privatised administration of Australia's detention regime in 1998, and from 1998 to 2003 Australasian Correctional Management (ACM), owned by the US Wackenhut corporation, ran the centres (see Chap. 8). Three months after publishing the above story I was again reporting on the privatisation process as Wackenhut announced its merger with Group 4 Falck, one of only three other companies competing for Australian detention contracts. This merger meant that Group 4 Falck would be the largest private prison/detention company in the world. At the announcement of the merger, the president and chief executive of Wackenhut, Richard Wackenhut, pointed to the 'similar values and cultures' shared by both companies. In the following news article I introduced the company to the *AFR* readership.

So who are Group 4 Falck? According to the company's publicity, 'Group 4 Falck has activities in more than 50 countries with more than 140,000 employees and annual revenues of approximately $US2.5 billion. It has three core activities: security, safety and global solutions'.

However, like ACM, Group 4 has become better known for its failures than for its growth. In February this year, a UK detention centre run by Group 4, Yarl's Wood, was burned to the ground. This state-of-the-art £50 million ($134.8 million) complex was razed as Group 4 officers prevented firefighters and police officers from tackling the blaze. According to The

Guardian newspaper, fire brigade representatives claim there was a 'potentially catastrophic' delay of at least an hour when officers were barred from the site not by detainees, as reports claimed, but by Group 4.

Group 4 appears to have lost the contract for its other detention centre in the UK, Campsfield House. In 1998 Group 4 accused nine asylum seekers of riot and violent disorder after a 'riot' in Campsfield House. However, all nine were acquitted of charges after it was proved that evidence from the Group 4 staff was false and unreliable. Video evidence produced at the trial showed Group 4 officers tearing their own clothes and smashing phones and furniture.

Closer to home, Group 4 came to the attention of the Australian public when a coroner, Graeme Johnstone, found Group 4, operator of Melbourne's private Port Phillip Prison, contributed to the suicide deaths of four inmates during the jail's first six months of operation. Apart from failing to remove hanging points within the cells, the coroner also found problems with information management, inexperienced staff, training, emergency procedures and cell design. (Macken, 2002)

The week before this article was published, *The Age* reported that management had almost completely broken down at the Woomera detention centre in South Australia, calling it 'a war zone full of fear, brutality and the walking wounded', while *The Australian* reported that 'some ACM guards were in the habit of taking a slow walk to avoid helping detainees who tried to hang themselves. They made comments such as, "if only they'd use rope, they might succeed"' (Williams, 2002).

The privatisations began with the camps onshore, but after the Pacific Solution (see Chap. 2), private companies also ran the camps in Nauru and on Manus Island in Papua New Guinea. They were briefly closed in 2008 by the Rudd Labor government but reinstated by the Gillard Labor government in 2012. The companies involved in the offshore detention system since 2012 include: G4S, Broadspectrum (formerly Transfield Services), IHMS and Wilson Security. In 2021, *The Guardian* reported that another company, Canstruct, is now running the camp in Nauru. Canstruct has been paid more than 1.4 billion dollars over the past five years despite no new asylum seekers arriving in Nauru since 2014. Canstruct, a Brisbane-based company and Liberal Party donor, won the contract by limited tender, meaning there was not an open and competitive process to secure the initial contract. The auditor general criticised the process, saying 'it is not clear why the department could not have secured a replacement supplier using a more competitive procurement method'. According to a report in *The Guardian*, Paladin, a company headquartered in a 'shack' on Kangaroo Island and with no experience with major contracts, received more than 500 million dollars in 2019 from the Morrison government to provide garrison services at Manus Regional Processing Centre without the contract going to open tender. In a scathing report, the auditor general assessed that the Australian taxpayer did not get 'value for money' (Doherty, 2021).

According to the director of legal advocacy at the Human Rights Legal Centre, Keren Adams, the Canstruct and Paladin cases raise serious questions about the Department's handling of offshore detention contracts. 'Canstruct, like Paladin, had next to no relevant experience when they were awarded the Nauru contract', Adams told *The Guardian*. 'One day they were building tunnels and the next they were managing welfare services for a group of highly vulnerable and traumatised people'. Adams said that as mainstream companies increasingly distanced themselves from the 'abject cruelty' of offshore detention, the government was having to cast their net wider to find contractors in Nauru and Papua New Guinea (Knaus & Davidson, 2019).

Was It Always Going to End in Tears?

Is there a causal relationship between the 'abject cruelty' practised within detention camps and them being run by private, for-profit corporations? I argue there is such a relationship, though it is complicated. Immigration detention was a cruel practice even before any camps were privatised because mandatory detention of potentially innocent people is an abuse of human rights.

However, comparison of private versus public immigration detention administration is possible. On 12 May 1998 the Human Rights and Equal Opportunity Commission (HREOC) released a report titled *Those Who've Come Across the Seas*. This is a line in the Australian national anthem, from a verse whose meaning is that the island continent of

Australia has plenty of room for everyone who might come here. The report contained the findings of the Commission's investigation into the policy of mandatory detention and conditions of detention in state-run centres in New South Wales, South Australia and Western Australia. HREOC began the investigation after receiving fifty-eight complaints against the Department (DIMIA) from or on behalf of people in immigration detention centres since 1990. The majority of these complaints alleged infringements of human rights under the *Human Rights and Equal Opportunity Commission Act 1986 (Cth)*. The major findings of the report were:

> that the mandatory detention for extended periods of almost all unlawful non-citizens who arrive by boat breaches Australia's human rights obligations under the International Covenant on Civil and Political Rights and the Convention on the Rights of the Child. The Commission has found that human rights under these international instruments are violated by
> - the conditions of detention
> - detainees' restricted access to services, including legal advice and representation
> - the practice and effects of long-term detention
> - restricted access to judicial review of detention. (p. 39)

The Commission recommended that the government and DIMIA develop and implement alternatives to detention of unauthorised arrivals and that the parliament amend the Migration Act accordingly. It also made a series of specific recommendations concerning conditions in the detention centres and emphasised the need to ensure that individuals deprived of their liberty are treated in a humane manner that respects human dignity (HREOC, 1998).

The detention regime under the control of the state was not perfect. Nevertheless, as compared to what occurred next under the control of private companies, this 1998 report contains an echo of a more decent, accountable state, if only in its expectations of better service, ethical treatment and compliance with international treaty obligations. Furthermore, the HREOC report was detailed, because the investigators had access to the centres and those detained within. Once the camps were privatised, contact with detainees became extortionately difficult. Especially, the camps in Nauru and Manus Island became completely isolated, and almost no media, lawyers or members of civil society were able to visit. It was from 1997 onwards, under the privatised regime, that the systemic abuse of asylum seekers began.

Torture Prevention

In 2016 two scholars, Richard Carver and Lisa Handley, published the first independent and global study of the impact of torture prevention measures, *Does Torture Prevention Work?*. Their reassuring finding is yes, torture prevention works. However, their study asserts that no single measure is sufficient to prevent torture because, as with every aspect of ongoing abuse, prevention operates within an ecology of practices. In short, the environment sustains either safety or its opposite, danger. They are cultural products.

Monitoring bodies (understood broadly to include National Preventive Mechanisms under OPCAT, the Optional Protocol to the Convention against Torture and other Cruel, Inhuman and Degrading Treatment or Punishment, and other international bodies and civil society organisations) have a direct effect in reducing torture. However, the global study found that the most effective way to reduce incidences of torture in detention is detention safeguards. These safeguards include abstaining from unofficial detention and ensuring, within the first few hours of detention, that relatives, lawyers and medical officers are notified and that detainees are able to contact them. The report also highlights the positive impact of reducing reliance on confessions, which for obvious reasons often involve coercion, sometimes torture. In Australia's detention regime this would translate as not using abuse to 'send a message' to other people who might potentially claim asylum. As we have seen, the body itself can be used as a 'confession' when it is abused and silenced. Other important safeguards are disciplinary sanctions against perpetrators of abuse and the absence of amnesty laws for perpetrators—Australia has not prosecuted a single person in relation to the abuse, or even murder, of asylum seekers in detention. Advocates and impartial assessors need the ability to carry out unannounced visits and to interview detainees in private. None of those strategies are currently in place within Australia's privatised system. Indeed, on 23 October 2022 the United Nations Subcommittee on Prevention of Torture (SPT) announced that it would suspend its scheduled visit to Australia due to obstructions it encountered in carrying out its mandate under the Optional Protocol to the Convention against Torture and other Cruel, Inhuman or Degrading Treatment or Punishment (OPCAT). The SPT delegation has been prevented from visiting several places where people are detained, it has experienced difficulties in carrying out full visits at other locations, and it has not been given all the relevant information and documentation it has requested (United Human Rights Commissioner 2022).

Australia's Privatised Immigration Detention Regime

HREOC's 1998 recommendation was that the authorities find alternatives to immigration detention and amend the Migration Act. But the Howard government had other ideas, calling instead for tenders from the private sector. The relationship between privatising the camps and the abuse that followed is best highlighted by two interventions of oversight, the Palmer Inquiry in 2005 and the Moss Review in 2015.

Rioting, lip-sewing, digging of graves and suicide attempts began in the camps in 1998 and continued, occasionally making headlines in the wider world. In response, a sinister new practice emerged in the now privatised camps—solitary confinement and 'punishment cells'. GSL, the company that had taken over the contract from ACM, labelled this a 'behaviour modification program' (detainees call it the GITMO system). It involved prolonged periods of solitary confinement over eight weeks. Detainees were first incarcerated in GSL's Management Unit (MU) for anything up to five days, where they would spend twenty-three and a half hours a day in a brightly lit cell with a mattress but no bedding or towels, wearing only a short gown. Security cameras were trained on the room, shower and toilet area. 'We had numerous reports of detainees detailing these conditions since GSL took over management', said Pamela Curr, then campaign co-ordinator for the Asylum Seeker Resource Centre in Melbourne. 'In some instances entry into the MU involved strip searching and cavity searches. Obviously this is distressing for people who have already been tortured, with rape being an integral part of that torture' (Macken, 2004).

The Royal Commission into Aboriginal Deaths in Custody (1991) had exposed the link between the use of isolation, and deaths and self-harm in Australian custody, and the Department of Immigration was well aware of the proven link. On 22 June 2004, Democrat Senator Andrew Bartlett asked Minister for Immigration Amanda Vanstone a simple question:

> Can the Minister specify whether it is legal within the current law and the existing guidelines for detainees to be put in isolation or separation from all other detainees as a specific consequence for particular behaviour such as non-co-operation with instructions?

The minister replied:

> I am not of the view nor do I have any advice that indicates that anything the Commonwealth does in this area or that its contractor does is outside the law. This is properly one of the most scrutinised Commonwealth programs in existence.[1]

Four days before Bartlett asked his question of the minister, a detainee who was subjected to the GSL behaviour modification programme was airlifted to Royal Adelaide Hospital Intensive Care for a drug overdose. Two months prior to Vanstone's and Bartlett's exchange, the legal status of the behaviour modification programme had been challenged before a Full Bench of the Federal Court.[2] This hearing, a case concerning an Iranian man held in a GSL MU, was opened by Judge Bradley Selway.

---

[1] SENATE Official Hansard No. 8, 2004 TUESDAY, 22 JUNE 2004.
[2] Secretary, Department of Immigration and Multicultural and Indigenous Affairs v. Mastipour, 2014.

> What is surprising is that there are virtually no provisions, either in the Act or in the migration regulations which purport to regulate the manner and conditions of [private] detention … It is usual when powers of detention are conferred for the parliament to make provision for the manner of the exercise of those powers. … It would not appear that any such regulations have been made.

Judge Paul Finn added:

> I wish to make only two additional comments. The first is to associate myself with the observations of Selway J concerning the absence of a statutory regime regulating the manner and conditions of immigration detention. The present legislative vacuum is, in my view, potentially unfair both to those involved in the conduct of detention centres and to the detainees.

The comments of both judges reflect the liminal nature of Australian detention centres. That the Howard government failed to make provisions, either in the Act or the migration regulations, to regulate conditions of detention is a story of partial incompetence but also of deliberate denial and obfuscation. As will be discussed further, clearly defining 'provisions' and 'migration regulations' would have revealed clearly what the Howard government was willing to do or not do to maintain the *phantasie* of 'them' and 'us', and to keep control of both.

Reporting on developments, interviewing Ruddock and Vanstone (successive immigration ministers), I often received the impression that they were making decisions 'on the fly' and 'testing the waters'. As 2004 drew to an end, advocates and journalists began hearing about the strange case of a woman called Anna in Baxter Detention Centre in South Australia. She was a German and Australian citizen who, as a result of mental illness, fell victim to Australia's policy of mandatory, indefinite detention of asylum seekers and undocumented people.

> I remember a friend in Baxter telling me he thought there was an Australian woman being held in detention, but that she was very sick. … I started ringing the German Embassy in November 2004 to see if they could get her out. But they told me that she had already been removed. Then she reappeared in January 2005. (Pamela Curr, personal communication, 2019)

In fact, the woman's name was Cornelia Rau. Rau was unlawfully detained for a period of ten months in 2004 and 2005, both in Brisbane and in the Baxter immigration camp. During that time, she was subjected to bewildering and brutal neglect by both the DIMIA and GSL and spent long stretches of time in isolation and the feared MU.

Fortunately for Rau, when it was revealed that a young *Australian* woman (one of 'us') had been held—indeed, lost—in Australian detention, the public outcry was instantaneous. By 9 February 2005, Vanstone as immigration minister had issued the terms of reference for what became known as the Palmer Inquiry. Mick Palmer, previously commissioner of the Australian Federal Police, was appointed to investigate the circumstances around the detention of Cornelia Rau—and then he was forced to ask for an extension of time when it was revealed that in 2001 DIMIA had also deported an Australian citizen, Vivian Alvarez Solon, to the Philippines because they had assumed she was a Filipina sex slave. The department had realised the error in 2003 but failed to tell her family, who had listed her as missing, until 2005.

At this time DIMIA had a contract with GSL to run the immigration camp in Baxter. The 2005 Palmer Inquiry (p. xiii) found a 'serious cultural problem' within the department and the way the contract between GSL and DIMIA was managed, or not managed. Its findings included weak leadership, with untrained and incompetent staff given 'exceptional, even extraordinary powers'. Palmer noted that the Baxter camp had been modelled on prison facilities and that its operations were based on prison norms. Most of its guards had worked in prisons. 'There is an enduring tension between containment and care, and the emphasis at Baxter is on containment'. Palmer found the care and management of Rau, a mentally ill person, was 'disjointed, fragmented and poorly co-ordinated' and that this was not an exceptional state of affairs in the Baxter centre. A fundamental conclusion of the Palmer report was that detainees suffered 'not so much incompetent management but an absence of management'. No one was managing the managers. 'Nobody was in charge'.

Despite this parlous state of affairs within the detention centre, the Palmer recommendations meant that GSL was able to renegotiate a more lucrative contract. Steven Brown, the UK-based managing director of GSL, explained this to me in 2005 (Macken & Morris, 2005): 'I don't know if it will increase our budget, though that may be the outcome. But we're working with DIMIA to find the best value for money'.

The treatment of Cornelia Rau almost perfectly illustrates the opposite of what is needed to prevent abuse and torture. No one was contacted—not family, lawyer or doctor—when she arrived at the facility. Her detention was illegal yet there were no disciplinary sanctions against GSL, DIMIA or the government. Monitoring bodies did not have easy access to the isolated site, nor were they able to carry out unannounced visits or interview Rau in private.

Following the Palmer Inquiry life improved for a period of time in the detention camps, according to HREOC. Then, the last detainee was removed from Manus Island in 2003, and on 8 February 2008, with Kevin Rudd as prime minister, the Labor government announced that all remaining asylum seekers in Nauru had been transferred to Australia. On that day Senator Chris Evans, Minister for Immigration and Citizenship, said,

> [T]he Pacific solution was a cynical, costly and ultimately unsuccessful exercise introduced on the eve of a Federal election by the Howard Government. (Evans, 2008)

At that time, I was part of a movement-wide discussion about how those of us who were critical of Australia's refugee policy should respond to the closures. The main question debated was, should this change made by Labor be taken as the end of the issue, or should the movement continue to campaign for necessary changes in policy and law, to ensure that mandatory offshore detention and its attendant human rights violations never happened again? Should we now be demanding that our detention services return to public administration? On the whole, campaigners were both tired and full of hope that the tide of popular opinion had turned and that now, knowing all that we knew, these abusive camps were gone for good.

We were wrong.

The Gillard Labor government reopened Nauru Regional Processing Centre on 14 August 2012 and Manus Island Regional Processing Centre on 21 November 2012. The government has access to the international recommendations for Detention Guidelines established by the United Nations High Commissioner for Refugees (2012), but they did not implement them when they reopened these centres. What followed in abuse, humiliation, murder, suicide, death through neglect and profound mental illness was as horrifying as it was predictable.

Despite previous commitments to bring detention back into public administration, Gillard contracted Broadspectrum to re-establish the facility in Nauru. Broadspectrum's obligations were extended in further contracts up to February 2016. The private company was responsible for providing 'garrison and welfare' services, security and escort services in both Nauru and Manus Island. It sub-contracted some of its obligations to Wilson Security Nauru.

In Nauru, the physical layout of the camp, issues in the surrounding Nauruan community and the powerlessness of asylum seekers all but ensured violence. Detainees were housed in vinyl tents on a small island that regularly records temperatures higher than 35 degrees Celsius. Complaint management and incident reporting did not meet required standards, as shown in extensive evidence provided by the 2015 Moss Review and the Senate Select Committee on the Recent Allegations Relating to the Conditions and Circumstances at the Regional Processing Centre in Nauru (Senate Select Committee, 2015a), among other reports. The Senate Select Committee noted, for example:

> Wilson Security and Transfield Services [are not] properly accountable to the Commonwealth despite the significant investment in their services. The committee has found that the Department of Immigration and Border Protection does not have full knowledge of incidents occurring in Nauru, owing to their inability to scrutinise their contracted service providers. A representative of the department acknowledged that 'the current contract does not provide as strong an abatement regime as the proposed contract' and told the committee that no financial abatements or penalties have been triggered under the current Performance Management Framework. The committee believes that the shortcomings of the current framework offer no reassurance that the department is fully aware of events in Nauru. (2015a, p. 125)

As the detainee population grew, so did reports about the sexual assault of women (Bacon et al., 2016) and abuse of children. On 10 August 2016, *The Guardian* published The Nauru Files (Evershed et al., 2016). Its eight thousand pages reveal over two thousand leaked incident reports from Nauru detailing allegations of assaults, self-harm, suicide attempts, child abuse, sexual abuse and squalor endured by asylum seekers in the 'care' of private companies. The reported incidents range from a guard allegedly grabbing a boy and threatening to kill him once he was living in the community, to guards allegedly slapping children in the face. In September 2014 a teacher reported that a young classroom helper had requested a four-minute shower instead of the usual two minutes. 'Her request has been accepted on conditions of sexual favours. It is a male security person. She did not state if this has or hasn't occurred. The Security officer wants to view a boy or girl having a shower'. According to another incident report from September 2014, a girl had sewn her lips together, and guard who saw her merely laughed at her (Farrell et al., 2016).

Immigration Minister Peter Dutton claimed that some of the reports were 'false allegations' by asylum seekers attempting to get to Australia. He criticised both *The Guardian* and the ABC for the manner in which they'd reported the allegations, saying that their approach 'has been to trivialise the very serious issues by trying to promote the 2,100 reports as somehow all of those being serious when they're not' (Farrell & Karp, 2016). In fact, the contrary was true: on 6 September 2015, a senior manager of non-government organisation Save the Children International wrote an email to staff of the Nauru centre explaining that Wilson Security had admitted they had been *downgrading* serious incidents when they reported them, without any clear justification (and that they had agreed to stop doing so) (Farrell & Doherty, 2016).

As allegations of abuse continued to surface through local advocates able to contact advocates in Australia, a new campaign was launched. On 12 October 2015, No Business in Abuse (NBIA) started targeting the private companies.[3] Its analysis and campaign were simple. Without

---

[3] No Business in Abuse (NBIA) was an independent, non-profit, non-government initiative that sought to end the complicity of corporate entities in human rights abuses perpetuated within Australia's immigration system.

investors the companies running the camps would fold. These companies had been invested in by large global funds that had ethical and human rights screens on their portfolios that should screen out Broadspectrum and Wilson Security. NBIA wrote a report detailing the abuses and calling on superannuation funds and global funds such as the Norwegian sovereign wealth fund to divest. Political scientist Claire Parfitt (2020, p. 9) has highlighted this campaign as one of the most comprehensive examples ever of using corporate boycott and divestment campaigns to secure political and humanitarian outcomes.

Human Rights Commissioner Gillian Triggs has called for investors to demand better corporate performance on human rights compliance (Rose, 2016), stating that investors 'have the power in their hands' to require corporations to comply with the United Nations' guiding principles on human rights. The commissioner was responding to, amongst other things, the recalcitrance of the Australian Government with regard to its obligations to people seeking asylum under international human rights law.

What If …?

Would public administration stop this culture of abuse? Yes, potentially it would. It might not stop the abuse entirely, but public administration would change the culture of the detention system for several reasons. First, the location of the camps would change. The processing centres in Nauru and Papua New Guinea are private businesses operating in foreign countries. There is no reason to think that either Nauru or PNG would be willing to have another country's public administration setting up a carceral system on their land, because there would be neither employment opportunities nor financial advantage in such an arrangement. Further, the legislative and regulatory standards required by Australia's public accountability might not sit comfortably in Nauru or PNG. Relocating the camps to the Australian mainland under public administration does not guarantee complete safety or humane treatment, as Australia's jails attest. But it would change the culture of secrecy, the lack of transparency and end the liminal, lawless nature of the camps.

Secondly, as noted by Australian scholars, Nethery and Holman (2016, p. 6), as an extra-judicial form of incarceration, immigration detention camps are not subject to the same regulatory framework as Australia's prison system. That has implications for the conditions under which people are held, their length of detention and their avenues for appeal. Bringing them back into public administration would begin the process of reinstituting a regulatory framework around what is currently 'a zone of indistinction between outside and inside, exception and rule, licit and illicit, in which the very concepts of subjective right and juridical protection no longer made any sense' (Agamben, 1998, p. 96).

Third, when detention camps are private businesses operating in foreign countries that have weak human rights protections, and when they are shielded by commercial-in-confidence contracts, distance, isolation and the complexity of sub-contracting, there is little transparency and a high level of secrecy. A Senate Inquiry (2015b) in August 2015 found a 'pervasive culture of secrecy' in the offshore camps, citing instances where Wilson Security officers had regularly destroyed incident reports, including reports of staff mistreatment of detainees. There is an anecdote of staff jokingly filing their incident reports in what they referred to as File 13, their codename for the paper shredder (Senate Select Committee, 2015a). Shredding important documents is a very serious matter in the public service if it becomes known; exercise of public power on behalf of the government by the public service is governed by law. Destruction of documents is likely to be an offence under the *Archives Act 1983* and therefore grounds for dismissal. It is thus much less likely to happen under public administration than private.

Fourth, the opportunity for an asylum seeker to contact their relatives, see a lawyer or receive treatment from a doctor in the early phase of detention opens up under public administration. It has been severely foreclosed in the privatised regime. Moreover, in the public realm, while Section 42 of the *Australian Border Force Act 2015 (Cth)* imposes a penalty of two years' jail for a whistle-blower who makes a disclosure in relation to a detention camp, section 42(2)I exempts disclosures 'required or authorised by or under a law of the Commonwealth, a State or a Territory'.

Fifth, anyone who died in a camp under public administration would need to have a coronial inquiry into their death.

Finally, a move back to public administration would transform any detention camps from being sites of economic activity, to sites of political contest, a move with some practical potential for public oversight through the various forms of media.

Cruelty and Denial Are the Point

John Howard and successive prime ministers have argued that privatising the camps is cheaper for the country, because private enterprise is more efficient at delivering services. The facts give lie to that. The per annum cost of holding a person in the Nauru or Manus camp at the Mid-Year Economic and Fiscal Outlook in December 2015 was AUD574,111 (Australian National Audit Office, 2021). Refugee Action Coalition (2016) reported that

> [d]etaining a single asylum seeker on Manus or Nauru costs $400,000 per year, according to the National Commission of Audit in 2014. Amnesty put it at $570,000 per person in a 2016 report. Detention in Australia costs $239,000 per year. By contrast, allowing asylum seekers to live in the [Australian mainland] community while their claims are processed costs just $12,000 per year, one twentieth of the cost of the offshore camps, and even less if they are allowed the right to work.

A Save the Children/UNICEF report, *At What Cost? The Human, Economic and Strategic Cost of Australia's Asylum Seeker Policies and the Alternatives* (Button & Evans, 2016) found that the Australian Government's refugee deterrence policies—boat turnbacks, onshore and offshore detention, and other programmes—cost AUD9.6 billion between 2012 and 2016. As at December 2016, about 3.4 billion of this was going to private companies with contracts for security, cleaning, catering, recreational/education and health in PNG and Nauru. The bill for chartered flights alone to Manus and Nauru came to 45 million.

Given that privatised camps are approximately twelve times more expensive than community-based detention and that the camps have proven to be chaotic, controversial and cruel, why does each successive government continue the practice? If not money or excellence of care, what is the attraction? Australian economist Richard Denniss barely contains his frustration when the question of cost comes up in progressive political circles. In conversation with me in 2021, he argues that the Left is missing the point by railing against the economic contradiction at the heart of Australia's neoliberal practice of privatising immigration camps—the fact that far from being cheaper, they are by a factor of twelve more expensive to run than community detention. He reiterates his observation that neoliberalism is not an economic project, but it is about transforming the Australian community.

> And they will waste as much of your money on their project as they want. So stop saying they're ideologues. Stop saying they're in the small governments. Stop saying they're free marketeers. Stop saying that it's head versus heart. All they are trying to do is reshape our entire community.

The Australian Government is 'performing' economic rationality while pursuing distance and control. Saving money is not what privatising the detention regime is about or ever was about. Dennis continues

> You can't take seriously their stated objectives. Imagine if, when Scott Morrison was immigration minister, he'd said to the electorate, 'look, privatising these camps is going to cost a shit-ton, but that's okay because cruelty is the point, and the lack of accountability is the point, deniability is the point – saving money has never been the point of this privatisation'. But that construction of reality is impossible to share, so he argues the private sector can do it better and cheaper.

This performance of economic rationality can most recently be seen in the associated performance of maintaining strong borders in northern Australia. Border security and national security are flagship justifications for cruel immigration policies. For instance, the Australian National Audit Office (ANAO) has examined the government contract for fixed wing aerial surveillance to 'prevent' people smuggling and manage other maritime threats across the north-west approaches of Australia. The initial 2009 contract with private company Surveillance Australia was valued at 1187 million. Twelve years later, ANAO found:

The contract has not been managed to secure delivery in line with the planned cost, scope and delivery timeframe. The contract has been varied on 40 occasions as of March 2021 with the effect of significantly changing the scope of the services to be delivered and increasing the term and value of the contract. The department has recognised that variations to the contract have significantly reshaped it and those variations have increased the cost by more than 29 per cent. Over the life of the contract, there has been a high turnover of officers responsible for the management of the contract and the department has not ensured that each of its contract managers had appropriate training or experience. (ANAO, 2021, summary, point 11)

Denniss argues that these contractual failures underscore as fraudulent the argument for national security concerning deterring, deflecting or detaining those who seek asylum by sea.

> No one in the national security community actually thinks that some refugees showing up on a boat has any impact on our national security. And none of them think for a minute that the failure of some guy in assessment to spot one of them is of any significance to our national security. This is not about national security – if it was, someone would be very worried about this scathing assessment from ANAO. The government's actions reveal the reality.

A privatised regime also provides the state with the benefit of deniability. Protection from scrutiny provided by commercial-in-confidence contractual arrangements between corporations and the government is complemented by a notional transition of authority whose details are contained in a memorandum of understanding, or MOU, between national governments. During the 2015 Senate Inquiry into conditions at the detention centre in Nauru, the secretary of the Department of Immigration and Border Protection, Michael Pezzullo, asserted:

> The Australian government does not run the Nauru regional processing centre, or RPC. It is managed by the government of Nauru, under Nauruan law, with support from the Australian government. The government of Nauru operates the RPC, assesses asylum claims and, where persons are found to be in need of protection, arranges settlement. The government of Nauru is specifically responsible for security and good order and the care and welfare of persons residing in the centre. (McKenzie-Murray, 2015)

This rhetorical (and contractual) distancing from the *management,* or *running,* or *operation,* or *'good order'* of the processing centre, on its distant soil, creates the fiction that the *existence* and the *ethics* of the centre are no longer the responsibility of anybody in Australia.

When the Private Was Made Public

Public things and places are where we experience others and ourselves as citizens within a democracy and where we are taught to recognise ourselves in the humanity of those around us. Pushing up against them, creating them, nurturing and challenging them strengthen the muscle and sinew supporting democracy. Public things democratise and humanise us. An extraordinary embodiment of this transformation was seen in the Manus Island camp.

In 2016, Papua New Guinea's Supreme Court ruled that Australia's indefinite detention of asylum seekers on Manus Island was illegal because it breached potential refugees' fundamental human rights. In response to this ruling, the Australian Government said that the camp that had housed asylum-seeking men for four years would be torn down and its men moved to new camps, divided between three different locations on Manus Island. However, these new camps were not finished and construction on one of them had not even started when the Australian Government ordered the men to leave the existing camp and move to the incomplete, and dangerous, new sites. The Australian Government also removed every Australian citizen working onsite in the PNG camps.

There followed an extraordinary three-week stand-off between the asylum seekers and the PNG navy and police force, as the PNG state stopped feeding the men at the initial camp and used its forces to try to remove them. Many of the men resisted being split up and moved, both for personal safety and to call attention to the ongoing abuses of their rights and bodies. The high-stake situation had all the ingredients for a bloody disaster. The fact that disaster was averted is testament to the power of these asylum seekers' commitment to non-violence and to their own respect for human rights.

Behrouz Boochani is a Kurdish journalist and writer from Iran. At the time these events unfolded, he had been in detention on Manus Island for four years. Boochani was often the spokesperson for the detainees in communicating with the world outside the camp as much as could be managed. In a letter from Manus Island in 2017, Boochani described a situation in which, as the private corporation withdrew its workers to safety, the camp became a small public, a body politic, and the interred, besieged men operated as a political unit or demos.

> In reality, it was a resistance that was completely democratic. By democratic I mean that every day, right at 5pm, at one fixed location in Delta prison, we gathered and everyone had the chance to express their opinion with the group and discuss. If anyone had a new suggestion, they could outline it and then we would put it to a vote; as a group we would consider whether the suggestion should be put into practice or not. Debates surrounding how to manage the tasks inside the prison and the rules pertaining to the prison were also resolved by voting.

Service to each other and care for their non-human companions were central to the demos they created.

> Sometimes, during this period, we smuggled into the prison a limited amount of food in the dead of night, and this food would be distributed equally among the prisoners. This principle also applied to the dogs that live among us: we factored them in. In our meetings we were adamant about the fact we had to show even more compassion to these dogs than before. Feeding them was imperative. These principles applied to the sick, too; we cared for them now more than ever before.

Because the men were in such a vulnerable position and because they were aware of the state's ongoing moves to divide and conquer, they avoided conflict and maintained solidarity by insisting everyone was responsible for their own choices and that those choices would be respected and supported.

> Throughout these three weeks, the gates were completely open and anyone could leave the collective resistance at any moment. They were totally free to go to the new camps and acquire food and water. We were particularly committed

to the following point: no one had the right to reproach another for leaving us. In fact, we all had to thank anyone who left the community because they stood with us for as long as they were capable, and we were all grateful for that.

After three weeks of ongoing non-violent resistance, the men were overwhelmed by the violence of the PNG police and forcibly moved to two of the three new camps. Boochani concluded the letter to Australia:

> Our resistance was an epic of love … Resistance in its purest form. A noble resistance. An epic constituted by half-naked bodies up against a violent governmentality. All this violence designed in government spaces and targeted against us has driven our lives towards nature. Towards the natural environment, towards the animal world, towards the ecosystem. (Boochani, 2017)

In the illegal absence of freedom to participate in any public spaces, places and voices, the refugee men held on Manus continued to care for each other, mourn each other and call out Australia's brutality. They continued to act with non-violence and to hold fast to their own humanity and love. It is not clear whether Australia can make the same bold claim.

Their solidarity, discipline and resistance transformed a private prison into demos. They created a place of political action that had at its heart the capacity to reconstitute that which had been reduced to bare life. It is important to note the neoliberal ideology has not only colonised our public lives, but it has also impoverished our imagination and language. Boochani (2017) succinctly asserts:

> Our resistance is the spirit that haunts Australia. Our resistance is a new manifesto for humanity and love.

References

Agamben, G. (1998). *Homo Sacer: Sovereign power and bare life* (D. Heller-Roazen, Trans.). Stanford University Press.

Aulich, C., & O'Flynn, J. (2007). John Howard: The great privatiser? *Australian Journal of Political Science, 42*(2), 365–381. https://doi.org/10.1080/10361140701320075

Australian National Audit Office. (2021). *Management of the civil maritime surveillance services contract.* Department of Home Affairs. Auditor-General Report No. 6. ANAO. https://www.anao.gov.au/work/performance-audit/management-the-civil-maritime-surveillance-services-contract

Bacon, W., Curr, P., Lawrence, C., Macken, J., & O'Connor, C. (2016). *Protection Denied, Abuse Condoned: Women on Nauru at Risk.* Australian Women in Support of Women on Nauru. https://www.awsnn.org/the-report

Blewett, N. (1999). *A cabinet diary.* Wakefield Press.

Boochani, B. (2017, December 9–15). A letter from Manus Island. *The Saturday Paper.* https://www.thesaturdaypaper.com.au/news/politics/2017/12/09/letter-manus-reynoldsisland/15127380005617

Briskman, L., & Dimasi, M. (2010). Not quite Australia: Asylum seekers on an exceptional Island. In S. Perera, G. Seal, & S. Summers (Eds.), *Enter at own risk?: Australia's population questions for the 21st century* (pp. 141–159). Black Swan Press.

Brown, W. (2015). *Undoing the demos: Neoliberalism's stealth revolution.* Zone Books.

Butt, R. (1981). Mrs Thatcher: The first two years. Interview. *Sunday Times.* https://www.margarehatcher.org/document/104475

Button, L., & Evans, S. (2016). *At what cost? The human, economic and strategic cost of Australia's asylum seeker policies and the alternatives.* Save the Children Australia & UNICEF, United Nations Children's Fund. https://resourcecentre.savethechildren.net/document/what-cost-human-economic-and-strategic-cost-australias-asylum-seeker-policies-and/

Denniss, R. (2018). Dead right: How neoliberalism ate itself and what comes next. *Quarterly Essay, 70.*

Doherty, B. (2021, April 10). Brisbane company paid $1.4 billion to run offshore processing on Nauru despite no arrivals since 2014. The Guardian. https://www.theguardian.com/australia-news/2021/apr/10/brisbane-company-paid-14bn-to-run-offshore-processing-on-nauru-despite-no-arrivals-since-2014

Evans, C. (2008, February 8). *Last refugees leave Nauru* [Media release]. Department for Immigration and Citizenship Australian Parliament. https://parlinfo.aph.gov.au/parlInfo/search/display/display.w3p;query=Id%3A%22media%2Fpressrel%2FYUNP6%22;src1=sm1#:~:text='The%20Rudd%20Government%20pledged%20to

Evershed, N., Liu, R., Farrell, P., & Davidson, H. (2016). The Nauru files. *The Guardian.* https://www.theguardian.com/news/series/nauru-files

Farrell, P., & Doherty, B. (2016, August 12). Nauru files show Wilson Security staff regularly downgraded reports of abuse. *The Guardian*. https://www.theguardian.com/australia-news/2016/aug/12/nauru-files-show-wilson-security-staff-regularly-downgraded-reports-of-abuse

Farrell, P., & Karp, P. (2016, August 18). Peter Dutton attacks Guardian and ABC over reporting Nauru files. *The Guardian*. https://www.theguardian.com/australia-news/2016/aug/18/peter-dutton-says-he-wont-be-defamed-by-guardian-and-abc-over-nauru-files

Farrell, P., Evershed, N., & Davidson, H. (2016, August 10). The Nauru files: Cache of 2,000 leaked reports reveal scale of abuse of children in Australian offshore detention. *The Guardian*. https://www.theguardian.com/australia-news/2016/aug/10/the-nauru-files-2000-leaked-reports-reveal-scale-of-abuse-of-children-in-australian-offshore-detention

Human Rights and Equal Opportunity Commission. (1998). Those who've come across the seas: Detention of unauthorised arrivals. HREOC. https://humanrights.gov.au/our-work/asylum-seekers-and-refugees/publications/those-whove-come-across-seas-detention

International Detention Coalition. (2022, July 25). *Alternatives to detention*. https://idcoalition.org/alternatives-to-detention/

Knaus, C., & Davidson, H. (2019, February 19). Paladin controversy prompts renewed scrutiny of $591m Nauru deal. *The Guardian*. https://www.theguardian.com/australia-news/2019/feb/19/paladin-controversy-prompts-renewed-scrutiny-of-591m-nauru-deal

Macken, J. (2001, December 15). The detainers. *The Australian Financial Review*.

Macken, J. (2002, March 22) Capturing the prison business. *The Australian Financial Review*.

Macken, J. (2004, June 24). Detention in need of some attention. *The Australian Financial Review*. https://www.afr.com/policy/health-and-education/detention-in-need-of-some-attention-20040624-j7238

Macken, J., & Morris, S. (2005, April 4). Detained earnings. *The Australian Financial Review*. https://www.afr.com/politics/detained-earnings-20050804-jkgv9

McKenzie-Murray, M. (2015, August 29). Nauru's systematic dysfunction'. *The Saturday Paper*. https://www.thesaturdaypaper.com.au/news/immigration/2015/08/29/naurus-systemic-dysfunction/14407704002306

Nethery, A., & Holman, R. (2016). Secrecy and human rights abuse in Australia's offshore immigration detention centres. *The International Journal of Human Rights, 20*(7), 1018–1038. https://doi.org/10.1080/13642987.2016.1196903

Palmer, M. J. (2005). *Inquiry into the circumstances of the immigration detention of Cornelia Rau: Report* [PDF]. Department of Immigration and Multicultural and Indigenous Affairs. https://www.homeaffairs.gov.au/reports-and-pubs/files/palmer-report.pdf

Parfitt, C. (2020). ESG integration treats ethics as risk, but whose ethics and whose risk? Responsible Investment in the Context of Precarity and risk-shifting. *Critical Sociology, 46*(4–5), 573–587. https://doi.org/10.1177/0896920519868794

Perera, S. (2002). What is a camp…? *borderlands, 1*(1). https://webarchive.nla.gov.au/awa/20021021000639/http://www.borderlandsjournal.adelaide.edu.au/vol1no1_2002/perera_camp.html

Refugee Action Coalition. (2016). *Detention costs*. https://www.refugeeaction.org.au/?page_id=3447

Rose, S. (2016, May 10). Gillian Triggs urges super funds to take up the fight on human rights. *The Australian Financial Review*. http://www.afr.com/news/policy/gillian-triggs-urges-super-funds-totake-up-the-fight-on-human-rights-20160509-gopw7d

Senate. Select Committee on the Recent Allegations Relating to the Conditions and Circumstances at the Regional Processing Centre in Nauru. (2015a). *Final Report. Taking responsibility: Conditions and circumstances at Australia's regional processing centre in Nauru*. Select Committee on the Recent Allegations relating to Conditions and Circumstances at the Regional Processing Centre in Nauru. https://www.aph.gov.au/Parliamentary_Business/Committees/Senate/Regional_processing_Nauru/Regional_processing_Nauru/Final_Report

Senate. Select Committee on the Recent Allegations Relating to the Conditions and Circumstances at the Regional Processing Centre in Nauru. (2015b). Submission 95. https://www.aph.gov.au/Parliamentary_Business/Committees/Senate/Regional_processing_Nauru/Regional_processing_Nauru/Submissions

United Nations High Commissioner for Refugees. (2012). *Detention guidelines on the applicable criteria and standards relating to the detention of Asylum-Seekers and Alternatives to Detention*. UNHCR. https://www.unhcr.org/publications/legal/505b10ee9/unhcr-detention-guidelines.html

Whyte, J. (2008). Its silent working was a delusion. In J. Clemens, N. Heron, & A. Murray (Eds.), *The work of Giorgio Agamben: Law literature life* (pp. 66–81). Edinburgh University Press.

Williams, T. (2002, March 18) New protests put Wommera on high alert. *The Australian*.

8

Mania or Mourning

Political action has the power to transform what was once experienced as personal into something understood as political. In Chap. 6 I quoted medical professionals who have made a connection between political action—however visceral that may be—and maintaining mental health and the sacred core of the person. Dr. Peter Young suggested that the government hated hunger strikes in the camps because they had little control over the personal political action. Dr. Jon Jureidini described three phases of adaptation to life in the carceral immigration system: (1) optimism and engagement with camp activities on arrival; (2) anger and protest at the system's inertia (often framed as a manifestation of madness); (3) resignation and withdrawal (such as retreating into sleep or a form of resignation syndrome), a stage from which people rarely recover. In the face of the deathly shallowness of melancholia, almost any form of political resistance brings a vitality and reality that is otherwise absent. Personal political action that resists the dissolution of one's 'sacred core' and refuses to accept the unreality of the camps, is an anathema to the melancholic state.

Here, understanding that the personal suffering being experienced is a consequence of political desire for control and coercion can liberate energy and agency and provide a frame by which to confront the locus of power.

If this is true for the person incarcerated in Australia's detention regime, could it be true for the nation more broadly? Could it be that the recent resurgence we have seen, of political action driving headlines and rallies, is the nation leaving its melancholic state for another more lifeful and reality-based state? Since 2019 there has been a groundswell of organised actions, protests and demands for a different politics and more transparent government. Foregrounding violence against women, Black deaths in custody, climate change and more, there is a revived contestation of ideas about what kind of country Australia should be: what is the 'sacred core' of the nation?

This disputation is currently taking the form of accusing the Albanese Labor government of surrendering Australian sovereignty to the interests of the North American defence and intelligence bureaus and forgoing its own professed values to support Israel in the violence in Gaza. Unfortunately, it must be said that these two debates are mostly conducted by Muslim and Indigenous Australians, climate activists and women: they remain marginal while the dominant groups in politics, the media and the corporate sector continue a business-as-usual narrative of largely uncritical acceptance of the US–Australia alliance and Israeli claims of self-defence, punctuated by, for instance, wild postulations as to whether climate protestors should be jailed for interrupting the Aussie morning commuter peak hour.

After two hundred and thirty years of colonisation Australia remains unformed, lacking consensus let alone enthusiasm for the symbols of a cohesive nation state. There is no agreement on what a National Day should be. Indeed, Australia Day on 26 January is also described as Invasion Day or Survival Day and remains contested as a date of national unity. We have yet to create a flag that represents the nation. The emergence of the Aboriginal and Torres Strait flags alongside the Australian flag at post-2022 election national press conferences was certainly a sign of hope, but it is also a reminder that we still need three flags to describe the nation. And as a person of Irish Catholic heritage, a small part of my soul dies every time I spy the Union Jack centre stage on the Australian flag.

We are ruled by a King born on the other side of the planet—distant, marginal, but with the constitutional power to sack an elected prime minister. Then there is our national anthem … few know the words beyond the first verse though most mutter something about being girt, or girth, whichever, by sea. And despite over two decades of almost a national obsession with the borders and boundaries of Australia, we retain the same under-developed understanding of sovereignty that was contained in a constitution written over a century ago. An example of this confused and superficial understanding is the Howard government's decision to excise thousands of kilometres of the Australian coastline while posturing as the leader who would defend borders, literally at all costs. Australia is also the only Western democracy that has no Charter or Bill of Human Rights. In sum, it is a country that has yet to find the symbols, songs and structures to hold it together as a cohesive nation. And as we are reminded by Jessica Whyte points, the constitution itself is mired in the splitting of the paranoid-schizoid nation with exclusion enshrined in the Australian Constitution, while citizenship is not a fact 'that gave legal sanction to Australia's mandatory detention regime'. The job of nation-building remains unfinished as the twenty-first century progresses.

This inability to cohere and progress reflects the 'stuck' nature of melancholia, with its compulsive repetition that ensures little is resolved, and its abhorrence of the symbolic, metaphoric and imaginative as being beyond a constricting, dictatorial control. It is hard to build an inclusive and abundant community when melancholia holds sway and complexity is exiled, through splitting, from the primitive psychological position of the paranoid-schizoid nation. Splitting is the central motif of almost every election. When the good nation can only be constructed out of the bad Other, a mature nation is still out of reach.

A Changing of the Guard

Paul Keating once said that when we change the government, we change the nation. It's possible he may have had this backwards: perhaps we change the government when, and because, the nation has changed. On 22 May 2022 I held my breath and hoped one of us was right. That's the day Australians went to the polls to elect another federal government. The conservative state of Queensland elected three candidates from the progressive Australian Greens, and across the country the Liberal Party lost seven traditional 'blue-ribbon' (conservative) seats to the Teal Independents—women who ran as independent candidates on a ticket of action on climate change, justice for refugees and the introduction of a federal anti-corruption commission. The centre-left Australian Labor Party won government. I breathed out.

But as I watched the results roll in on election night, I asked myself if this outcome represented an overblown, manic response to the lifelessness of melancholia—a response that would soon sputter and die and let denial and disavowal reassert their presence. Or, could it signal a substantial return to reality, a shift of the psychological terrain of the nation? Something like a return to the unfinished national project of mourning.

Moments of Fear and Love

The recognition of harm done and the shame that follows, are tender, frightening, fragile moments. These moments need to be nurtured, contained and respected. This is when, according to Melanie Klein (1946), the infant enters the depressive position. It is a psychological state that closely resembles Freud's description of mourning (1917), a moment that hangs suspended between fear and love. This is when the little one—the wounded nation—leaves the narcissistic *phantasie* of the split all-good/all-bad world, the paranoid-schizoid position, and makes the painful realisation that good and bad are inseparable. They live in the same person, they inhabit the same nation, we are all capable of both. It is in this moment that the infant/nation develops the ability to love. The world is revealed as neither right nor wrong, neither them nor us, redolent of transcendence and of something entirely new.

There was a glimpse of this recognition and remorse in 2019, when an Australian gunman shot dead fifty Muslims at prayer in Christchurch, New Zealand. In a moment of shame, Australians watched New Zealand's Prime Minister Jacinda Ardern tell the world that the White supremacist who committed the atrocity was not one of 'them'. Australian novelist Richard Flanagan finished her sentence at a Palm Sunday Rally for Refugees in Canberra, Australia:

> He is one of us. And the terrible truth is that we are him. We are our media, which too often promotes neo-Nazis. We are our parliament, which voted for a neo-Nazi slogan, resolving that it's 'OK to be white'. We are our Senator [Fraser Anning], who called for a 'final solution' to the so-called problem of immigration … Christchurch proves one thing; national security does not lie in the fairy tale of border security; it does not repose in the ongoing torture of free human beings; it exists in tolerance and human decency. (Flanagan, 2019)

During that 2019 federal election, shared grief and shame over what happened in New Zealand was enough to briefly curb the usual demonisation of refugees and the aggressive, tough-on-borders speeches that had become a hallmark of Australia's political campaigning. But without an appreciation of what was at stake in the national psyche and soul—with insufficient attention to the difference in tenor of the national discourse—the moment slipped away. Our relatively young national psyche can, like an infant, fail to thrive for want of care. The development of imagination and empathy are stunted or delayed. Grief, shame and mourning are acts of care and of self-care.

Here I begin the journey back with an example of seeing, imagination and love from a person I knew very well. This is a story about what can happen, what can be imagined and proposed when someone considers the humanity and hurt of the Other as vitally important to themselves.

Body Swap

On 1 September 2016, *Guardian* journalist Ben Doherty reported on what Jim Macken, my father, had just proposed to both the federal Coalition and the Australian Labor Party.

Changing Places
Retired judge, 88, offers 'body swap' with a refugee on Manus or Nauru
'I would consider it a privilege to live out my final years in either Nauru or Manus Island in his or her stead,' Jim Macken says. An 88-year-old retired judge has offered to swap places with a refugee held in offshore detention, volunteering to live the rest of his life on Manus or Nauru in exchange for one refugee being sent to Australia.

Jim Macken, a former justice of the industrial court of New South Wales, union official, and a member of the Order of Australia, has written to the immigration minister, Peter Dutton, offering a 'body swap' with a refugee held on one of Australia's two offshore detention camps.

Macken has conceded his proposal 'could be considered too novel for government' but says it is 'perfectly possible'. 'I understand this is an unusual request but I offer it in complete sincerity. My reason for making this proposal is simple. I can no longer remain silent as innocent men, women and children are being held in appalling circumstances on Manus Island and Nauru. It is even worse that they are being held in these dangerous and inhospitable conditions in order to ensure no other asylum seekers and refugees attempt to come to Australia for protection. The Australian Government is essentially treating refugees in these camps as human shields and this is utterly immoral. As this is being done in my name I cannot remain silent.' (Doherty, 2016)

Three years later I asked dad why he did it.

> I don't know where the idea came from, but once it arrived, I knew I had to act. I didn't think my offer was really that shocking, but the political response was. I think it was Martin Luther King who said, 'it's not the words of our enemies that we remember, but the silence of our friends'. That's what shocked me, the silence of our friends. It made me realise I don't know my country anymore; I don't recognise this Australia.

While the silence of his friends in the Labor Party and the union movement shocked my father, it probably did not surprise asylum seekers and many First Nations people. These kinds of silences have been woven through the DNA of this colonised nation for hundreds of years. My father realised then that the indifference had been compounding over time.

Perhaps you only hear the silence when it's directed at you. I understand that getting one person out of those terrible camps won't solve the problem for the hundreds of people left behind. But in the end, life has got to matter, even one person's life has got to matter, and that's as much my responsibility as it is Peter Dutton's, in a way. I have been in almost every big political stoush over the last seventy years, but nothing prepared me for this new Australia. Only a schism in the soul of a nation can explain why tolerance of wrong can become worse than the wrong itself.

My father died four weeks after this conversation was recorded. I include part of his story here for a few reasons. First, because I am psychically footsore and heartsick and in need of cause to believe change is possible however haltingly she comes. Then, to highlight that the last twenty years have witnessed pockets of resistance. My father's resistance complements the extraordinary feat of the men imprisoned on Manus Island as described above; the work of academics, nurses, psychologists, doctors, lawyers, teachers, social workers; the dedication of nuns, priests, brave activists young and old; and of course, the endurance of the women and men who have the lived experience of this regime, who have kept all our spirits going even as we failed. There have been days of wonder like when in 2007 it seemed the camps were being permanently closed and we might soon be able to atone, to count ourselves as people of honour.

I include my father's comments because I want to stress, 'it's not the words of our enemies that we remember, but the silence of our friends'. We are all implicated in this inertia: there are no innocent bystanders who just happen to keep voting for a policy that continues to destroy children, teenagers, adults, whole families. Finally, I include it to consider whether it is possible to repair a schism within the soul (of a nation) by refusing to tolerate an egregious wrong. For a nation submerged in a state of melancholia with its attendant denial of reality, of the pain of others, of the need to mourn, with its cold and feeble grip on the erotic energy of life, I wonder what might shatter this silence and bring us back to tears?

Mourning Requires More than Death

If death was all that was needed to create a state of mourning, we would have been well on our way to creating it. The past few years have been years of death on an historic scale for Australia and indeed for the world. In 2019 wildfires consumed the east coast of the country. Thirty-four people died, over a billion animals burnt to death or died of starvation in the devastated landscape; millions of hectares were destroyed and over two thousand buildings burnt to the ground. Then, as the rain finally came, Covid-19 arrived in Sydney onboard the Ruby Princess, an ocean liner that deposited hundreds of sick and infected travellers on the wharf at Circular Quay—death and disaster followed. The global death toll of Covid-19 continues to climb as does Australia's national toll. These have been cruel deaths as families were kept away from the aged-care homes that became scenes of utter devastation. The elderly and sick spent the last days of their lives fighting to breathe in almost complete isolation. Their deaths were marked by funerals bereft of family, friends, community and comfort. If death guaranteed mourning, we would now be a nation deeply immersed in it.

But, as Freud witnessed during the First World War, death does not always produce mourning. Sometimes it produces a deeper melancholia, deeper denial, disavowal and splitting. The deaths of forty-two people in Australian immigration detention and the relative lack of a national reaction are evidence that we need more than deaths to trigger mourning. These forty-two people remain ungrievable because they were not considered lives as Judith Butler describes it: 'An ungrievable life is one that cannot be mourned because it has never lived, that is, it has never counted as a life at all' (2016, p. 38). While the deaths of so many are unacknowledged or not considered important, they cannot be properly mourned.

To find the lifefullness of mourning we need to work through and into death psychologically, honestly and symbolically. We need to face our history with the terrifying tenacity of courage and love, following fragile ant-trails of connection between an impoverished present to a chaotic, creative and lifeful future at peace with the past, having acknowledged the necessity to do the hard labour of admitting fault and burying the dead. It is a journey that, Butler suggests, leads us back to ourselves.

Who 'am' I, without you? When we lose some of these ties by which we are constituted, we do not know who we are or what to do. On one level, I think I have lost 'you' only to discover that 'I' have gone missing as well. (2004, p. 22)

It is a roughly sketched map that points the way back to the national project of mourning—to find the nation that has gone missing and that for so many, like my father Jim Macken, is no longer recognisable as Australia.

Reality Interrupts Relaxation

If political action is in a sense a mental health strategy for asylum seekers in the abusive conditions of detention, could it be that political action might also restore ethical vigour to the entire nation? Indeed, even losing a political fight is more energising than staying alone and mute in the face of abuse and injustice. That is why governments right, left and centre abhor hunger strikes and direct action. From the state's perspective it is far better to accuse someone of personal failure and individual criminality than attempt to analyse racism as a part of the ongoing colonisation of Australia, or abuse of refugees as riding on a racist undercurrent.

Since 2019, I have felt and occasionally glimpsed an Australia I recognised from the 1980s and early 1990s. In the process I have found a 'me' and a 'you' fighting fires, laughing and yelling in both public spaces and formerly private places. It may be that from these little things, big things grow, that this melancholic state is being overturned by the sheer power of reality and the mourning it has carried with it. Curiously, all my experiences of collectivity have been in the flesh. The clicktivism of online petitions and auto-generated letters to local members of parliament has never felt transformative nor has it led to a sense of solidarity despite, or perhaps because of, its no-cost delivery. In these darkening days I am relieved to see online campaigning based on clicktivism go the way of the dodo, quietly schlepping into oblivion.

These are personal reflections shared by many thousands of other Australians. It is a long road that I believe will eventually transform

Australia's brutal immigration detention regime. It begins for me with the experience of being part of a thousand-strong army of volunteer firefighters during the 2019 Australian summer of fires. This showed me what it was like to rely almost exclusively on the support of the community to avert disaster, even as the prime minister denied the nature of the crisis and his need to return from holidays in Hawaii (Macken, 2020, p. 13). As we entered properties, emptied swimming pools and used dressage rings as staging areas, the idea of private property collapsed under the weight of public need. The state was largely irrelevant as the community self-organised and supported each other through this darkness.

Even among so much destruction, there was an aliveness and connection as the fire revealed our interdependency on each other to fight the fires, feed the strike teams and rescue both vulnerable families and creatures. This was relational work with moments of blistering clarity like when the firefighter driving a fire truck, looking exhausted and covered in soot, pulled up alongside a media team and yelled, 'Are you from the media? Well tell the Prime Minister to get fucked' (Schaffer, 2020). He spoke for thousands of exhausted firefighters.

In January 2020, as the east coast of Australia continued to burn, Lorena Allam, a *Guardian* reporter descended from the Gamilaraay and Yawalaraay nations of north-west New South Wales, wrote an opinion piece that articulated the interrelationship between peoples' mourning, reality and the ability to act.

> We have to help each other mourn for what we all love and are losing day by day ... We know what it feels like to lose everything, and we know the rage of helplessness in the face of government indifference. Maybe this summer is the turning point, where our collective grief turns to action and we recognise the knowledge that First Nations people want to share, to make sure these horrors are never repeated. Our precious country needs us. (Allam, 2020)

This slippage—the potential to move from one psychological state to another—arose again the day I joined the March4Justice in Canberra (Gorman, 2021). As thousands of women demanded an end to violence against women, I was aware that our image of who we were was undergoing a shift. Giving voices and names and backstories to the violence inflicted by men on so many women, the public performance of that rage and pain was, and remains, a vital source of hope for many. Anger and fury have been making increasing appearances in recent years as Aboriginal and Torres Strait Islander families also say enough is enough, thousands of men and women of all races protesting and demanding that BlackLivesMatter.

In March 2022, communities coalesced to literally rescue hundreds of neighbours from the rising flood waters across northern New South Wales (Kurmelovs & Tondorf, 2022). This time we witnessed a muddy new kind of community: a courageous, cranky and self-organising community. These people were not consumers but citizens demanding both action and a seat at the decision-making table. Reality with its teeth and claws—fire, smoke, flooding rain—would not be denied in these places of pain, loss and death. Here, a public performance of mourning was being conducted in relief centres, news interviews and disseminated photos of heroic efforts or of small children cradling their beloved dogs in tears.

Most recently I have found 'you' and 'me' in the weekly marches in Australia in support of the people of Palestine, calling for a ceasefire, return of hostages and an end to genocidal violence. These actions are not perfect. It is not enough, yet. But with reality sliding in from the margins to demand its central place in this country's discourse, I think we are attempting to shake off our melancholia with each of these explosive incursions of reality.

Imagine This!

I believe that finally facing the truth of Australia's colonisation will transform the nation sufficiently to change its treatment of asylum seekers, because this abuse of asylum seekers has roots in the denial of colonial violence. To face that truth will break our collective heart, as it should. We will understand ourselves as a people capable of extreme cruelty and we will finally feel sorrow and shame. This collective sorrow is our ticket out of the crippling narcissism that enables the state to subject children, women and men to degrading and humiliating treatment. Denial of colonial violence and each of our parts in it creates a state capable of torture. It also severs the possibility of living in right relationship with each other and with this extraordinary old country. And yes, even with the shift to a professedly progressive political platform we have collectively fallen at the first hurdle, but more of this failure shortly. For now, let's imagine (with Keating) that it were otherwise.

Imagine White Australians finally hearing the truth about our shared history from its beginning. Imagine in that storytelling we meet the little ones stolen, the young women destroyed by the sexual violence of the colonisers, the old women and men and children poisoned by the flour White settlers gave them, the communities wiped out by poisoned waterholes, the children and women driven off the cliff, the young men who had almost no defence against flintlock musket fire. Imagine hearing the stories of each nation from each different country, the stories of songlines and boundaries, the complexity of kin, the love and creativity of Sorry Business, of music and culture, language and art lost and now remembered. Imagine learning all the things we don't know because we have knowingly denied them.

Imagine learning how a people continue to survive and grow in the face of the White onslaught. Imagine if we, non-Indigenous Australians, saw the tears, the hurt howling down through the past that remains so very present. Imagine if we were all finally bought to tears as we recognise our collective complicity. Imagine being able to ask for forgiveness for harm done by our own people, for debts not paid, for lives cut short, for land, children and language stolen and destroyed. Imagine if, after all that truth-telling and the necessary restitution that would consequentially follow, we were forgiven. Imagine if we were all truly and finally welcomed to this country. If we were all able to live in right relationship with this extraordinary country and her First Peoples.

This is the promise of Makarrata:[1] the coming together after a struggle. It could be that fulfilment of the promise in the Uluru Statement from

---

[1] Makarrata is another word for treaty or agreement making. It is the culmination of First Nations peoples' agenda. It captures their aspirations for a fair and honest relationship with government and a better future for their children based on justice and self-determination.

the Heart would transform the lives and futures of Aboriginal and Torres Strait Islanders, but White Australia's people also have much to gain. It holds the promise of uniting the nation and humanising those who now come to Australia seeking a new life under our protection. Recognition and respect for the First People leads to respect for the Last People.

An integral part of that reality and the awakening of our collective spirit is recognising the harm done to those who—like non-Indigenous Australians—dared to come by sea; those who have come seeking nothing but protection. Once reality is reasserted by acknowledging the truth of colonisation, the harm done to asylum seekers and refugees will not be denied or disappeared. It is not possible to live in right relationship with this country's First Peoples and at the same time abuse, humiliate and degrade those who come more recently looking for protection. These two things cannot co-exist because the fear of those who come by sea is the fear we harbour about our own destructiveness. We cannot ask for forgiveness of Aboriginal and Torres Strait Islander people and continue to traumatise and degrade those who come looking for our protection. To finally be awake to the violence that made the colonisation of Australia possible, is to be awake to the violence imposed on asylum seekers and all the Others.

Behrouz Boochani (2017) was prophetic when he said from the ruins of his former prison on Manus Island. 'Our resistance is the spirit that haunts Australia. Our resistance is a new manifesto for humanity and love'. Australia is sorely in need of a new manifesto for humanity and love.

Operationalising Imagination

Imagine if federal Labor fulfilled its own platform and brought immigration detention centres back into public administration. With the centres back onshore, detainees would have access to lawyers, family communications and the media. Those on the outside would be able to bring the powers of the Public Service Act to bear; Community and Public Sector Union (CPSU) mechanisms of protection would again cover the rights and safety of centre workers. Taxpayers would no longer spend billion dollars per year on keeping wretched people detained in private jails that continue to operate as black sites.

To a greater or lesser extent, Labor, the Independents and the Australian Greens, all of which have to varying degrees raised the prospect of more humane immigration policy and practice, all surfed the wave of political protest into Parliament House for the next three years 2022–2025. These years may reveal this outcome to be yet another manic response to the lifelessness of melancholia—a waste of the energy that drove these parties and individuals into power—or they may reveal new forms of restoration, imagination, empathy. It is difficult, and sometimes foolhardy, to speak with certainty about the nature of the historic moment we occupy. We are groping in the dark to understand where we are and who we are. But I believe it is possible to look at events and results and to divine from them a reasonable idea of our collective psychological state. Certainly, our recent path is possible to apprehend psychologically.

On 29 January 2017, Prime Minister Malcolm Turnbull announced that US President Donald Trump had confirmed that he would honour a 'refugee swap'[2] deal with Australia agreed upon by the Obama administration. The leaked transcript of the conversation included Trump's interjection when Turnbull explained how Australia discriminated against arrivals by sea, saying: 'That is a good idea. We should do that too. You are worse than I am'. And over the next five years, how true that became! Following Turnbull's prime ministerial term, we had the bizarre occurrence of new leader Scott Morrison secretly making himself minister of five other portfolios; we saw neo-Nazis protesting on the steps of the Parliament of Victoria; we sat through the dissolution of the public service and concurrent elevation—to the tune of 20 billion dollars a year—of consultants who took on that work; we experienced a vicious policy called Robodebt literally cost lives as the government persecuted people accused—incorrectly—of owing thousands of dollars in welfare payments. By 2022, with the poverty of policies on display and the Coalition in disarray, the majority of the Australian electorate had had enough and hoped for better.

Scott Morrison had taken over leadership of the Liberal/National Coalition in 2018 and was voted in as prime minister in his own right in 2019. The majority of Australians then thought he reflected their values

---

[2] The "deal" was that in return for the United States agreeing to vet up to 1250 asylum seekers in Australia's detention centres, with the "good faith" agreement that those who passed would be accepted, Australia would accept Central American refugees the United States can't settle.

and was the best person to lead the nation. However, he was described by one colleague as being 'completely unencumbered by belief and values – which makes him so effective'. A text message sent by Barnaby Joyce (National Party) to a third party described Morrison as 'a hypocrite and a liar [who] I have never trusted'. Morrison 'rearranges the truth to a lie', Joyce said in the short message text. Malcolm Turnbull (Liberal Party) said: 'Scott has always had a reputation for telling lies'. It says a great deal about the intrinsic denial of the Australian electorate that this kind of dishonesty was considered suitable in the nation's highest office.

However, by the time the 2022 federal election rolled around, the nation had tired of the government disfunction and Scott Morrison.

Given that 2022's victorious candidates campaigned on a broad platform of transparency in government, action on climate change and better treatment of refugees, there was good reason to hope for a new politics when the election not only produced a Labor victory but also a potentially new political force in the Teal Independents, Independent Senator David Pocock, and increased Green representation. When the incoming prime minister, Anthony Albanese, stressed in his first announcement that his government was committed in full to the Uluru Statement from the Heart and the three principles of Voice, Truth and Treaty, it seemed reality was making more than a guest appearance in the national story. The election of the Albanese Labor government was welcomed by asylum seekers and refugee activists, and by a large number of Aboriginal and Torres Strait Islander people.

Both groups would be disappointed before the prime minister's term was halfway through. At first glance the causes of that disappointment appear diverse, but I believe they emanate from the same place—a denial of the foundational truth and reality that has ravaged the capacity, imagination and coherence of the nation.

Albanese made a referendum for an Indigenous Voice to Parliament the priority of his first term. Its uptake would mean, simply, that Aboriginal and Torres Strait Islander people would have a legal, yet non-binding avenue to getting their concerns heard by Parliament. It was a humble ask. Early canvasing suggested that the carrying of the Voice was a safe bet. In August 2022 polling suggested 64 per cent of people would vote 'Yes' and 34 per cent would vote 'No'. But fourteen months later, after a racist and hostile campaign, only 40 per cent of people voted 'Yes'. Nine million Australians voted 'No'; they did not think Australia's First People could have a legislated body with a direct, consultative-only line to the ear of the governors of the nation.

Like so many others I had assumed that the idea of an Indigenous Voice to Parliament would be easily supported. While many criticised it for its apparent timidity, others believed for that reason alone it would be supported. It is too early to settle on a reason why the failure was so overwhelming, but clear divisions arose around the notion that First Nations people were asking for a special deal and that Whiteness would be thereby devalued, less special. Here again we can draw from Ghassan Hage's (2003, p. 21) observation (see also Chap. 4) about those he calls 'paranoid nationalists' who feel themselves becoming 'newly marginalised'. Hage compares this envious state to a 'child whose mother has stopped feeding her' yet who remains codependently attached to the non-feeding mother (the nation) and will defend it/her viciously and territorially in the hope that she will unconditionally feed them again as she once did.

This is the psychological regression Melanie Klein warned of when she noted the paranoid/schizoid position was never fully consigned to early life but would reassert itself when the subject felt anxious or threatened. This infantilised state was extremely apparent in the compelling slogan adopted by the 'No' campaign: 'If you don't know, vote no'. In the protective, defensive, hoarding anxiety of this statement, gone was the idea of an aspirant nation where being clever was a goal and getting educated was a matter of course, and in its melancholic place was a hollow enshrinement of cultural negation.

The day after the referendum a group of Indigenous leaders called for a week of silence and mourning. Their statement said:

> This is a bitter irony. That people who have only been on this continent for 235 years would refuse to recognise those whose home this land has been for 60,000 and more years is beyond reason.[3]

---

[3] https://alc.org.au/newsroom/media-releases/a-statement-from-indigenous-australians-who-supported-the-voice-referendum/

Unlike other nations with similar histories of colonisation, such as Canada and New Zealand, Australia has not formally recognised or reached a treaty with its First Peoples. 'It's very clear that reconciliation is dead', Marcia Langton, an architect of the Voice, said on National Indigenous Television (NITV). 'I think it will be at least two generations before Australians are capable of putting their colonial hatreds behind them and acknowledging that we exist'.

As for the failure of the 'Yes' campaign, certainly there is plenty of blame to go around. But perhaps Gangulu man Mick Gooda, a 'Yes' campaigner and former Human Rights Commissioner, gives clearest expression to the state of the nation afterwards.

> So here we are, four months after the referendum and at the federal level things seem to have come to a complete standstill. It's almost as if some form of paralysis has taken over. I have heard of vague rumours that some local or regional structure will be established; we have heard the Prime Minister's Close the Gap statement last week about more jobs in remote Australia and a revamped Community Development Program; but what we are not seeing is a narrative, a vision of where we go to from here. (National Press Club, February 24, 2024)

That vision of where to go next is precisely what is not possible for the melancholic. The narrative and vision for a shared future depends on being able to manage the symbolic, the metaphoric and to do so with love, empathy and imagination. This is nowhere visible in the current political leadership of Australia.

In light of the Voice referendum's result, we might have predicted what would become of the immigration policy under the current Labor government—whatever was promised and hoped for during their election campaign. Perhaps because of the empty words of hope, the sense of betrayal felt by so many refugees and advocates is acute.

In a policy sense, the only real difference between contemporary Australian Labor and Coalition immigration policy is that Labor committed to ending the temporary protection visa class and thus granted nineteen thousand people permanent protection. But, in terms of the 'social license' that Labor immigration minister Andrew Giles said he was committed to building, Labor has done untold damage. There was the spectacle of the Minister for Home Affairs, Claire O'Neil, shouting in Parliament House that she would like to hold 'these people in detention forever'.

At time of writing the Albanese government has, on 28th November 2024, just passed the most brutal anti-asylum seekers legislation yet. Late Thursday night the *Migration Amendment (Removal and Other Measures) Bill 2024*, the *Migration Amendment Bill 2024* and the *Migration Amendment (Prohibiting Items in Immigration Detention Facilities) Bill 2024* were all passed by both Labor and the Coalition. In doing so the Albanese government has expanded its powers to deport refugees to third countries, cut off lifelines for people in detention by seizing mobile phones and can now conduct invasive, unwarranted searches in immigration detention. The new laws impose severe penalties of up to five years' imprisonment on individuals who fail to assist with their own deportation, as well as empower the Government to impose country-wide travel bans on as-yet unknown countries.

Zaki Haidari, Amnesty International Australia's Strategic Campaigner for Refugee Rights, responded saying:

> It is a deeply shameful time for Australia. Once again, politicians from both sides of the political spectrum have devised increasingly punitive and racist laws targeting the most vulnerable people in our society—refugees and people seeking asylum. In doing so, they have not only undermined Australia's international obligations but also eroded the very foundation of our multicultural society's social cohesion. These actions are a betrayal of the principles of fairness, humanity, and compassion that should define us as a nation.

Labor under Albanese has continued to employ boat turnbacks, mandatory detention and offshore detention in Nauru. The Albanese government contracted a US prison operator with a controversial human rights record to run the Nauru camp (Doherty & Knaus, 2022). In Labor's first Federal Budget, the allocation for offshore processing (2022–2023) was increased by 150 million to 632.5 million, with onshore detention receiving an astounding 1.3 billion plus over one billion yearly thereafter

(Kaldor Centre, 2022); Asylum Seeker Resource Centre, 2022). Both decisions dishonour Labor's election promise that immigration detention would return to public ownership (Refugee Council of Australia, 2022). Indeed, while the Labor platform has supported the return of immigration detention to the public service for twenty years, the party has never yet taken the opportunity of government to implement that transition.

In early April 2024, the Asylum Seeker Resource Centre (ASRC) (2024) began reporting on the growing number of men being transferred to the Nauru Regional Processing Centre. The Nauru centre began filling again when four boats arrived off the coast of Western Australia carrying sixty-four people from Pakistan, Bangladesh, India and China. Now, every boat that arrives delivers asylum seekers straight to Nauru. The ASRC is in contact with thirty-eight detainees who arrived in early 2024 from Bangladesh, India and Pakistan. Case manager Heidi Abdel-Raouf said the men were in shock to have found themselves imprisoned on a remote foreign island.

> The people we've spoken to in Nauru are reporting to us that they're experiencing high levels of distress, anxiety, depression, sleeping issues, isolation, and some are expressing suicidal feelings. They are saying they have had their smartphones removed and replaced by basic phones, so they've got no ability to access apps like WhatsApp to message or video call their loved ones. It's causing a great deal of anguish and distress.

The men are described as traumatised by being denied communications, including access to human rights information and avenues. There are also currently seventy refugee men in Port Moresby (PNG) too mentally unwell to manage a safe life in an environment where they have no jobs, no accommodation and no hope of moving forward or back. Australia's Department of Home Affairs paid 80 million dollars to Papua New Guinea's government to look after refugees left there when Australia's Manus Island Regional Processing Centre closed, but according to Papua New Guinea that money has been spent, and Australia refuses to do anything further to help these men despite its 2017 payment being an acknowledgement of a degree of responsibility for their fate.

The Rudd Labor government promised in 2007 there would be no Pacific Solution under Labor. 'The Pacific solution is just wrong. It's a waste of taxpayers' money. It's not the best way to handle asylum seekers or others' (O'Brien, 2007). Rudd's government had closed offshore camps by February 2008. However, as discussed in Chap. 4, under Julia Gillard, Labor reopened them in 2012 and by 2013, back under Kevin Rudd, they were in full swing with even more draconian and punitive operations. The policies that have led to so much abuse have not changed under Anthony Albanese nor has the framing of asylum seekers as a threat to the equilibrium of the nation. The influence of independent MPs (Teal, etc.) has so far failed to produce any difference. Australian Greens in the House of Representatives have increased in number from one to four and they hold more influence than ever in the Senate, but there is no guarantee they will exhaust their political capital in ending the torturous regime, nor can they without the support of the mainstream, or hope to create a sustainable, publicly run, humane and legal regional system for asylum seekers.

The rhetoric and gesturing of the Rudd government and now the Albanese government are manic responses that seek to manage profoundly complex issues with superficial redress. Even during the camp closures there was no substantial national conversation about changing Australia's overarching detention policy and attitude, no admission of harm done or attempt to reframe asylum seekers as people in need of a humanitarian response. In short, this crisis of humanity was not—and is not—worked through psychologically, symbolically or with public policy. In keeping with a melancholic diagnosis, Australia's 'efforts' in this regard are vapid, self-absorbed and bereft of imagination and love. At the first sign of boat numbers increasing, the state snapped back into its defensive paranoid-schizoid position, and without any attempt to destroy or discredit the established social licence for the harsh policy, it was only a matter of time before abuses began again. With the referendum on the Indigenous Voice to Parliament defeated and the privatised detention regime again cranking back into life, the nation remains in the grip of a melancholic state.

References

Allam, L. (2020, January 6). For first nations people the bushfires bring a particular grief, burning what makes us who we are. *The Guardian*. https://www.theguardian.com/commentisfree/2020/jan/06/for-first-nations-people-the-bushfires-bring-a-particular-grief-burning-what-makes-us-who-we-are?

Asylum Seeker Resource Centre. (2022, October 26). *ASRC'S response to the 2022–23 Federal Budget: A budget of failed expectations*. [Media release]. ASRC. https://asrc.org.au/2022/10/26/asrc-bugdet-response/

Asylum Seeker Resource Centre. (2024, April). Cruel neglect of refugees abandoned in PNG continues as more people threatened with eviction. (Media Release) ASRC. https://asrc.org.au/2024/10/28/cruel-neglect-of-refugees-abandoned-in-png-continues-as-more-people-threatened-with-eviction/

Boochani, B. (2017, December 9–15). A letter from Manus Island. *The Saturday Paper*. https://www.thesaturdaypaper.com.au/news/politics/2017/12/09/letter-manus-reynoldsisland/15127380005617

Butler, J. (2004). *Precarious life: The powers of mourning and violence*. Verso.

Doherty, B. (2016, September 1). Retired judge, 88, offers 'body swap' with a refugee on Manus or Nauru. *The Guardian*. https://www.theguardian.com/australia-news/2016/sep/01/retired-judge-88-offers-body-swap-with-a-refugee-on-manus-or-nauru

Doherty, B., & Knaus, C. (2022, September 21). Australia to pay controversial US prisons operator $4.6m for 52 days of transition work on Nauru. *The Guardian*. https://www.theguardian.com/australia-news/2022/sep/21/australia-to-pay-controversial-us-prisons-operator-46m-for-52-days-of-transition-work-on-naurus

Flanagan, R. (2019, April 14). Have we, Australians, become a country that breeds mass murders with our words? *The Guardian*. https://www.theguardian.com/australia-news/2019/apr/14/have-we-australia-become-a-country-that-breeds-mass-murderers-with-our-words

Freud, S. (1957). Mourning and melancholia. In J. Strachey (Ed.), *The standard edition of the complete psychological works of Sigmund Freud* (Vol. XIV, pp. 237–258). Hogarth Press. (Original work published 1917).

Gorman, A. (2021, March 15). 'Enough is enough!' Where, when and why March 4 justice protests are taking place across Australia. *The Guardian*. https://www.theguardian.com/australia-news/2021/mar/15/march-4-justice-where-when-womens-march-protests-australia-march4justice-sydney-melbourne-canberra-brisbane

Hage, G. (2003). *Against paranoid nationalism*. Pluto Press.
Kaldor Centre for International Refugee Law. (2022, April 26). *The cost of Australia's refugee and asylum policy: A source guide*. https://www.kaldorcentre.unsw.edu.au/publication/cost-australias-asylum-policy
Klein, M. (1946). Notes on some schizoid mechanisms. *The International Journal of Psycho-Analysis*, 99–110.
Kurmelovs, R. & Tondorf, C. (2022, February 28). Lismore flood: Hundreds rescued and thousands evacuated as NSW city hit by worst flooding in history. *The Guardian*. https://www.theguardian.com/australia-news/2022/feb/28/lismore-flood-worst-history-nsw-floods-2022-rescued-evacuated
Macken, J. (2020). Melancholia in fields of fire. *Arena Quarterly, 1*.
O'Brien, K. (presenter) (2007, November 21). Interview with Kevin Rudd. *7.30 Report* [TV series]. ABC.
Refugee Council of Australia. (2022, August 2). *ALP refugee policy commitments in their 2021 National Platform*. https://www.refugeecouncil.org.au/alp-refugee-policy-commitments-in-their-2021-national-platform/
Schaffer, A. (2020, January 18). The firefighter whose denunciation of Australia's prime minister made him a folk hero. *The New Yorker*. https://www.newyorker.com/news/as-told-to/the-firefighter-whose-denunciation-of-australias-prime-minister-made-him-a-folk-hero

9

Conclusion: What Is to Be Done?

In the face of such violence, lifelessness and cruelty, what is to be done? I believe it is possible, and urgent, that we find our way into a state of mourning as a nation, or at least enough of a nation, and that mourning will again liberate the erotic energy necessary to live fully. We can become a place and a people that refuses to treat the most vulnerable with cruelty and contempt: we can stop torturing asylum seekers. To do this we must honestly and psychologically confront the truth of the violence of colonisation; we must finally bury the lie of the kindly settler and terra nullius and make amends for harm done. Nothing less will spring the trap we have created for ourselves and our children. We *may* be seeing the beginnings of such a transition right now.

Pursuing an answer to how Australia became a nation that tortures asylum seekers taught me three things. One: imagination matters; it is the vehicle that carries us to the threshold of empathy and identification. Two: it is possible—and vitally important—to read the nation as a psychological subject and to do that through the stories we tell ourselves and each other and by our actions. Three: political action is a mental health strategy individually and collectively.

The previous chapters portray a nation captured by the destructive psychic forces of melancholia with its denial, disavowal and splitting being unleashed over the last twenty-five years. They analyse how the refusal to stay with the project of mourning Australia's violent colonisation, to finally bury the myth of the kindly settler, has resulted in almost unimaginable suffering for Aboriginal and Torres Strait Islanders and, most recently, asylum seekers. They discuss how this refusal created the psychic ground from which practices of abuse emanated; how asylum seekers were made into torturable subjects and how the privatisation of the immigration detention camps created both deniability for the state and the ecology for this abuse. They reveal how the medical professionals tasked with the protection of the 'sacred core' and ongoing care of asylum seekers attempted to hold on to both the humanity of their patients and their own amidst desperate cruelty and how this treatment constitutes the cruel, degrading and humiliating treatment that devolves into torture. And they make clear that it all began with the original sin of colonisation, and later, its denial, as the British took control of the country through flintlock muskets, poison, disease, rape and the phantasie of Terra Nullius.

The changes wrought by this national failure are not limited to the persecution of asylum seekers. They can also be found in the brutal 'No' campaign that accompanied the referendum for an Indigenous Voice to Parliament; in the nation's stalled political capacity; in the inability to reach mature reconciliation with First Nations people; in the apparent disinterest in decisive action to prevent extreme climate change, catastrophic species extinction, desertification, salination of once productive land; in the historic collapse of trust in institutions. These are political problems emanating from the shadowland of melancholia.

Freudian melancholia, with its compulsive repetition, its inability to imagine, love and empathise, its shallow, narcissistic hold on life, has had profound impacts on a range of national projects beyond the abuse of asylum seekers. As melancholia has severed the nation from reality, it is not surprising to see it writ large in our national leadership. A national leadership that has continually failed to deal with many other aspects of reality: the impacts of fire in 2019, taking effective action to lower Australia's carbon emissions and build climate resilient communities and economy, surging inequality, homelessness and the rising numbers of species extinction. It can be seen in stalled moments of national reconciliation with First Nations peoples, in the narcissism of a political culture that circles around itself in constant self-referential posturing, and in the ongoing violence against women. The entire Australian community has experienced the consequences of this bleak pyscho-affective state.

Finding Our Way Back to Mourning

For all that, I believe there are signs of hope, perhaps moments of restitution when we recognise the potential for the transformation of sites of guilt into a drive for reparation and love (Klein, 1952/1975). This moment holds the potential to imagine a time when the defences of splitting, introjection and projection fall away and reality reasserts itself. When we understand those previously split-off parts of people—the all-good, all-bad Australian/refugee—can finally be seen as whole, complicated, interrelated people. This is the moment when absence is experienced as a loss rather than a persecutory attack. Instead of anger, the wounded nation feels grief. At this point the baby/nation begins to cry real tears.

Now is that moment of recognition when we see we are, as a nation, 'in the midst of the collapse of collective values' (L. Newman, personal communication, 12 January 2020). Potentially, Australia can trade in its superficial and sanctimonious self-righteousness and finally go through a necessary withdrawal from 'the moral antidepressant it's on because it is numbing the state's capacity to take responsibility for this behaviour'. This may be the moment when Australia can begin to 'face up to the bad things it's done' (J. Jureidini, personal communication, 9 March 2020).

On polling day of the 2022 federal election, the Morrison government began texting voters in marginal seats: 'BREAKING – Aust Border Force has intercepted an illegal boat trying to reach Aus. Keep our borders secure by voting Liberal today'. Campaigning in his coastal south-east Sydney electorate of Cook, named after the coloniser James Cook, Prime Minister Morrison reminded the Australian electorate: 'I've been here to stop this boat. But in order for me to be there to stop those that may come from here, you need to vote Liberal and Nationals today' (Galloway,

2022). It could have been that the boat, which was said to have been intercepted off Christmas Island far north-west of the mainland, came too late in the day or that voters saw through the ploy; in any case, the election result indicates it didn't turn the intended political trick, even as the announcement itself highlights the attempt to extract political and propagandistic value from those seeking asylum in Australia.

At the time of writing, the Australian Government has agreed to allow New Zealand to take four hundred and fifty of our asylum seekers for resettlement. Domestically, the Refugee Council of Australia (2022c) gives details of people held in what the Department of Home Affairs calls 'alternative places of detention' (APODs):

> According to the Department, APODs can be hospitals, hotel accommodation, aged-care facilities, or mental health in-patient facilities. Sometimes parts of detention facilities can be reclassified as 'alternative places of detention'. In response to a Senate Question on Notice, the Department of Home Affairs revealed that from 1 January 2018 to 31 January 2021, 170 APODs were used in Australia at any time, with the highest number being in Queensland. As at 31 January 2021, 56 APODs were classified as hotel-type APODs.

The number of people in APODs has been decreasing as young men are shipped off under the deal brokered between the previous administrations of President Obama and Prime Minister Turnbull. Despite the collapse of Afghanistan and the war in Europe, there are almost no refugee boatloads coming into view and those that do are sent straight to Nauru. The most recent arrivals were forty-three men originally from Bangladesh and Pakistan who were found wandering about 10 kilometres from Beagle Bay, an Aboriginal Nyul Nyul community around 150 kilometres from the far north-west coastal town of Broome. While this incident sparked a war of words between Prime Minister Albanese and opposition leader Peter Dutton, Beagle Bay Futures Indigenous Corporation chairperson Henry Augustine said the best thing his community could do as the men came into town was 'just be nice'. 'They were just people needing help I think', he said.

However, the almost-empty camps and images of men leaving the APODs after almost a decade in detention should not be read as a change of heart. They could be more a hunch that, for now, the electoral advantage of persecuting asylum seekers isn't what it was. But no one should repeat the mistake almost everyone made in 2007 when activists and organisations assumed White Australians were ready to mourn their deeds. They weren't. Nor does it appear they are now. In an attempt to neutralise the threat of the Coalition using a tough-on-borders election strategy, the Albanese government pre-emptively passed into law the most brutal and extreme anti-asylum seeker legislation yet (see Human Rights Law Centre).[1]

Return to Mourning

The nature of mourning is chaotic, erotic/cathectic and at times frightening. There is the sense of thrashing around in the memories and ideas of the loved one that keeps the mourner/nation in a state of not-knowing and off balance. This was what the electorate found so disturbing as the Keating era drew to a close and demands for settling the question of who or what was Australian became loudest.

By collapsing into a melancholic psycho-affective state, the authentic question of national identity was subverted. Having refused to accept the death of the foundational myth of the peaceful settler in light of the reality of violence in Australia's colonisation, the state was able to create new images of what is Australian by creating the un-Australian. Images of those who would throw their children overboard, who would try to jump the queue, who come to Australia 'illegally'; these are the 'non-Australians' who make the 'Australians'. As Whyte (2008) has succinctly put it, exclusion precedes belonging. In the melancholic Australia, exclusion of the Other may be the only way to feel a sense of belonging.

But reality will have its day. Widespread climate denialism has not stopped the climate heating and delivering ever more frequent heatwaves,

---

[1] Human Rights Law Center brief.

floods and fires, and the failure of the Voice referendum has not prevented some stories of colonisation being told. As discussed in Chaps. 2 and 3, Aboriginal and Torres Strait Islander peoples first coaxed the nation to try to mourn its young history in the period from the 1970s to the mid-1990s, after which it collapsed into its melancholic state with the majority of the electorate signing on for a 'comfortable and relaxed life' contingent on not looking back. Then in 2017, once again First Nations peoples threw White Australia a lifeline out of its melancholia via the Uluru Statement from the Heart.

The Statement extends the lineage of the Aboriginal League in 1933; the 1963 Yirrkala bark petitions; the Freedom Ride of 1965; the 1966 Wave Hill Station walk-off by Gurindji, Mudburra and Warlpiri workers; and the formation of the Aboriginal and Torres Strait Islander Commission (ATSIC) in 1990. It remains the nation's most powerful ticket out of melancholic malaise. In its call for establishing a Makarrata Commission for the purpose of treaty-making and truth-telling, it has the potential to finally free White Australia from the lie of the peaceful settler (and the hypocrisy of the abuse of asylum seekers).

The Statement from the Heart is a living document with the energy and strength to be contested even as it is loved by many. It was bought to life at Uluru by debate, consultation and gathering together of many Aboriginal and Torres Strait Islander leaders. Discussion, debate and challenges to the Statement continue within Aboriginal and Torres Strait Islander nations today. How could it be otherwise? As a White Australian I respect that debate and the story that is continuing to unfold; as the Statement says, we are all at base camp in this journey. Importantly, debates and discussions on the Statement have not shown the petty meanness of melancholia nor the vindictive exclusion as practised by Australia's White state. Because of the document's vitality, honesty and elegance, because it offers non-Indigenous Australia an extraordinary invitation and roadmap, we hear echoes of Vincent Lingiari's generosity when he said to Gough Whitlam in 1975 (McKeon, 2016): 'We want to live in a better way together, Aboriginals and white men, let us not fight over anything, let us be mates'.

Policy as Healing

Just as the psycho-affective state of melancholia made current asylum seeker policy and practice possible, a return to mourning will change it. Maturation and mourning is a process of reintegrating the split unknown/known into the conscious world. That is one reason why it is imperative the immigration detention camps currently located in 'not-Australia' be reintegrated into the known and conscious public space of the nation. Moving the processing centres back into public administration is both psychological work and the work of public policy. Even more effectively, moving asylum seekers out of the camps and into the community will give more protections to those in dire need of them and provide much-needed evidence of Australians' capacity for empathy, imagination and progress. Making the most vulnerable people safe means everyone is safer, enabling people to trust themselves, their community and their state.

Mandatory detention will end when the policy has lost its social licence to operate. As any marketing department will confirm, a social licence can be created and also destroyed; once it is gone, it is almost impossible to recover. Australia's policy of mandatory detention breaches the right not to be arbitrarily detained under article 9(1) of the International Covenant on Civil and Political Rights (ICCPR), and children's right not to be arbitrarily deprived of liberty under article 37(b) of the Convention on the Rights of the Child. Many people clearly believe that some form of detention is necessary during the processing of refugees and asylum seekers. This is not a view I share, but even for those that do, upon confronting reality there should be no more argument for a mandatory, arbitrary carceral immigration system to operate in Australia's name.

The atomisation of a privatised, for-profit system must also be reversed in the interests of becoming whole. As Bonnie Honig argues, we relate to public services and places differently than we do to private industries: '[w]ithout public things, action in concert is undone' (2017, p. 4). That's why a recovery process must be embedded in this policy revision, in rebuilding the connections between all of us. In the words of Wendy Brown: 'When the domain of the political itself is rendered in economic terms, the foundation vanishes for citizenship concerned with public things and the common good' (2015, p. 39). Bringing these services back into the realm of accountability of the citizenry, and structuring them so that each is interdependent on the success of the rest in *integrating* asylum seekers back into the world, are necessary to facilitate our public healing.

Restoring public administration of the camps would help change the framework of Australian immigration detention. It would thwart creation of an ecology of torture. When detention safeguards are in place, the opportunities and culture that lend themselves to torture are curtailed. Detention itself loses much of its power to 'send a message' if it is conducted in a legal, humane fashion. There is also a greater likelihood of disciplinary action against perpetrators of abuse and for monitoring bodies[2] to conduct unannounced visits and interview detainees privately, which are known have a direct effect in reducing torture. Asylum seekers in camps under public administration on mainland Australia could have access to lawyers and doctors, if not relatives, within a few hours of arrival. And putting the centres back into public administration removes the avenues of deniability currently available to the state and ensures the immigration minister is held directly to account for entire programme.

Further, the detention camp as a 'zone of indistinction' (Agamben, 1998) would be transformed. These places would no longer be the spilt-off, denied and disavowed repository of Australia's abjected psychic material. They would be inside (not outside), governed by explicit rules (not exceptions), and subject to juridical protection and inspection. Public administration would see all offshore camps eradicated because they must be built and staffed by Australian public servants, removing incentive for foreign countries to enter into such arrangements. Anyone employed by the Commonwealth in connection with immigration detention would be covered by the Australian Public Service Act and related statutes including the *Freedom of Information Act 1982* and could be called before the Senate and the Human Rights and Equal Opportunity Commission. They would be subject to review and governed by the APS Code of Conduct. Moreover, the Commonwealth would also be liable for their unlawful acts or acts of omission. Finally, the camps would not be protected by commercial-in-confidence contracts.

---

[2] Understood broadly to include National Preventive Mechanisms under the OPCAT, civil society organisations and international bodies.

It's worth noting that according to government figures (Kaldor Centre, 2022), it costs nearly twelve thousand dollars a day to detain a refugee in Nauru, for which amount it would be possible to put them in a six-star mainland resort and still make considerable savings. The public administration of immigration detention centres has the potential to turn an economic non-place into a clear social contract wherein political traction and accountability are possible.

Creating Subjects of Care

To begin this journey we need to see people seeking Australia's protection as deserving of care as opposed to torturable subjects. Australian musician Missy Higgins was nursing her infant son when she first saw the photo of Alan Kurdi. Alan was the little Syrian boy whose body washed up on a Turkish beach in September 2015. It was the photo of his lifeless body, with his bright red shirt, blue shorts and carefully tied shoes, his little body lying tossed on the shoreline, that caused a momentary pause in the ongoing slaughter of Syria's civil war. Everything about the little boy told a story of love and care and attention. A mum who dressed him so well, a brave father who led his family to what he hoped was safety. Higgins' response to that heart-shattering picture was the song, 'Oh Canada'. Her video for the track uses animated images drawn by refugee children, beginning with the image of the soldier who lifted Alan's lifeless body from the beach, and continuing from the perspective of Alan's father, Abdullah, who was the only survivor in his family of four. Higgins' hope for the song and video was simple: she wanted people to stop turning away from calamity and cruelty. This one calamity, contained in a photograph and explored through the symbolic power of music and art, was enough to pressure Prime Minister Tony Abbott to increase by twelve thousand Australia's intake of asylum seekers from Syria.

The transformation of asylum seekers from people deserving compassion and protection, to torturable subjects posing a threat to national security, took time and strategy as well as the collusion—wittingly or unwittingly—of the mainstream media. It took the disappearance of those seeking Australia's protection into offshore and isolated immigration detention camps. It took the removal of their faces and their humanity. Reversing this corrosive narrative will take time. To date, one campaign in particular offers an example of just such a powerful, tenacious strategic reversal.

#LetThemStay and Why Names and Faces Matter

In early February 2016, the High Court rejected a challenge to the constitutionality of offshore processing and upheld Australia's right to detain asylum seekers in Nauru and Papua New Guinea. A majority of the full bench found that section 198AHA of the Migration Act, which was passed by the Turnbull government in 2015, allowed for the Commonwealth's participation in the plaintiff's detention in a foreign country. The court's decision gave the Coalition government the green light to remove two hundred and sixty-seven asylum seekers, including thirty-nine children, from the mainland to Nauru. Of this group, the majority had been transferred to Australia from Nauru because of serious medical conditions that could not be treated there. The group included thirty-three babies born in Australia to asylum seeker mothers. They had never been to Nauru.

In my interviews with psychiatrists (se Chap. 5), they referred to the restorative power of political action which, by offering a sense of agency, ameliorates the brutalising effect of powerlessness. The decision to send the sick asylum seekers (back) to Nauru, along with their defenceless infants, prompted activists and advocates to accelerate an enormously successful political campaign called #LetThemStay. It began with *The Sydney Morning Herald* running the headline: 'The faces of the babies Australia wants to send back to "hell" on Nauru' (Gordon et al., 2016). On the front page of the newspaper was the chubby face of little Samuel, who came into the world 'a miniature wrestler who, eight months on, has just produced his eighth tooth'. Two days later thousands of people rallied around Australia, demanding the Turnbull government let the asylum seekers, their babies and their children stay in Australia. Christian churches across Australia began invoking the concept of sanctuary, opening their doors to asylum seekers facing removal to offshore detention centres. The Anglican Dean of Brisbane, the Reverend Dr. Peter Catt, said he was offering up St John's Cathedral in Brisbane to the asylum seekers.

> Many of us are at the end of our tether as a result of what seems like the Government's intention to send children to Nauru. So we're reinventing, or rediscovering, or reintroducing, the ancient concept of sanctuary as a last-ditch effort to offer some sense of hope to those who must be feeling incredibly hopeless. (Edwards, 2016)

A week later, on 12 February 2016, medical doctors at a Brisbane hospital refused to release a one-year-old girl, badly burnt in Nauru, until a 'suitable home environment is identified' (Tapim, 2016). Asha (not her real name) was injured when boiling water was accidentally spilt inside the tent she was living in with her parents. She was flown to Brisbane and admitted to Lady Cilento Children's Hospital. The medical staff asserted their right to treat their young patient according to her medical needs, not according to the political desires of the Turnbull government. Baby Asha's cherubic, slightly pixelated face made national frontpage news for the following week. When activists became concerned that Border Force would take the baby from the hospital and fly her back to Nauru before she was well enough, people gathered outside the hospital keeping watch day and night. Eight days later, hundreds of people had surrounded the exit points of the hospital, holding candle-lit vigils, with local businesses feeding the crowds.

Australian doctors began discussing a boycott of the immigration detention system. Dr. John-Paul Sanggaran, who worked at Christmas Island Immigration Detention Centre, argued the system is 'a form of systematic child abuse ... a form of torture'.

> The only course left to us is to refuse to participate ... The AMA [Australian Medical Association]'s own code of ethics states: 'regardless of society's attitudes, ensure that you do not countenance, condone or participate in the practice of torture or other forms of cruel, inhuman, or degrading pro-

cedures, whatever the offence of which the victim of such procedures is suspected, accused or convicted' ... By continuing to work within immigration detention we merely provide legitimacy to those that would lie and mislead the public into believing healthcare of a respectable standard is being delivered. (Doherty & Davidson, 2016)

As a result of all this action, baby Asha and her family were released into the Australian community, an exceptional change of heart by the Turnbull government. A combination of photographs of Asha, humanising stories of the family's plight, solidarity of medical health workers, churches and activists, energetic crowd support and the prospect of a doctor boycott was enough to convince the state it needed to act in the interests of (itself and) the baby's welfare.

The media played a critical role. Asha's example demonstrates the power of media in shaping the perceptions of the public and, conversely, dispels any doubt about the role played by mainstream media in the creation of asylum seekers as torturable subjects. Asha's face, disseminated nationwide, activated the meta-ethics described by Emmanuel Levinas, who said that the encounter with the human face 'orders and ordains' us, calling us as subjects into 'giving and serving' the Other (Marcus, 2010, p. 16). We, the on-lookers and perpetrators, are saved by the relationship with the Other. Baby Asha and her family were able to get the help they needed, and the protests protected them from returning to Nauru. But the protestors, the hospital workers, the community that looked on were also briefly restored to hope in the knowledge that should they ever need it, there was a public that would stand up and protect them and theirs. Despite being literally an exception to a rule, there was a mutuality in the movement of protest to keep little Asha as one of 'ours'.

Disturbance as Transcendence

Reality, with its haul of ungrieved deaths, is slowly being asserted in Australia. It will be ferocious and disparate, a diversity of voices, faces and performances carrying the signature of mourning. The splitting and denial that has characterised us for twenty-five years will end. But how will we know when it does—what are the signs? Freud described the sometimes-psychotic destabilisation that comes with mourning, with staying connected to the reality of love and loss and shame. Do we look for moments where we slip our moorings, moments of being undone? There is certainly a sense of the world being unmade right now through wars in Gaza, in Ukraine and elsewhere, in global epidemics of mutating disease. The imperative to mourn is building.

Klein describes the movement beyond the paranoid-schizoid position as moving into a depressive phase. While this is not appealing, it nevertheless signals learning to love, to live in relationship with the world. The transition is perilous:

> The infant is physically and emotionally matured enough to integrate his or her fragmented perceptions, bringing together the separately good and bad versions. When such part-objects are brought together as a whole they threaten to form a contaminated, damaged, or dead whole object. (Hinshelwood, 1998, p. 138)

Striving not for the deadened psycho-affective state of melancholia but for the spacious, vital and harrowing world of mourning takes courage and endurance. It also requires staying alive to the nuanced and reciprocal nature of forgiveness. It will not be either/or; it will not be Left/Right. It will not be 'us' and 'them'. It is a transcendent space of a new thing. That's why it disturbs.

I first heard Australia accused of state-sanctioned torture in September 2002 when Professor Michael Dudley reported the findings of his studies saying, 'What all of this describes is state-sanctioned torture. Australia is torturing refugees in these camps'. This was followed by my colleagues' suggestion that 'Australia doesn't torture people. It's not who we are'. I knew that was not correct. It is who we are. Australia does torture people. The Australian people now know what we are capable of doing to another person, what we are capable of doing to a child. However vociferously the claims are denied, Australians now know we are collectively capable of voting for policies that destroy the sacred core of another person. We know ourselves as capable of both inflicting torture and of turning away from such abuses. But we were not always that nation and we are capable of change.

Nationally, we should not delude ourselves, however, that this next period of reconnecting with reality will be easy or that reality will look like it did when we aborted national mourning in the mid-1990s. There have been three major decisions made by the state that have transformed and then set the course of post-colonial Australia. They are the proclamation of *Terra Nullius* in 1835, the creation of the White Australia policy in 1901, and the introduction of mandatory immigration detention for anyone who arrived by boat in 1992. Since then, as the previous chapters have detailed, people who come seeking Australia's protection have regularly been targets of cruel, degrading and humiliating abuse that often devolved into torture. The Australian electorate knew this abuse was going on and its majority continued to uphold the policies through their vote at every federal election from 2000 to 2019.

Asylum seekers are not the only people continuously damaged by this racist policy. While the link between the colonisation of Aboriginal and Torres Strait Islander people by settler colonisers and the present-day rejection of refugees may often elude the colonisers, the link is clear to many First Nation peoples.

> Aboriginal Peoples have never been accepted in this land, even though it is OUR land. We have never been treated as equals. I will finish by reminding everyone that this is not John Howard's country, it has been stolen. It was taken over by the first fleet of illegal boat people. (Wadjularbinna, 2001, capitalisation in original)

Ray Jackson, an activist, Wiradjuri elder and president of the Indigenous Social Justice Association, wrote compellingly about the relationship between the state's treatment of Aboriginal and Torres Strait Islander people and recently arrived asylum seekers.

> First, these governments rule over the stolen lands of the traditional owners and yet firmly believe that they have some moral right to dictate who comes seeking refuge on stolen Aboriginal lands. I do not accept that they have that right. Our lands were invaded 223 years ago and Australia has become most wealthy on our sequestered resources. The asylum seekers being imprisoned in isolated privately managed-for-profit incarceration camps, with the singular exception of Christmas Island, are all on Aboriginal

lands. And I, as a Wiradjuri man, say to those asylum seekers, you are most welcome to our lands. I realise, of course, that other Aborigines may have different views to mine and, of course, that is their right. But I will state most strongly in their defence that these refugees did not invade us, they did not steal our lands, they did not suppress our culture and language, they did not commit genocide, they did not steal our children, they did not steal our wages, they did not steal our human rights as a first people to exist and to grow. The parliaments of the invaders have done all that and more. Again, I say to the asylum seekers, you are welcome to our lands. (Jackson, 2011)

Jackson wrote a letter to Prime Minister Kevin Rudd in 2013 titled, 'A Cruel and Crass Act of Colonialism', in which he

names and identifies the material reality of this foreign/domestic nexus as crucial to the operation of the Australian settler-colonial state: 'The invasion of the Aboriginal Nations that began in January 1788 continues to this day but after time it also allowed, under statute, a xenophobic and racist Law that was used against my peoples and immigrants/refugees'. (Pugliese, 2015, p. 90)

Compounding the genocide committed from 1788 on, the Law that Jackson speaks of, when wielded against asylum seekers, has shattered the lives of thousands of people, including hundreds of children.

Having turned our face from this task in the mid-1990s, we now confront the twofold task of mourning the death of Australia's foundational narrative and the loss of our innocence. We cannot continue to believe we are wholly good and decent people, incapable of treating those considered foreign in cruel and degrading ways to assuage our own anxieties and psychic enfeeblement. The nation-building work of mourning, of reconnecting with reality, awaits us all. Melancholic denial of life and love has already cost and killed so much, so many. It is time to transition out of this deadly psycho-affective state.

Of course, as Freud outlined, there are no guarantees when we take the path of mourning, only this one—that we will emerge with the capacity to live and love again.

References

Agamben, G. (1998). *Homo Sacer: Sovereign power and bare life* (D. Heller-Roazen, Trans.). Stanford University Press.

Brown, W. (2015). *Undoing the demos: Neoliberalism's stealth revolution.* Zone Books.

Doherty, B., & Davidson, H. (2016, February 19). Doctors to propose boycott of Australian immigration detention system. *The Guardian.* https://www.theguardian.com/australia-news/2016/feb/19/doctors-to-propose-boycott-of-australian-immigration-detention-system

Edwards, M. (2016, February 4). Churches to offer sanctuary to asylum seekers, AM. [radio broadcast transcript]. *ABC.* https://www.abc.net.au/am/content/2015/s4400000.htm

Galloway, A. (2022, May 21). Asylum seeker boat stopped off Christmas Island as Morrison trumpets border security on election day. *The Age.* https://www.theage.com.au/politics/federal/asylum-seeker-boat-stopped-off-christmas-island-as-morrison-trumpets-border-security-on-election-day-20220521-p5anb1.html

Gordon, M., McKenzie, N., & Baker, R. (2016, February 2). *The faces of the babies Australia wants to send back to 'hell' on Nauru.* The Sydney Morning Herald.

Hinshelwood, R. D. (1998). *A dictionary of Kleinian thought.* Free Association Books.

Honig, B. (2017). *Public things: Democracy in disrepair.* Fordham University Press.

Jackson, R. (2011). Indigenous leader to asylum seekers: 'You are welcome here'. Green Left Weekly, 896. https://www.greenleft.org.au/content/indigenous-leader-asylum-seekers-you-are-welcome-here

Kaldor Centre for International Refugee Law. (2022, April 26). The cost of Australia's refugee and asylum policy: A source guide. https://www.kaldorcentre.unsw.edu.au/publication/cost-australias-asylum-policy

Klein, M. (1975). Some theoretical conclusions regarding the emotional life of the infant. Envy and gratitude and other works 1946–1963. Hogarth Press and the Institute of Psycho-Analysis (Original work published 1952).

Marcus, P. (2010). *In search of the good life: Emmanuel Levinas, psychoanalysis and the art of living.* Karnac Books.

McKeon, N. (2016, March 2). Vincent Lingiari & Gough Whitlam: The story behind the image. *NITV.* https://www.sbs.com.au/nitv/article/vincent-lingiari-gough-whitlam-the-story-behind-the-image/t0m0ejh6i

Pugliese, J. (2015). Geopolitics of Aboriginal sovereignty: Colonial law as 'a species of excess of its own authority', Aboriginal passport ceremonies and asylum seekers. *Law Text Culture, 19*, 84–115. https://ro.uow.edu.au/ltc/vol19/iss1/4

Tapim, F. (2016, February 12). Brisbane's lady Cilento children's hospital refuses to release badly burnt Nauru baby. *ABC News.* https://www.abc.net.au/news/2016-02-12/brisbane-hospital-refuses-to-release-nauru-baby/7165470

Whyte, J. (2008). Its silent working was a delusion. In J. Clemens, N. Heron, & A. Murray (Eds.), *The work of Giorgio Agamben: Law literature life* (pp. 66–81). Edinburgh University Press.

Epilogue

We, Us, Ours

The silence surrounding my father Jim Macken's offer to swap places with a refugee in detention was not total. He sent a letter to every member of Australian Parliament, all two hundred and twenty-seven of them. He heard nothing by way of reply from the Greens, the Liberal Party, the National Party or any of the Independents, but he did receive four responses. These were from the Labor Party's Senator Lisa Singh and Senator Linda Burney, and Tanya Plibersek MP and Matt Keogh MP of the lower house. I asked him if he was surprised by these responses at all and he said: 'No – of course it was mainly women that responded. They can still imagine what it would be like if it was them, or their own kids, in those camps'.

We must all imagine that it could be us; it could be ours.

Index[1]

Abandonment, 15
Abbott, Tony, 81, 128, 201
ABC, xiii, 62, 71, 84, 103, 117, 117n3, 120, 124n4, 127, 130, 131, 132n6, 158
Abdile, Hani, 4
Aboriginal and Torres Strait Islander peoples, 1, 2, 7, 11, 16, 18, 19, 21, 24, 36, 37, 39, 42, 43, 46, 48, 50–52, 54, 65, 110, 183, 185, 198, 206
Aboriginal Land Rights, 51
Aborigines Progressive Association, xiii, 41, 41n3
Abuse, 2, 4, 10, 20–21, 30, 38, 67, 78, 83, 84, 88, 90, 95, 98, 100–102, 104, 108, 112–114, 134, 138, 141, 143, 145, 149, 151, 152, 156–159, 179, 181, 183, 190, 194, 198, 200, 203, 206
ACM, xiii, 85, 87–89, 144–148, 152
Affective states, 34
AFR, xiii, 3, 87, 95, 120, 132, 147
Agamben, Giorgio, 142
Aggression, 10, 60
Albanese, Anthony, 29, 185, 190
Albanese-Labor, 30
Allan Patience, 6
All-good Australian, 22
Alternatives to Detention Database, 138
Amnesty International, 4, 71, 92, 107, 188
An empty land, 15

---

[1] Note: Page numbers followed by 'n' refer to notes.

Analysis, 6, 10, 93, 108, 132, 158
Anderson, Benedict, 10
Annihilation, 14
Anxiety, 10, 14, 23–25, 43, 44, 60, 61, 65, 91, 92, 97, 114, 115, 119, 186, 189
Anxious nation, 7, 25
Apathy, 6
Archetypes, 12
Article 15 of the Rome Statute, 93
Asylum seekers, 3, 4, 7, 10, 18, 20, 21, 24, 25, 27, 30, 35, 42, 68–71, 73, 78, 82, 87, 89–91, 93, 94, 97–100, 104, 108, 111, 112, 114, 115, 117–122, 124–126, 128–130, 132, 133, 138, 142–144, 148, 151, 154, 156–158, 161, 164, 176, 179, 181, 183, 185, 188–190, 193, 194, 196–202, 204, 206, 207
Atkinson, Judy, 33
Australasian Correctional Management, xiii, 85, 144, 147
Australian Aborigines League, xiii, 40
Australian Border Deaths Database, 94
Australian Broadcasting Corporation, xiii, 62, 110, 117
Australian Constitution, 2, 11, 47
Australian Council of Heads of Schools of Social Work, 85
Australian Council of Trades Unions, 60
Australian Financial Review, xiii, 3, 87, 146
Australian Human Rights Commission, 37, 83

Australian mainstream, 65
Australian Protective Service, 139
Australian Reconciliation Convention, 19, 37, 64
Australian Solution, 21

Bad, 6, 14, 45, 46, 66, 69
Banal, 6, 83, 121
Behrendt, Larissa, 37
Blemishes in its past history, 64
Blewett, Neal, 141
Boochani, Behrouz, 4, 29, 165, 183
Bringing Them Home, 38, 53, 55
Briskman, Linda, vii, 4
British, 9, 11, 15, 16, 37–39, 42–44, 47n4, 52, 63, 140, 194
Broadspectrum, 90, 148, 157, 159
Brown, Wendy, 28, 140, 199
Bully, 6
Burke, Anthony, 10
Butler, Judith, 5, 26, 34, 36, 178

Cameron, Archie, 37
Canstruct, 148, 149
Capacity to love, 6, 18, 27, 36, 67
Catt, Peter, 203
Celermajer, Danielle, 83
Children overboard, 124, 125, 127, 128, 128n5
Christmas Island, 21, 128n5, 130, 146, 196, 203, 206
Citizenship, 9, 12, 22, 23, 41n3, 112, 117, 141, 173, 199
Clewell, Tammy, 28

Climate change, 18, 21, 64, 97, 172, 174, 185, 194
Coalition, 5, 5n2, 61, 69, 116, 121, 128, 138, 144, 161, 175, 184, 187, 188, 197, 202
Collective national denial, 2
Colonial violence, 7, 35, 37, 64, 181
Colonisation, 2, 6, 7, 12, 15–17, 24–26, 30, 33, 34, 36, 38–43, 48, 49, 51, 100, 172, 179, 181, 183, 187, 193, 194, 197, 198, 206
Comfortable and relaxed, 17, 62–64, 100, 198
Community Public Sector Union, xiii, 139
Compulsive repetition, 13, 70, 173, 194
Convention against Torture, xiv, 80, 82, 91, 151
Convention on the Rights of the Child, 89, 90, 150, 199
Cook, Captain James, 42
Corrections Corporation of Australia, 144
Covid-19, 30, 178
Cruel/inhuman/degrading treatment, 93
Cruelty, 5, 30, 34, 50, 72, 86, 128, 149, 162, 181, 193, 194, 201
Curiosity, 5, 6, 10, 12, 34, 35
Curr, Pamela, 71, 152, 154

Day of Mourning, 40
Death, 6, 14–16, 18, 26, 30, 37, 40–42, 51, 63, 64, 71, 81, 83, 86–89, 94, 107, 157, 160, 178–179, 181, 197, 207
Defense mechanism, 24
Demonise, 20, 46
Denial, 2, 6, 11, 14, 16–19, 26, 34, 42, 46, 48–50, 53, 60, 62, 64, 90, 100, 137, 154, 161–164, 174, 177, 178, 181, 185, 194, 204, 207
Denniss, Richard, 140, 162
Department of Immigration and Multicultural Affairs, xiii, 66, 66n1, 144
Department of Immigration and Multicultural and Indigenous Affairs, xiii, 87, 139, 153n2
Depravity, 10
Depressive position, 23, 97, 174
DIMA, xiii, 66, 144, 145
Disavowal, 17, 64, 137
Disintegration, 14, 25, 59, 99
Dispossession, 2, 11, 16, 51, 61, 64
Doherty, 81, 116–118, 121, 149, 176, 188, 204
Doherty, Ben, 116, 175
Dotson, Kristie, 112
Dudley, Michael, 3, 101, 205
Dutton, Peter, 24, 158, 176, 177, 196

Envy, 23, 24
Erotic energy, 6, 55, 177, 193

Face, 5–7, 16, 48, 70, 84, 96, 97, 100, 101, 113, 122–124, 130,

158, 171, 178–182, 193, 195, 202–204, 207
Fear, 6, 7, 10, 13, 14, 25, 33, 44, 45, 51, 52, 59, 61, 65, 67, 71, 92, 131, 148, 174–175, 183
Federal election, 11, 17, 18, 29, 62, 68, 108, 112, 124, 127, 137, 139, 175, 185, 195, 206
Federal Parliamentary Press Gallery, 125, 127, 133
First Nations people, 1, 1n1, 2, 7, 17, 30, 34, 40, 42, 47, 51, 176, 180, 186, 194, 195
Flanagan, Richard, 175
Foley, Gary, 51
Foundational myth, 15, 51, 53, 63, 197
Fragile, 7, 43, 114–115, 174, 178
Frances Peters-Little, 42
Fraser, Malcolm, 50
Fraser, Malcom, 115
Freud, 6, 7, 13, 14, 16–20, 26–29, 36, 41, 42, 50, 55, 67, 72, 97, 109, 119, 174, 178, 205, 207
Freud, Sigmund, 6, 13, 59

G

Galbraith, Janet, 4
Genocide, 37–41, 79, 207
Gibson, Ross, 45
Giles, Andrew, 138, 187
Gillard, J., 4, 70, 71, 81, 90, 128, 148, 156, 157, 190
Gillespie, Liam, 36
Gilroy, Paul, 27
Global Legal Action Network, 82, 93
Glynn-McDonald, Rona, 39
Goddard, Chris, 4

Good, 4, 6, 14, 53, 69
Gooda, Mick, 187
Grieve, 14, 36
Group 4 Falck, 147
GSL, 152, 153, 155, 156

H

Hage, Ghassan, 10, 60, 65, 186
Hanson, Pauline, 22, 66, 68, 69, 73
Hawke, Bob, 50–52, 60
Headland Speech on National Identity, 61
Higgins, Missy, viii, 201
Hoenig, Ron, 67, 111
Honig, Bonnie, 199
Howard, John, 12, 17, 18, 21, 22, 37, 61–63, 81, 89, 111, 121, 128, 133, 161, 206
Human rights abuse, 10
Human Rights and Equal Opportunity Commission, xiii, 52, 84, 139, 149, 200
Human Rights Law Centre, 30, 197

I

Illegal maritime arrival, 116
Illegals, 81, 113, 116, 117
Imagination, 10, 11, 13, 18, 30, 50, 55, 114, 133, 166, 175, 183–190, 193, 199
Immigration Detention Advisory Group, 84
Immigration detention camps, 4, 81, 139, 160, 194, 199, 202
Immigration detention complex, 5
Immigration policy, 20, 30, 66, 90, 103, 143, 184, 187

Indigenous Voice to Parliament, 1, 34, 185, 186, 190, 194
Indigenous Voice, 1, 34, 185, 186, 190, 194
Infantile, 6, 65
Inhumane, 7, 35, 72, 78, 79, 83, 89, 91, 109, 137, 142
International Covenant on Civil and Political Rights, 90, 150, 199
International Criminal Court, 78, 93
International Health and Medical Services, 82
Introjection, 15, 22, 195
Irregular maritime arrival, 116
Isaacs, David, 97
It's OK to be White, 73
It's Time, 50

Joint Standing Committee on Foreign Affairs, 84
Jureidini, John, 7
Jureidini, Jon, 86, 98, 171
Jus cogens, 79

Kaldor Centre, 189, 201
Keane, Bernard, 2
Keating, Paul, 17, 50, 60, 133, 173
Khanna, Ranjanna, 28
Klein, Melanie, 6, 14, 15, 22, 36, 46, 59, 174, 186
Known/not known, 72
Kociumbas, Jan, 37
Kurdi, Alan, 123, 201

Labor Party, xiii, 5, 30, 120, 174–176
Lacan, Jacques, 67
Lambing Flat riots, 47
Langton, Marcia, 187
A Last Resort?., 85
Latham, Susie, 4
Lepenies, Wolf, 28
Lévinas, Emmanuel, 122, 123
Lifeless, 6, 201
Lingiari, Vincent, 49, 198
Lip-sewing, 85, 152
Loss, 6, 13, 16–18, 23, 26–28, 30, 34, 36, 40, 41, 48, 53n6, 64, 67, 83, 121, 122, 181, 195, 205, 207
Love, vii, 6, 13, 14, 18, 23, 27, 29, 30, 34, 41, 42, 59, 67–73, 97, 98, 166, 174–175, 178, 180, 182, 183, 187, 190, 194, 195, 201, 205, 207

Mabo Case, 52
Mabo, 52, 55, 61
Macfarlane, Ingereth, 42
Macken, Jim, vii, 9, 86, 89, 96, 109, 124, 125, 133, 148, 153, 155, 175, 176, 179, 180
Macken-Horarik, Mary, vii, 109, 125
Makarrata, 182, 182n1, 198
Mandatory detention, 199
Mania, 19
Manic, 19, 174, 184, 190

Manus Island, 29, 70, 71, 89, 90, 94, 138, 148, 151, 156, 157, 164, 165, 176, 177, 183, 189
Marr, David, 127
Masoumali, Omid, 94, 107, 123
McGrath, Ann, 42
McKinnon, Crystal, 35
Media, 10, 17, 20, 26, 44, 48, 62, 63, 69, 70, 72, 103, 108–114, 116, 117, 119–122, 124, 126–134, 138, 145, 147, 151, 161, 172, 175, 180, 183, 201, 204
Medical neglect, 4, 71
Melancholia, 6, 7, 12–22, 24, 26–31, 34, 36, 42–44, 46, 53, 54, 62–67, 71, 73, 98, 103, 114, 171, 173, 174, 177, 178, 181, 184, 194, 198, 199, 205
Melancholic denial, 6, 15, 49, 103
Melancholic malady, 7
Melancholy footnote, 42
Mendez, Juan, 3
Mendiola, Ignacio, 108
Mental Health Alliance for Refugees, 3, 102
Metaphorically, 12, 65
Moreton-Robinson, A., 36
Morrison, Scott, 19, 81, 92, 113, 116, 128, 129, 162, 184, 185
Mourner, 14, 42, 197
Mourning and Melancholia, 13, 27, 29
Mourning, 1, 6, 12–19, 23, 25–30, 34, 36, 39–42, 47–55, 59, 60, 63–65, 73, 97, 114, 115, 174, 175, 178–181, 186, 193–199, 204–207

MTC, 138
Multicultural, 17, 27, 65, 66, 188

Narcissism, 6, 13, 15, 18–20, 22, 27, 65, 67, 72, 73, 109, 181, 195
Narcissistic, 6, 29, 30, 103, 174, 194
National security, 20, 69, 78, 82, 119, 120, 122, 124n4, 128, 132n6, 162, 163, 175, 201
Nauru Regional Processing Centre, 89, 90, 156, 189
Nauru, 4, 9, 24, 25, 70, 71, 73, 89–92, 94, 97, 100, 107, 108, 108n1, 113, 123, 138, 148, 149, 151, 156–159, 161, 163, 176, 188, 189, 196, 201–204
Neoliberal, 60, 63, 140, 141, 162, 166
Newman, Louise, 7, 95
No, 1, 2, 6, 185, 186, 194
"Non-alien," 23
"Non-citizen," 22
Non-Indigenous Australians, 2, 182, 183
'No' Vote, 1
Non-White, 6
"Not-Australia," 137
Notes on Some Schizoid Mechanisms, 14

O'Donoghue, Lowitja, 35
O'Neill, Margot, 131
Object relations, 14, 36
Office of Multicultural Affairs, 66

Offshore, 4, 5, 12, 20, 21, 24, 29, 45, 70, 84, 89, 90, 93, 102, 108n1, 112, 137, 138, 148, 149, 156, 160, 161, 176, 188, 190, 200–203
On water matters, 108, 128, 129
One Nation, 59, 60, 68, 69, 121
Onshore, 12, 94, 112, 137, 148, 161, 183, 188
Optional Protocol to the Convention against Torture, 152
Other, 17, 20, 25, 36, 46–47, 59, 65, 67, 70, 80, 82, 97, 98, 108, 110, 111, 122–124, 151, 173, 175, 188, 197, 204

Pacific Solution, 21, 30, 70, 89, 90, 148, 190
Paladin, 149
Palmer Inquiry, 83, 100, 152, 155, 156
Papua New Guinea, xiv, 29, 70, 73, 89, 148, 149, 159, 164, 189, 202
Paranoia, 10, 61
Paranoid/schizoid position, 15, 186
Paranoid-schizoid phase, 22–23, 46, 64, 69, 73, 104, 137
Paranoid-schizoid position, 6, 46, 112, 119, 126, 174, 190, 205
Parliament House, 63, 184, 188
People's Inquiry into immigration detention, 85
Perera, Suvendrini, 21
Persecution, 20, 21, 68, 70, 93, 104, 108, 111, 121, 133, 138, 194

Peterie, Michelle, 69
Pezzullo, Michael, 163
Phantasie, 14, 17, 64, 71, 154, 174, 194
Politics, 3, 5n2, 6, 10, 25, 26, 36, 43, 46, 72, 114, 124n4, 132n6, 172, 185
Practical reconciliation, 67
Privatisation, 63, 72, 137, 139, 141, 142, 145, 147, 162, 194
Privatised immigration regime, 10
Privatising, 20, 137, 145
Projection, 15, 24, 25, 65, 69, 195
Protection Denied, Abuse Condoned, 91
Psyche-splitting, 14
Psychic life, 15
Psycho-affective, 2, 12, 26, 46, 197, 199, 205, 207
Psychoanalysis, 5, 34, 36
Psychoanalytic, 10, 25, 26, 36, 68
Psychoanalytically, 12, 25, 34, 42
Psychologically, 2, 16, 18, 26, 29, 55, 97, 114, 115, 178, 184, 190, 193
Psychotherapeutic, 6
Psychotherapy, 5
Psychotic, 12, 13, 87, 100, 205
Public ownership, 63, 189
Public Service Act, 138, 139, 183, 200
Pugliese, Joseph, 22

Queue jumpers, 81, 116

Rape, 15, 71, 81, 90–92, 153, 194
Rau, Cornelia, 155, 156
Reconciliation, 2, 18, 21, 23, 50, 64, 67, 187, 194, 195
Redfern Speech, 17, 53, 133
Referendum, 2, 21, 49, 185–187, 190, 194, 198
Refugee Council of Australia, 4, 116, 189, 196
Refugees, 2–4, 10, 12, 20, 25, 35, 42, 66, 68–70, 72, 73, 79–83, 91, 92, 97, 104, 112, 114, 115, 117–121, 124, 126, 131, 133, 141, 163, 164, 174–176, 179, 183, 185, 187–189, 199, 205–207
Relaxed and comfortable, 30
Resistance, 5, 7, 29, 38, 40, 48, 52, 79, 103, 123, 165, 166, 171, 177, 183
Richardson, Dennis, 116
Rosen, Jay, 110
Royal Commission into Aboriginal Deaths in Custody, 153
Rudd, 4, 70, 81, 90, 128, 148, 156, 190, 207
Ruddock, Philip, 68, 103, 145–147
Rutherford, Jennifer, 10, 59

Sacred core, 7, 80, 171, 172, 194, 205
Sadism, 12, 20
Sanggaran, John-Paul, 83, 203
Save the Children, 113, 158, 161
Schamberger, Karen, 46
Seeking asylum, 3

Seeking protection, 9, 10, 69, 94, 115, 116, 119
Self-immolation, 4
Senate Select Committee on the Recent Allegations Relating to the Conditions and Circumstances at the Regional Processing Centre in Nauru, 157
Sexual assault, 90–92, 145, 158
Sexually assaulted, 4, 92, 96
Shallow, 6, 30, 46, 62, 119, 194
Singh, Charandev, 88, 145
Solitary confinement, 96, 152
Sorry Business, 1, 39–41, 182
Sovereignty, 13, 20, 21, 36, 42, 43, 51, 118, 120–122, 142, 172, 173
Standing, Guy, 63
State propaganda, 20
State-sanctioned torture, 3, 205
Steel, Zachary, 84
Stillborn, 15
Suicide, 3, 4, 71, 87, 88, 93, 96, 102, 132, 148, 152, 157, 158
Superficial, 18, 173, 190, 195
Symbolic gesture, 18
Symbolic, 5, 12, 18, 19, 49, 64–65, 67, 173, 187, 201

Tampa, 69, 82, 89, 120–122, 124, 127, 132
Temporary Protection Visas, 68
Terra Nullius, 11, 16, 43, 49, 52, 194, 206
Thom, Graham, 71
Tofighian, Omid, 4

Torturable subject, 108
Torture of asylum seekers, 10, 79
Torture, 3, 4, 10, 35, 65, 67, 68, 72, 78–83, 91, 93, 95–98, 101, 102, 108, 138, 151, 153, 156, 175, 182, 193, 194, 200, 203, 205, 206
TPVs, 68
Transfield, 90, 113, 148, 157
Trauma, 3, 12, 25, 39, 53, 53n6, 68, 79, 84, 86, 95, 97, 104, 121
Treaty, 42, 43, 52, 70, 115, 150, 187, 198
Trust, 21, 95, 98, 104n3, 130, 194, 199
Truth-telling, 6, 16, 182, 198
Turnbull, Malcolm, 81, 128, 184, 185

Uluru Statement from the Heart, 30, 43, 182–183, 185, 198
UN High Commissioner for Human Rights, 84
UN Special Rapporteur, 91
Un-Australian, 22, 44, 197
Unconscious, 5, 10–14, 20, 110
United Nations Convention Against Torture, 80
United Nations High Commissioner for Refugees, xiv, 21, 115, 157
United Nations Report on Mandatory Detention, 90
United Nations Special Rapporteur, 3
United Nations Subcommittee on Prevention of Torture, 152

Vanstone, Amanda, 153
Victim-complex, 6
Voice to Parliament, 21, 49

Wackenhut, 144
White Australia policy, 46, 47, 47n4, 50, 102, 206
White Australia, 10, 16, 17, 42, 43, 45–48, 47n4, 50, 52, 53, 63–65, 69, 72, 102, 183, 198, 206
White Australian, 9, 17, 47n4, 64, 67, 198
White fantasy, 2
White, Patrick, 44
Whitlam, Gough, 16, 49, 50, 198
Whyte, Jessica, 22, 173
Wilkie, Andrew, 93
Wilkinson, Marian, 127
Wilson Security, 90, 92, 148, 157–160
With baseball bats, 62
Wolfe, Patrick, 37
Woolridge, Michael, 68

Yes, 1, 2, 30, 185, 187
Yes' vote, 1, 30
Young, Peter, 82, 100, 171

Zion, Deborah, 83

GPSR Compliance
The European Union's (EU) General Product Safety Regulation (GPSR) is a set of rules that requires consumer products to be safe and our obligations to ensure this.

If you have any concerns about our products, you can contact us on

ProductSafety@springernature.com

In case Publisher is established outside the EU, the EU authorized representative is:

Springer Nature Customer Service Center GmbH
Europaplatz 3
69115 Heidelberg, Germany

www.ingramcontent.com/pod-product-compliance
Lightning Source LLC
LaVergne TN
LVHW020344260326
834688LV00045B/1522